The
OUTRAGED
TIMES OF STRIFE

Aditya Sudarshan is a novelist. Author of *A Nice Quiet Holiday, Show Me A Hero, The Persecution of Madhav Tripathi* and *The Outraged: Times of Ferment,* he won the Hindu Metroplus Playwright Award in 2011 for his play *The Green Room.* He has been a scriptwriter for NDTV's political satire show, *The Great Indian Tamasha,* and a columnist in *The Hindu*'s Literary Review. His literary criticism and book reviews have been published in various newspapers. He currently manages the Writing Centre at FLAME University, Pune.

The
OUTRAGED
TIMES OF STRIFE

ADITYA SUDARSHAN

RUPA

Published by
Rupa Publications India Pvt. Ltd 2019
7/16, Ansari Road, Daryaganj
New Delhi 110002

Sales centres:
Allahabad Bengaluru Chennai
Hyderabad Jaipur Kathmandu
Kolkata Mumbai

ISBN: 978-93-5333-492-5

First impression 2019

10 9 8 7 6 5 4 3 2 1

The moral right of the author has been asserted.

Contents

Prologue

This is a story of Versova, a sliver of a suburb that yet vies for centre stage, where buff young hopefuls and shop-soiled innocents strut and pick their way down Mumbai's degraded streets, in the immemorial quest for glory. I was there, just plain Dhruv, a lad from Delhi trying to make it as an actor—or indeed, any way I could.

I had one star in my sky, by which I took my bearings—Ahishor Frances. His first film was the philosophical masterpiece (everyone said so) called *Schrodinger's Cat*. His second was to be a documentary about Indian god-men—until the day he was attacked by goons, and the hour his family betrayed him. I do not mean only his famous stepfather and stepbrother, but that whole tribe of the elite and educated and (one used to think) courageously forward-looking, who decided to look the other way. Some, however, were up for the fight. These included my former boss, Jatin Khanna, a man who loved to scrap for justice, and also others, young and old, whose motives were strange—more eager and more unnerving. And this web of supporters had a spider at its centre.

But I am getting ahead of myself. The sharpest cut of all

had come from Maithili Krishna, the girl Ahishor loved (but so did many others), who cared for no one's opinion; whose eyes were fixed, not on the stars of the screen, but on the secret lights of a higher plane. Neither a mother's tears nor a girlfriend's plight nor a man's frantic curses would keep her from walking that esoteric way.

And then there was Sasha. Why had he come to live among us, this strange young man with shining eyes and a haunted past, who aimlessly walked the broken pavements, yet went like an arrow to the broken people and could not seem to count the cost?

Times of Ferment, Book 1 of *The Outraged*, has set the stage for the present story. Ahishor has resolved to embark on a radical new movement, a project far greater than any mere film. He must advance the liberal cause by first purging it of the disloyal and the hypocritical, who, as it so happens, the times are identifying by one means above all: their sexual misdemeanours. Meanwhile, he retains in his sights the enemy without—those skilled charlatans who call themselves god-men—and all that they stand for.

None who enter the swirl of this revolution, whether to help or hinder or merely to gaze upon it, will ever be the same again.

The Guru of Reality

Two figures stood on the sand, in the minutes before sunrise. Majestic and overpowering beauty lay before them. No painter could have bettered, by design, the flaming layers of the pre-dawn sky, while, like an angelic audience in attendance, discrete and flaxen clouds hovered unto the horizon. The morning was profoundly still, but the sea rippled mysteriously everywhere, and near the shore, it came racing to wash the women's feet.

They resembled each other greatly. Like Maithili, Shonar too was slimly built, with cropped hair and an oval face from which stared cool and steady eyes. She was darker of skin and there was silver in her hair (she was fifteen years older), but they might yet have passed for sisters. They both wore sarongs—one white, one orange—and they each held their sandals in their hands.

Minutes later, there rose on the horizon the brightest spot in the conflagration, the red-gold orb from which all dazzle emanated, and into which, once again, it would soon converge. Shonar breathed deeply and clasped her hands together.

'What do you see?' she intoned.

They were the first words that had been spoken on that

stretch of the beach for a long time. Even now, as far as the eye could see, the sands were clean and devoid of people.

Shonar continued:

'Sadhguru says we see beauty to the extent that we are liberated. The freer we are, the more beauty we perceive. Until finally, there is nothing but beauty.'

Maithili nodded, for it was a familiar and beloved thought to her.

'When will I see him?'

'Tomorrow itself! He'll talk to you personally. He's very keen to meet you. He's spotted your potential.'

'That's your doing! What if he's disappointed?'

They both smiled fulsomely, their eyes narrowing in mirth. They were almost the same height.

'Sadhguru doesn't go by my opinion.' Shonar shook her head meaningfully. 'You think? He spotted your powers himself.'

'Just from the photograph you sent him?'

'Yes—and I told you, I sent him that only because he asked who I was spending time with in Boston. I didn't even talk up your spiritual side. He spotted everything himself.'

Maithili looked away, towards the daybreak, her heart tightening with nameless emotions. She moved her hand to her pocket.

'Smoke?'

'I quit, you know that,' said Shonar. She stared with wonderment and faint disapproval as Maithili lit up. 'It interferes with your kriya[1], you know. But I guess it doesn't for you.'

'I'll quit too if he tells me.'

---

[1] In yogic practice, kriyas are cleansing techniques meant to purify the body and mind, for a specific result.

'Just like that? You wouldn't argue?'

Maithili shook her head. Her eye fell on the wooden fishing boats, painted with red and green stripes, which were tied to the coconut trees that were beginning to sway in the breeze. She thought suddenly of her mother. Once, years ago, the whole family had visited Auroville for a weekend. She recalled everyone drinking coconut water on one of the beaches, and becoming upset because there was less water in her coconut than in anybody else's. The rest of that afternoon had dissolved into tears and angry punches at her mocking brother.

She felt no pangs. The memory passed as something silly and fleeting from the remote past—and even in itself, reminding her that she had always been different.

'How do you do that though?'

It was Shonar, cocking her head curiously.

'I mean, how do you manage to just commit? I can't do it, I'll be honest with you. I try! I really, really try! I want to believe in Sadhguru. I *do* believe in him, I do! But even now I'm afraid of what he will ask me to do. I talk the talk, but I can't walk the walk! I can't give up my comforts. And he knows that. That's why he tells me I'm not ready.'

'What is more comforting, Shonar,' said Maithili, 'than the Truth and the whole Truth?'

Her eyes were gleaming with that unnameable sensibility that I had once mistaken for irony (though perhaps at the time it had indeed been just that).

'Obedience does not mean you give up your comforts. It means you receive the only comfort there is.'

'Yes, yes,' the older woman nodded, grinning happily. 'When you say it, I believe it. But then the doubts come back! I think—well this is just a man, how can he be a god? What if he… You see? My faith is just not strong enough! Even though I've known him for so long now. I know he's not like the others. There's nothing…*religious* about him… You know? He's very *secular*. But…'

'It's normal to have doubts,' smiled Maithili. Yet a subtle tension had gripped her; there was something dislikeable in Shonar's eager gaze. She did not, therefore, say how (just as he had recognized her from her picture), so she too, on the very first sight of Narayanan's photograph, had known that he was The One. In silence, she thought of him, with his topknot, like Shiva's, and the long, curly locks that framed the unforgettable face, almost Mongoloid in its features.

They were no longer alone. A dark-skinned man in a dhoti was moving silently across the sands. Soon the fishermen would arrive in force. The sky was still riotously beautiful; the waters deep, swelling with mystery; the air bracing and bountiful. But the most intense magic of the dawn had passed already.

'I guess you're younger too, that's an advantage.' Shonar was smiling in a knowing way. 'One grows more tentative with age… Unfortunately, when I was your age, I was still going along the conventional route. I must have just begun on my PhD! Ha! Later of course, I broke the mould. Himachal happened… growing apples and milking cows… then I spent a whole year hiking up and down various mountains—that's the year I became a seeker!—I told you about that.'

Maithili, who was not listening, merely nodded. She liked Shonar and was grateful for the part she was playing in her story. But sometimes she was tiresome.

She began to walk along the surf, balancing in the undertow and looking at the foamy patterns that swirled about her feet.

'My father was a writer,' said Shonar, following her. 'He

wrote novels in Bengali. Really sweet, genuine man, but he wanted me to have a full education, lots of degrees, and then to join the IAS. He was a big believer in education. By which, I mean our English-medium, anglicized education. Now I think that ended up harming me. It's made me too attached to my intellect. Anyway, that's what Sadhguru says. I—'

'He is right!' exclaimed Maithili. Not noticing the brief, wounded smile that came flashing her way, she continued with conviction. 'They are such bores! There is nobody more tedious than our intellectuals and pundits. Pundits—that's what they call themselves.' She looked up gravely, before training her gaze toward the curving fringe of greenery that beckoned in the breeze. 'My parents are like that. I used to imagine, that with all their reading and writing, they would have had some answers. But they only had words.'

It seemed she would say more, but she did not; only her eyes burned, as though with dark flames. Shonar, however, was grinning and nodding.

'I know what you mean! The best decision I ever made was to stop reading newspapers and stop watching TV. They talk about everything under the sun, except what really matters. Round and round they go in circles! Politics, economics, art, culture, history, yadda yadda yadda.'

'Yes,' said Maithili.

'But do they understand the soul of India?' queried Shonar. 'Not one bit. They are completely cut off from her soul. That's why all these so-called brilliant people just do more and more damage. And still, they are so full of themselves. Still, they keep talking! In love with the sound of their voices!'

'My grandfather was aware,' said Maithili. 'He was in the government. But he knew how petty it all was. He was a seeker himself, at heart… You remind me of him, a little bit.'

'Really?' Shonar was surprised and pleased.

'Yes—a little bit.'

'Oh… I just wish I could let go! You know? I can't seem to let go! I guess it's also because of the bad experience I had at Auroville. It really shattered my faith. I thought they were building a new world in there. But it was the same old one after all—even worse, in fact! Petty politics and power struggles and people being taken advantage of. Brazenly! No wonder there's barely a thousand people living there now. When Aurobindo and the Mother began it, it was supposed to have fifty times that!'

The light was strengthening all about them. More figures were emerging onto the beach. One man, wearing a yellow lungi, appeared drunk. He walked with a strange gait and shouted raucously at no one in particular.

'Sadhguru is special,' continued Shonar. 'He's so different from those trishul[2]-wielding fanatics; he's intelligent, he believes in rationality and debate. He's a man of the world as well as being a guru. He's genuine; he doesn't take advantage of people. He's respectful towards women! I'm telling you that just in case you are worrying… I know *I* worried before I met him. But even though I know all this, I still struggle to commit!'

She looked at Maithili with a despairing smile. But on Maithili's own lips lay only the faintest smirk—or perhaps nothing. Shonar persevered.

'Sometimes I think that there is no other world possible at all. All we get is brief moments of bliss. Like the dawn today… And then reality returns… There! There you go! Shoot! Will you look at that, Thalia? I swear, when I first moved to Pondy,

---

[2]trident

this beach was clean!'

Her gaze was trained on a knot of discarded plastic wrappers—garbage that had snagged on a stone—which was now being worried continually by the waves going to and fro.

Maithili looked, but showed no reaction. She was not perturbed. She had not expected, on returning to India, to find it altered, devoid of dirt and chaos. But she had understood why it was India, after all, where her answers lay.

'India...' she began to say—her voice was calm, though this was a conclusion that had come to her arduously, and had reversed, bit by bit, her desperate conviction when she had fled to Greece—'is a cauldron of spiritual energy. It's been stored up over centuries. We are lucky to have it, even if it's a mess right now. It's totally missing in the West. People there are totally blocked, because they are too content with their material achievements. They only want to *dabble* in the spirit, nothing more.'

Shrugging suddenly, she stared down the beach, at the dark figures on the yellow sands.

'All that is needed for India is the right spiritual principle—the right principle of arrangement—to bring order to chaos. When that happens, then India, and *only* India, will be the leader of the world—the jagat guru.'

'That's exactly what Sadhguru says!' exclaimed Shonar. 'Did you read it from him? You read it on his website, right?'

After a short silence, during which the other woman continued to gaze eagerly, Maithili answered—'No.' It was a deliberate lie. She had researched Sadhguru extensively, reading his essays and listening to his speeches, many days in succession, ever since she had learned of him. But, although there was no reason to have lied, she did not regret it—and was even pleased.

'That's amazing,' whispered Shonar.

For both of them, the crash of the waves was now a compelling rhythm, like a mantra in their heads. Shonar closed her eyes, and her perception, it seemed, only sharpened. *This was reality*, she reminded herself, *this, without distractions, was more real than what had been before. She could feel it all—the waves, the wind, the trees huddled close, the gulls calling, the sand catching between her toes, that delicious grittiness... And what greater reality waited beyond? How infinitely sparer, how infinitely more elegant was the Truth itself?*

'Sadhguru literally means the Guru of Reality,' she murmured aloud, and then half-blushed, for fear that Maithili would think she was instructing her.

But when she looked, the other girl was simply stepping forward, staring at nothing, and yet—it seemed to Shonar— staring at secrets, brimming with secrets herself, like a full vessel that is guarded from prying eyes. And her heart beat fast to be near her.

'I can't wait to make you meet him,' she said. 'I'm so glad I met you, Thalia.'

'I'm glad too,' smiled Maithili, glancing at her companion. Then her eyes widened.

It was not Shonar's face she had seen in that moment, but the reptilian snout of her demon, atop the woman's body—the very same creature that had been with her ever since her teens, appearing to her sometimes in one form, sometimes in another. Then the demon disappeared, even as Shonar kept talking, and Maithili too turned away, the familiar thrill of recognition fading into a strange fatigue. What an ordeal it was to glimpse and not behold, to taste and not consume, to have power and lack knowledge. Suddenly, more intensely than ever, she wanted to know God; to hold Him to her breast; to consume Him, if that were possible. How could she endure the wait till the morning?

'Oh—I wrote your parents that letter,' Shonar was saying. 'The one you asked me to.'

'Yes. Thank you,' said Maithili, a moment later.

'I think I wrote it well. I'm sure they must have got it… Isn't it miraculous! I didn't post the letter; it just disappeared off the table. I mean to say… I don't know if someone else picked it up and posted it! But I believe in His powers. He can make things happen. I know that!'

Maithili was looking steadfastly into the distance, her stride never breaking.

'You know, this was one of the things Sadhguru wanted me to do, which I couldn't. I just *couldn't.*'

'What thing?' asked Maithili. There was an edge to her voice, but Shonar, perhaps, did not notice it.

'This—this thing. Cutting off one's parents.'

Then Maithili swivelled, with narrowed eyes flashing with displeasure.

'It's not about cutting off one's parents!' Her voice, all of a sudden, was shot through with irritation. 'It's about doing what you have to, to get to the next level! If you can't understand—at least be quiet for some time!'

Breathing harshly, she quickened her pace, marching briskly away. Shonar was shocked, yet more wounded than offended at the younger woman's tone. She was careful not to return to the subject, neither on that day, nor the next, when the two women took the morning bus to Mahabalipuram, the ancient, legendary town where the Guruji was waiting.

Mentor's Mentor

In Versova, Jatin's car was stuck behind a massive bus that was backing out of a tiny gate, off the main road. He cursed profusely, slamming his fist on the horn. His black mood had lately been further soured by my informing him that I couldn't meet for coffee (and the rant that he wanted), because I wasn't in the city. I had left Mumbai indefinitely for my parents' home in Delhi, though 'two to three weeks' was what I was telling everyone. The truth was that I felt isolated and overwhelmed by all that was happening in Versova. But I will speak of myself later.

The weather, at the time, belied the goings-on. It was wonderfully mild and cool, all day and night. And there were happy faces too, among the vendors and the shopkeepers, the watchmen and the rickshaw drivers. The new year had left a sense of gaiety lingering on the streets; one felt it in the quick strides of pedestrians in mufflers (worn, I think, from pride or habit, more than necessity), and the alert stares of the stray dogs that sat upright in the bracing cold. But inside the apartment towers, behind the posh and the crumbling facades where our little 'fraternity' hid and lived, a great consternation was building.

No sooner had the debates over Ahishor's 'retirement' peaked, than the allegations against Pankaj Pande arrived like a fresh wave, lifting the general excitement even further, and adding the froth of sexual transgression. And who could fail to notice Ahishor's own involvement in this matter, his retweeting of everything Ruhi put out, and the quote (accurate or not) that appeared beneath his name in the *Mumbai Mirror*: 'It's a shocking incident, because Pande is considered a progressive man. Then again, we have many counterfeit progressives.'

It had not taken long for Jatin to dash off an excitable email to Ahishor, expressing (by Jatin's standards) a cautious astonishment that the young man should have been so quick to doubt his venerable elder. 'You are too intelligent and brilliant,' he reminded him, 'to be taken in by mere allegations and rumours—and that, at the moment, is all these are. I'm not saying Ruhi is lying. Sadly I'm not in touch with her any longer—which is not my own doing. She is unreliable and has issues. As you know, she was working with me on the YouTube videos, before leaving that in the lurch in a thoroughly unprofessional way. But you're certainly aware of how unique a film-maker Pankaj Pande is, even if he never quite achieved his potential—a fate that, by the way, can easily befall any of us. I know exactly what you mean about counterfeit progressives—but surely, Ahishor, you ought to know (if not, please take my word for it) that Pankaj Pande is not one of them!'

He received no reply. Pankaj himself, however, was not only keen to go into a huddle with Jatin, but appeared put out (in a distracted way) that he was not already present in his office.

I should recount for the reader, the bond that existed between these two men. I had experienced it as incessant exhortations from Jatin to watch and learn from Pankaj's work, but I had also witnessed the two of them together and listened with genuine interest to their talk. It seemed to me that Jatin's admiration, which was no doubt heightened by his affinity for father-son relationships (young men like me and his new assistant, Arvind, were at the flip side of this craving), possessed a sound objective basis too, while Pankaj's indulgence of his energetic admirer was also filled with real fondness and gratitude. It was to Jatin's credit that he championed this largely forgotten film-maker, who alone, among his elite, Nehruvian-liberal contemporaries, had continued to express himself via his chosen metier (shunning academic and institutional sinecures), and, through decades of social and cultural confusion, braved the box office.

This was not to say that he had emerged unscathed. One of Jatin's memorable descriptions of Pankaj had, perhaps, more grave truth to it than he realized. 'Pankaj Pande always looks,' Jatin would say, 'as though he has just been hit on the side of the head with a brick, you know?' He would then mimic a certain glazed-eyed head-lolling, and the room would be choking with laughter.

But there was little laughter in the great man's office that afternoon, in the quiet wilderness of Aram Nagar. Save for the guard at the gate, Jatin found the whole place deserted. A flight of wrought iron stairs went up to the second storey of the bungalow (the downstairs, owned by a businessman, was locked most of the year).

In the outer office was a singular absence of assistants and interns. Pankaj Pande sat by himself, on the sofa in his private room, his long legs crossed and his hands clasped behind his head. His collar and the two buttons below it were unfastened. But he always looked this unkempt. What was unusual was the bottle of whisky on his desk, with two empty glasses alongside.

'Hello Sir! Where is everybody?' demanded Jatin.

Pankaj, who had only moved his gaze to register the arrival, shrugged from where he sat.

'Where's the work? … I've given them all an off. You see, I'm not a tyrant like you.'

A gleam entered his eyes and his lips curled in mirth. Even with his white hair, deep-set eyes, and skin that resembled parchment, he looked boyish when he smiled. (I had observed a striking divide, among women, in their judgments on Pankaj's looks. He was delightfully mischievous to some; especially ugly to others.)

'If you'd come ten minutes later, you'd have found me drinking,' he declared. The booming voice was a mimic's delight.

'At least I wouldn't have found you drunk! Given the circumstances, that's quite creditable… You sit, I'll pour,' said Jatin, moving to the table.

'I'm not even sure about that,' said Pankaj thoughtfully.

'About what?'

'Both things. Whether I would have gotten drunk in ten minutes and whether it would have been alright to do that… or rather pathetic.'

'Boss, it's a crazy situation you're in.'

'It's not just me, you dick-head!' snapped Pankaj suddenly. 'We're all in a crazy situation! I just happen to be *alive* enough, to…' He pursed his lips contemptuously. Rising to his full height, tall and swaying (his distinctive carriage), he took the drink from Jatin's hand.

'I mean… more than anything…' He waited on his feet, staring abstractedly with his head cocked. Jatin felt a surge of sympathy and was about to speak when Pankaj raised his hand.

'More than anything,' he repeated, 'I'm disappointed. That's actually what I feel… I feel disappointed.'

'Disappointed in whom?'

'In whom? Well… In everyone who should know better!'

'Boss, what exactly happened? I mean, what's the deal?'

'It's good news for you, though,' Pankaj grinned. 'That film of yours will get attention now. Suddenly I'm hot news, you see! If you still want to make it, of course.'

Jatin had, for years, been talking about making a film on Pankaj Pande, using his life and career as a lens to explore the changing state of Indian cinema and Indian society itself.

'Of course I'm going to make it! This whole thing is just going to be a blip. It'll blow over soon.'

'Aah, you are not an artist, Jatin,' the elder man shook his head wisely. 'An artist would make *use* of this episode. I'm going to use it myself… You see, it's made me realize how shallow our talk of modernity is. Beyond the window-dressing of freedom and self-expression and what not, we still have the mentality of a… of a frightened little khap[3] panchayat! As for women's liberation and feminism and all that bloody discourse—pah!'

He slipped behind his desk, and sank into the familiar chair of authority; then he put his feet up on the table, and smiled lopsidedly at Jatin. The latter, grave and twitching, pulled up the chair opposite.

'Are you going to tell me what happened?'

'A physical relation happened. With no strings attached. She knew it just as much as I did. What happens is—I've been thinking about this—a girl imagines that she really owns

---

[3] A kind of community organization in Indian villages, usually in the north, infamous for their regressive judgments and violence.

her sexuality, imagines that she's finally capable of having fun with it. And a man respects that. He takes her at her own estimate. Later, you discover that it was a sham. She cannot actually handle the idea of sex for the sake of pleasure. There has got to be something attached. And when she finds there wasn't anything attached, she feels used. You see? She feels used because it *wasn't* the casting couch! You see how regressive this thing is—I mean, from her side! I mean, from the side of all the bleeding hearts and feminists—self-proclaimed feminists!'

'Yes, yes, I see perfectly! I've worked with her myself, and I wasn't exactly impressed by her ethics—her work ethics anyway. But that's not how it's being portrayed.'

'How is it being portrayed?'

'You know, boss! The allegation is that you forced her, without her consent.'

'And you believe that?' A smile spread over the old man's face.

'Of course I don't believe that!' said Jatin hotly. 'I'm just trying to figure out what to do about it! The cops—have the cops—'

'Yes, the case is with the cops now,' Pankaj waved his hand airily. 'They'll question me any day now. I'll tell them what happened. Let's see her prove this. My concern is not the police or any of the proper processes, you see. It's all this noise and— nonsense!'

His hand went to the glass of whisky, which tottered on the table. A moment later, his gaze had become hunted; his eyes turned up to the ceiling. The strain, for the first time, was showing.

Jatin looked at the open windows beyond the table. It was quiet all around, green and peaceful as few places in the city could ever be. But he knew well the 'noise' that the old man had spoken of. That was raging here, as everywhere. It only ever lessened, he reckoned, when one travelled somewhere exotic, but even then it never died, only bided its time.

'It's inside our heads,' Pankaj chimed in on Jatin's thoughts. 'You know? Nobody can think clearly. People are walking about like fucking zombies. Just spouting words! A whole lot of words! Twitter, Facebook, bloody television! And nobody knows what's true or false! Nobody can... because the noise never stops long enough to allow that—to allow that to happen! You see? ... Ask yourself! When are you ever alone? You can run off to Goa, but you're never goddamned alone anymore!'

He was gesticulating; his voice reverberating wildly about the room, carrying, as usual, thunderous confusion bestowed with flashes of clarity. He was enjoying the energy of performance and the pleasures of abstraction, which, however, were misplaced at such a time. But Pankaj Pande was an artist to a fault.

'You were right about one thing,' he wagged his finger. 'This new generation—they are a fucked-up bunch, Jatin. You're damn right about that! I'll tell you what. This is perhaps the first generation of independent Indians who don't believe in anything. I mean, absolutely nothing! They aren't even hedonists. They think they are, but they aren't. Because even *that* takes balls— which they don't have! Ruhi Khanna—she didn't have balls!'

At the back of his mind, Jatin felt the urgency of the situation being belied all the while. There was something specific they needed to talk about; the thought of it gnawed at him. But he never could resist Pankaj's pronouncements. Unconsciously, he slipped into the familiar role of the one unto whom pearls are scattered.

'True, very true... what do you and I believe in though?'

'Well, you and I are from different generations ourselves.' Pankaj twisted his body, now gesturing towards the other wall and turning his head for emphasis, whenever he desired it. 'Still, I suppose you're closer to mine than to theirs. Right? Now I'm not saying we believed in much—liberal socialism, the welfare State, as regards the government. A sense of restraint and culture in our art—a certain other-regarding quality—which came from a sense of duty that we felt as privileged people in this country... Maybe it was all wishy-washy crap! But at least we tried. What I'm saying is, even if our ideals were misplaced, at least we valued the *point* of ideals. You see?'

Then suddenly, he swivelled and ran his visitor through with a piercing stare.

'And this chutiya calls *me* a "counterfeit progressive"! Who the fuck does he think he is? Little fuck! Aren't you a great pal of his?'

Immediately, Jatin was filled with distress, but with the subject finally raised, he received a burst of energy.

'I don't know what he's doing!' he pleaded. 'Honestly, that's the part of this I can't figure out at all!'

'Everyone can see what he's doing,' roared Pankaj. He swung his feet off the desk, stamping the floor. 'He won't stop maligning me! I've never even met the little prick! In my fifty years in this town, I haven't seen such pettiness! I tell you what, he doesn't deserve half the sympathy he's been getting! Whoever beat him up that time was justified. I don't care what any of you say about it! I'd punch his fucking lights out myself!'

He let loose a volley of expletives in Hindi.

'You reckon he's doing this because of that thing you tweeted?' Jatin enquired desperately. 'About him being a drama queen?'

'God knows! Maybe he wants to fuck the girl himself! It's pathetic, whatever it is. And he was a damn drama queen! One producer drops out and you stop making films? Is that the courage of a film-maker? What are his credentials as a filmmaker anyway? One film—which was kiddish rubbish!'

'We can agree to disagree on that,' said Jatin, bridling; for in no circumstances could he pass over a difference of opinion. 'I think he is a wonderful talent, and I think he was very unfairly treated by Ritesh Azad. And he obviously didn't deserve to be beaten up by those god-man's goons. You know that too; you're just angry right now—which I understand. But that doesn't mean—'

'This is the reason you're a failure yourself.' Pankaj's smile was stirring with malice. 'You're a drama queen yourself, Jatin. You crib and complain about everything, and you always have. Naturally, you amount to nothing. You're a failed novelist, a failed film-maker.'

'You're angry,' said Jatin, his body trembling in the little chair that he occupied, while the older man watched fixedly from above. 'We can agree to disagree,' he said again. 'I came here to try to help you.'

'I'm not hearing anything helpful!' laughed Pankaj.

'I wanted to tell you that I'm going to take this up with Ahishor! If he is really just taking revenge for your tweet... well I can't believe that! I'm going to confront him!'

'Do that then. Call him to heel. He's mobilizing all the crybabies against me. It's driving me mad.'

'I will,' said Jatin. 'I'll do it.'

'Do it now!' Pankaj leaned forward, slamming his bare palms on the surface of the desk. The whisky shook and spilled. But his own mouth was quivering too. Wisps of white hair fell, straggling, about his gaunt face. In the seizure of his passion, he looked old and weak, as he never did in repose.

'Or are you a failure of a friend as well?'

Jatin reached quickly for his glass to down it.

'Go now!' Pankaj thundered on. 'Did you come here only to finish my whisky? You've got a nerve! You're the guy who's been talking this chap up! It's people like you who've emboldened him! I ought to curse the day I ever met you!'

Paralyzed, with his arm outstretched, Jatin Khanna looked close to tears. His voice emerged huskily and full of contrition.

'I'm going to find him right away. Please don't... I'll fix this for you. Trust me—please.'

The old man settled back into his chair, staring intently. He kept staring until, as though freshly whipped, Jatin started, and got to his feet. His gaze was rooted to the floor, like a guilty child's. Then he rushed to the door.

He was sweating by the time he was back in his car, in the shade of the trees outside the bungalow. Taking out his phone, he called Ahishor, and was informed (as he had been the previous day) that the 'number he was trying to reach was out of coverage area'. Jatin screamed and raised the instrument as though to smash it to pieces against the steering. Before he could do this, however, he looked up to see if the guard at the gate was watching, in which case he would divert his ire towards him. But the man, seated on his steel chair, had dozed off. He looked funny with his mouth open. For a moment, the watchman's cap dangled from his limp grip, and then dropped freely to the grass.

A breeze blew in from the direction of the road. Suddenly, Jatin reached a determination, which both surprised and somehow softened him. He decided to call Sasha.

A Conversion

Fifteen minutes previously, Sasha had stepped out of his flat on an aimless but necessary walk. Like every other day, he had been thinking furiously. And yet, he did not know whether he ought to be anxious at all, or whether it was only a pathological impulse that had been acting upon him for weeks.

For it had been weeks now. Outwardly, he had been entirely idle—yet he thought all day about Ruhi, Ahishor, Sushant, me, Jatin—about all of us—with a compulsiveness that alternately energized and drained him. (In a different category were his thoughts of Maithili. Those were blanketed by an overpowering pain.)

His feelings, I think, were analogous to those of an author who, in the midst of writing a book, broods over the fate of his or her characters. Yet the analogy only goes so far. Sasha took little aesthetic interest in any of us. His worry was somewhat maternal—though perhaps more analytical than that word suggests. Sitting by himself, staring at the sea, he would imagine, for example, what Ruhi was feeling, what Ahishor was doing, and why Jatin was given over to fits of rage. And then he would imagine what he might say to them if they were in front of him, which would be good for them. All the while he wondered if he was vastly presumptuous, a busybody whom everybody despised, and pathetic and dysfunctional, moved only by the movements of others, like floating weed. He did not, therefore, call or meet a soul. But he could not cease praying for each one.

His solitude was interrupted once every day, by the arrival of the maid. Her name was Kaushalya. She was a short and rotund Nepali woman who, in consequence of a malnourished childhood, early osteoporosis and having to fend for herself in a foreign country ever since her teenage, looked and behaved much older than she was. In the first few months at Sasha's flat, she had been strict and voluble, pointing frequently to a shortage of supplies in the kitchen and upbraiding him for his general lack of interest in housekeeping. He was too abstracted to pay her much heed; besides, she was meant to be working. But by and by, they had grown friendlier. Kaushalya's sternness had proved to be all on the surface, while her talkativeness was obviously an emotional need. She was soft-hearted and given to worrying about the well-being of everyone she worked for, as well as her own. She was never, in fact, far from tears. They spoke frequently about happenings in the area, though the news that she brought was invariably morbid and it was usually up to Sasha to bring to their conversations an antidote of cheer.

That morning, Kaushalya had entered the house in a weighty silence and turned to the kitchen without a word. Forty minutes later, Sasha was still reading in bed, when she entered the room with a broom and dustpan, and uttered a loud sigh.

'What's the matter?' asked Sasha dutifully.

'A man killed himself in Prestige Apartments. He jumped.'

'Really?'

'I'm not lying!' she exclaimed. 'You can check on the computer!'

'I'm just surprised,' explained Sasha. 'I'm not saying you're lying. You always talk about lying.'

'Because you think I'm lying always!' she cried.

Her speech was typically loud and excitable, in bespoke Hindi that was harshly accented. It took time to get used to; but Sasha was now accustomed to it.

'He used to do shooting work,' continued Kaushalya. 'The woman who works at his house lives next door to me. She told me herself. All the police was there yesterday.'

'Yes, that is sad,' said Sasha, sitting up among the pillows. 'Many people are sad, who work in films. It's an uncertain business. It's difficult to tell what's going to happen to you.'

'His friends ought to have helped him.' She was standing still; the broom just an appendage.

Sasha shrugged. 'In this city, it's not easy to have friends. I mean, there are lots of people, but not many friends. But you're right,' he said suddenly, 'his friends should have tried their best... What happened?'

She had collapsed onto the chair near the window, still clutching the broom and pan.

'My brother is leaving Mumbai,' said Kaushalya.

'You have a brother?'

'You know him; I brought him here that day to clean the fans. Yes, I call him my brother,' she nodded. 'He is from Kathmandu...' She sighed and looked at the floor, which her dangling feet did not reach. Her eyes were puffy.

'He's gone back now. I have nobody here... I have nobody here.'

'You have some people,' said Sasha.

'I haven't been to Nepal in eight years. I haven't spoken to anyone at home for the last four—no, five—it's been four or five years at least. Earlier I used to have their numbers written down and sometimes, I would phone them. Now all the numbers have changed.'

She began to mumble inarticulately, and then started to sob. Though he knew her mood would pass, Sasha was disquieted. Worry—like something forgotten, yet ever-present—was taking hold of him too. His heart tightened in his chest.

'Yes... yes...' he said gently. 'But Mumbai is your home now. You have to keep going forward.'

Kaushalya continued to sob. (It passed Sasha's mind that though she always talked loudly, she always cried softly.) After some time, she removed a handkerchief from the pocket of her dress and dabbed at her eyes.

'Your dress looks nice,' said Sasha.

He was not pretending. She was wearing a striking magenta gown with embroidered sequins, which he had never seen on her before. It was a grand, flowing piece of clothing, redolent of matriarchs and priestesses.

Kaushalya made a noise (he guessed) of thanks, with her face still averted. Soon he saw that she had begun to pray—her lips were moving; her eyes closed gravely. A few deep breaths later, she appeared composed. She turned her head and stared at the sea, sometimes glancing at the neighbouring building.

Men were at work there, renovating the old structure tearing down and fortifying the outer walls. Every now and then, the prolonged crackle of falling debris would strike through the rest of the day-time sounds. But it was a pleasant interruption—not unmusical, nor even unmeaningful (or so it seemed to Sasha).

'I have changed my dharm[4],' announced Kaushalya.

'What?' he wondered aloud. 'What do you mean, "changed your dharm"?'

'I'm a Christian now,' she said, mangling the word horribly. 'Yesterday, I took all my gods and goddesses to the sea and consigned them to the waters. I said to them, "Sorry, but you are not working for me, so please forgive me." And I said goodbye! Did I do wrong?'

Sasha shook his head automatically, though he was filled only with a curious amusement.

'I have been praying to them for so long. But I still keep falling sick. My body still aches. You know how much I am spending on medicine. So I thought, why not try something new? She told me about the pastor [it took Sasha another moment to parse this pronunciation]. So I went to see him.'

'"She" told you? Who's "she"?'

'Bhaiyya[5], you don't listen! The woman who works at Prestige.'

'Oh, the same one?'

'The pastor said I should stop praying to my old idols. He told me the truth about Isah. Now every Sunday, I will go to mass in Veera Desai. Veera Desai, yes, that's where the church is. The pastor said if I go for two months regularly, they'll give me one kilo rice, one kilo onions and tomatoes, and one litre oil for free. Isn't that nice? They are helpful people. They care.'

'Well, I hope so. Christianity is a great religion, it's true,' said Sasha. He was reminded suddenly of a sweet-smelling, yellowing copy of the Bible, that he had found in the bookshelf in the

---

[4]In this case, 'dharm' means 'religion'.
[5]Sir

living room of his father's old house in Dehradun. As a child, he had tried and failed to read it, but always particularly respected it. No doubt its dark red, textured cover and golden lettering had impressed him. Yet there had been other venerable books on that shelf, which he had not handled so carefully.

'Only you mustn't expect any magic cure for your health.'

'Yes, I know,' said Kaushalya. She was sounding enthusiastic now. 'Bhaiyya, I will have a Christmas dinner soon. You will come, won't you?'

'Alright! But Christmas is already over.'

'But I was not a Christian then. So I want to do something now. I'll tell you when I will do it. Alright?'

With renewed energy, she got up and began to sweep the floor.

He had expended no energy in judging Kaushalya's conversion, or the motives of her pastor. It seemed beside the point—though *what* the point was, he couldn't exactly say either. Nevertheless, something about the story elevated Sasha's mood. He felt, through the day, a layer of urgency and significance added to his worries about us all, which halted their descent into doubt and self-loathing. Perhaps it was that word—pastor—and what it signified. There had come upon him the distinct sense that he was on the right track, and, moreover, that a crucial moment of decision was near.

He was marching quickly down the pavement, walking off his excitement and fatigue, when his phone rang. Sasha stared at the name flashing on the display, but it disappeared before he could answer. He called back. After the third ring, came a gruff and hesitant 'hello'.

'Hi Jatin, you called?' asked Sasha.

'Yes, sorry, are you busy? You have a minute?'

'I'm taking a walk, but I'm not busy.'

'Are you sure? Otherwise, we can talk later.'

'We can talk now,' Sasha assured him. His step had slowed; he was near a fast-food joint with a pleasant hubbub of people outside. Their faces were animated, eager and involved in one another. He remained quiet while Jatin spoke.

'I just want to apologize for that day. I was out of line. I had no business to lose my temper to that extent. Yes, there are issues I have with you, Sasha. I find you, at times, unbearably sanctimonious. But I know you have issues with me too. And we should have been able to handle our disagreement in a reasonable way. And I take responsibility for that not happening. Listen, can you hear me, or should I call later?'

'I can hear you fine, Jatin,' Sasha was hurrying away from the knots of people; he lingered behind a bus stop, as though to shield himself from the traffic noises.

'Not to make excuses, but I have been going through a lot of shit. Work-wise, as you know. But most of all, in my personal life, which I haven't ever told you about. But I'll tell you in the future—when we meet; I hope we will meet. I want a chance to rectify this.'

'We will meet, of course,' said Sasha. He felt a flush coming over him and was flooded with emotion. 'Of course. Thanks for calling, Jatin.'

'One thing I want to say is that you're a very good person, and a very smart person. Though sometimes I doubt the "smart person" part! No, I'm just kidding! But honestly, you are one of the most decent people I know. You are really, exceptionally decent. And I'm a good judge of people, if nothing else! At least *usually* I am. But in your case, I *know* I am. I don't want to lose our friendship. So, I just wanted to call and apologize. Unconditionally... Wait, can you hear me at all?'

'Yes, very clearly,' Sasha replied. 'Thanks for saying that, Jatin. I value our friendship a lot as well. I also know what you mean about my being sanctimonious sometimes. I'm trying to fix that—or to avoid giving that impression.'

'I'm sure you will! That's where your smartness will help you! And let's meet soon. I just need to sort out a couple of things. By the way, have you spoken to Ahishor recently? You've been following what's happening, right? Where have you been anyway? What have you been doing?'

'I have—I've been following what's happening,' said Sasha. He felt a surge of excitement, and then, maintaining the discipline of restraint, was left teeming with anticipation. 'But I haven't spoken to anyone.'

'Well, let's meet soon. I could do with a dose of sanity in my life! How's Monday for you? Either Monday or Tuesday? I'll call and fix up, ok? Thanks… Thanks Sasha.'

'Thanks for calling,' said Sasha, once more.

'I'm glad I called. I feel better now. Thanks again, bye… Bye, bye!'

Putting away his phone, Sasha took a long, trembling breath. He sighed, feeling his heart lightening every moment. He walked forward without knowing it, effortlessly, as though he were walking on air. The smile on his lips refused to dislodge. He noticed himself being looked at strangely, and, still buoyant and breathless, found the pathway to the beach, where the open space dispersed the traffic of people. It was the sunset hour. A golden hue had fallen over the world. In Sasha's breast was occurring some magic play—such movements of his soul, as he wrote down, late that night, in his journal:

I felt as though some powerful essence had flowed into me—and just as a glass jar filled with water can withstand the weight of the ocean, so I now felt I could not be denied. I had a purpose among those faces on the road. They needed me, as the flock needs the shepherd. They may hate me for a time, but only as all authority is hated; yet ultimately, if it be real authority, it is respected and sought out. As I strode to the beach, my happiness was soaring. I felt I had only to speak to whomsoever I chose—and they would come around to my side, sooner or later. For in essence, they were putty in my hands. Such was my power. A power all the more profound for passing unrecognized and misunderstood. I would use it, of course, for good! I was determined to do good. I said so aloud, to the sea, as I reached it.

Then I gazed about at the rocks—the people sitting or strolling, the children playing, the horses standing, the big towers on the skyline, the sky enflamed by the setting sun, the waves gathering afar and ever beyond... A panic set upon me slowly. My great mood was deflating, as though leaking from some gap in me, which I could not stopper, though I was desperate. But I could not find it; I could not even begin to. I closed my eyes.

I prayed to you, oh God. You, who have given me everything, without whom I am nothing and am capable of doing nothing; no, not the slightest good at all! I prayed for your strength, to keep me from wretchedness and hubris alike. I thank you and ask for your forgiveness.

Afterwards, when Sasha walked by the breakers, memories of Maithili (I imagine) must have awakened within him. On just such an evening, by the setting sun, he had first caught sight of her. And sure enough, there, once again, was a pale young girl standing in the surf! His heart must have leaped for a moment, before he perceived that this was only a young child. She was dressed, however, like a woman, in a faded dress with flower patterns and curlicues, which showed her white neck and limbs. A bulky beige handbag was slung over her shoulder. She was standing still, with her head bowed—exactly as he had stood when he prayed.

Little Elena

She was crying. When she raised her head, her lips were still quivering and her mascara trailed from her eyes to her cheeks. She had full, white cheeks and big, glistening eyes with long lashes, which were, at present, hung with drops of tears. Her hair was light brown, and grew, thick with curls, to her shoulders. It was an angelic face; nonetheless for being unhappy.

Suddenly she caught sight of Sasha looking, and frowned and pouted furiously. He stepped forward at once.

'Are you alright?'

An angry remark seemed to fly to the girl's lips, but she said nothing, and instead, stared back at Sasha with silent and wary scrutiny.

'Are you alone?' he asked. The girl nodded, never shifting her stare.

'You're alone! Did something happen just now? What happened? Maybe I can help.'

'Bloody Indians,' she said distinctly. She spoke with a strong, East European accent. 'They are bloody cheats!'

It was impossible to be offended, for inconsistent with the

general denunciation was the plaint in her eyes, that she held out to him.

'What happened?' he asked.

The girl continued to stare, until her eyes (they were green, like little lakes) clouded over with confusion and pain. Soon her tears were returning, but she grimaced and kept them away. Then, biting her lip, she dropped her head. Sasha followed her gaze, which appeared suddenly to have become interested in a seashell stuck in the sand, just beyond the reach of the tide.

He bent to pick it up, and at the same instant, a phone rang. When Sasha looked up, the girl was rummaging through her bag, her face screwed up in impatience, which turned to exasperation when she discovered who was calling. Then followed the astonishment of hearing her speak in coarse, practised Hindi.

She was telling off the person at the other end of the line for calling belatedly and not giving her the time to do what she was being asked to.

'*Main baahar hoon; Internet slow hai! Tumhe rukna padega!*'[6]

No sooner was the call over, she immersed herself in some task on her phone. She was concentrating fiercely, oblivious to the world, including Sasha.

It was a very big world, from the sea to the city, and it was darkening by the minute. *She could not*, thought Sasha, *be older than fifteen or sixteen.*

'You can use the Internet at my house,' he told her.

She looked up askance, hopping simultaneously, for the water had surged up to where they stood. Sasha could not help smiling.

---

[7]I am out; the Internet is slow! You will have to wait!

'I live right here,' he explained.

'I need to send photos to the guy for event. Net on phone is slow!'

'Yes. So, come. It's no problem. By the way, my name is Sasha. And yours?'

'Sasha is a name from my country!' Her face had lit up, with a smile full of shyness and curiosity. 'You are not from Ukraine!'

'Oh no, I'm not! But my father was very fond of Russia. Especially… he loved Russian literature. So he chose this name for me.'

'Sasha!' She was thrilled. Even with the tears drying on her cheeks, she was suddenly bursting with delight, carried on fresh waves of vitality, the triumphant gift of her yet-present childhood. She gazed at Sasha and he half blushed at her frankness and innocence. Simultaneously, his heartbeat quickened. Till a moment ago he had been free, but he could not, any longer, walk away.

'You still haven't told me your name.'

'Oh sorry! I am Elena.'

'Nice to meet you, Elena.' He put out his hand, and she, suddenly bashful, shook it with endearing grace.

Enquiring eyes rested upon them as they made their way, among thickening traffic and the first lights of the night, to the gates of his apartment. She walked very quickly on high heels, with a grave, set expression visible in the midst of her make-up. *She was such an odd creature,* thought Sasha—*dolled-up, yet plainly a child, and a foreign girl to boot. It was startling to think of her alone in the city. But there were all kinds in Mumbai, and many children working the jobs of adults.* The passers-by only looked, and passed by.

Inside his flat, he led her straight to the computer. He then went to the kitchen to pour out two glasses of water. Elena was quiet until she had finished sending the email. Then she drank all the water, put down the empty glass and turned on Sasha's swivel-chair to face him.

'Thank you.' She made a brief bow.

'Finished your work?'

'Yes. I had to send pictures of girls to the coordinator, for event in Delhi. Bloody Internet wasn't working on my phone!'

'What kind of event?'

'Oh, a wedding. They need foreign girls to play the dhol. I coordinate from our end.'

'The wedding organizers want foreign girls to play the dhol? Do you play the dhol too?'

'Sometimes. Not just dhol. Sometimes holding flowers on trays, sometimes dancing. There are other events too. It's the season now. But it's nothing bad,' she added gravely. 'Foo! (her phone had rung, prompting the exclamation) Ankit, *maine photos bhej diye!*[7]' she screamed uninhibitedly into the instrument. '*Chaar ladkiyan arrange kiya hai maine! Check karo apna email!*[8]'

'It does sound a little bad,' smiled Sasha, a moment later, 'Arranging *chaar ladkiyan*[9] and all that!'

'But it's not like that!' Elena grinned merrily. A red tint was appearing over her cheeks. 'It's only events! But ya, sometimes it happens! I'm on the phone in cafe talking to coordinator, and everyone looks at me, like who is this girl!'

'How old are you?' asked Sasha.

---

[7] I have sent the photos!
[8] I have arranged for four girls! Check your email!
[9] four girls

She stopped smiling at once.

'Nineteen.'

'You're not nineteen.'

'Why are you asking? It's rude to ask this to a lady!'

Her eyes were flashing, and they began to dart around the flat, as though searching for a speedy getaway.

'You're right; I'm sorry.' He persisted, 'Why were you crying on the beach though? Was it because you needed to send this email and the Internet wasn't working?'

'Foo! No! How silly!'

'Then why?'

'Because... Because I came to Mumbai and now there is no work! Bloody casting guy cheated me!'

Gradually, she revealed the whole story. A man purporting to be a casting agent in Bollywood had found her on a social networking site, and urged her to come down from Delhi, where she lived, to Mumbai, for a week. He had promised several auditions for movies and ads, as well as a hotel to stay in. But having extracted half his quoted fee on the day she arrived, he had taken her to precisely one audition, and then disappeared.

Having confided this to Sasha, a sudden reserve passed over Elena's young face, quite altering it. She began, with a deep frown, to question him.

'What do you do? Are you also working in films? Do you have any work? Any friends who can give work?'

She spoke of 'work' with a terribly earnest regard, which was both droll and discomfiting.

'I don't work in films, but I have friends who do,' Sasha was thinking hard as he replied. 'Yes, I can introduce you to them... About me, what am I doing? Well, these days I'm mostly studying. Just studying by myself, I mean.'

'I've studied by myself too,' Elena put in eagerly. 'With my... my Indian uncle. We used to read many books at home.'

Suddenly, she jumped from the chair (it went gliding backwards from the shock) and went haring towards Sasha's bookshelf.

'Exupéry!' cried Elena, pulling forth his copy of *The Little Prince*. 'He is my favourite!' Her eyes roved greedily through the stacks of books. 'Wow, you have many good books! I was reading this one too!' She had extracted Simone De Beauvoir's *The Second Sex*. 'It's a sign of a person who has a pure heart!'

'Is it really?' laughed Sasha. 'I'm not sure that's true. I know plenty of well-read people who are not pure at all. Hey! Why are you looking like that?'

She had turned and fixed him with a strange, fierce glare, which, by and by, seemed to creep inwards, filling her face with doubt. Without another word, she began putting the books back into the shelves, and then collapsed, as though physically shoved, onto a mattress alongside. The muscles of her face were working visibly; it seemed she was holding back her emotions with enormous effort. Picking up a cushion, Elena hugged it to her breast.

Sasha did not know what to say, and so, remained quiet. He heard her breathing in a harsh rhythm. Her gaze had turned blank and hopeless, as of one staring into an abyss. He was flooded with the desire to comfort her, to tell her that never in this world were such expressions warranted! Eventually, he rose, picked up her empty glass and took it to the kitchen to refill it. When he re-entered the living room, he found her looking, expectantly, towards the kitchen door. His heart tightened with warmth.

'Drink some more water, Elena... Here... So this is your first day in Mumbai! I guess it's been quite a day! What about eating some food? Would you like some? You must be hungry.'

'I'll eat later, at my friend's house,' she said, after several thoughtful sips of water. 'I have friends in Malad; that's where I left suitcase in the morning. That time agent said I would shift to hotel in the evening, but now there is no hotel! So I'll stay in Malad I guess.'

'Are you sure? Are they people you trust?'

'Ya, ya,' she spoke absently. Uncertain, Sasha sat in front of her. He was straining forward, his gaze fastened upon her. He felt a wild urge to offer the girl every favour of board and lodging, but the fear of frightening her (and a certain dizziness of his own) restrained him. She was still thoughtful, swallowing at intervals and staring at nothing in particular.

Suddenly, she looked up at Sasha, focussing again, as though taking fresh stock of him.

'Alright, I'll eat,' she said. 'What do you have to eat?'

Her voice was patient and even indulgent. He answered eagerly, thrilling to this strange note in it. 'I have roti, dal and aloo ki sabzi. Dahi. Then there's also bread and cheese. And chocolate biscuits—but that you should have later.'

'Ok, I'll have roti and sabzi,' nodded Elena. 'Thank you, Sasha.'

'You're welcome!'

'Will you eat too?'

'No, I'm not hungry. I'll eat later.'

*   *   *

He watched her unabashedly. They had changed positions. Elena was up on the chair with a little table in front of her, where she could put her plate. Sasha sat cross-legged on the mattress, close to her feet, gazing up. She ate in a funny way, rolling up the roti and biting it, and scooping up the sabzi separately with her spoon. When he remarked on this, she uttered a sigh of resignation, though he had been smiling as he spoke.

'I know it's not how you eat,' she spoke sorrowfully, with a self-pity that was wildly unmerited and (by the same token) moving. 'I try to eat it my way. It all mixes up inside anyway... Happy?' she said, taking up a piece of potato in a piece of roti.

'Eat as you are comfortable,' said Sasha firmly.

When she had finished (she had eaten everything, leaving nothing on the plate), he brought her a chocolate biscuit. This she consumed with a relish that (like her many attitudes) was quite out of proportion. Licking her lips, she looked at Sasha, with delight pouring from her green eyes.

'This is a wonderful biscuit! Thank you very much! ... Oh no, one is enough, thank you, I'll have more later!'

'Tell me,' pleaded Sasha, 'what brought you here. To India, I mean. Tell me everything about yourself, please. Your whole story.'

Elena smiled and nodded wisely. 'Alright, I will,' she said, with the same air of bestowing largesse upon an unequal, which struck secret, thrilling chords inside Sasha. Knitting her brows as though straining to remember, she laughed suddenly, was embarrassed momentarily, sat tongue-tied, unsure of how to begin, and then, looking steadfastly down at the table, with occasional frank glances at Sasha, told him in a muddled but determined fashion:

'When I was little, I was performing on all the stages in Europe. Since I was eight. I was doing beauty pageants and dance performances. Dancing is my first love, even before cinema. I used to travel with my mother. My father didn't live with us, except for one year when my mother sent me to live with him. He had drinking problem. Then my mother started working at the Indian Embassy. In Kiev, my home town. So she started working there and meantime I was learning Indian classical dance, Bharatanatyam... Also at the Embassy, yes... But I already loved Indian movies by then. Both of us and my grandmom and my godmom also, we all used to watch them. At that time, I thought they were the best movies in the world! Foo! I was very young! Haanji[10], little bit—I learned little bit of Hindi from them! But then properly I learned Hindi in Delhi. So, like that... Actually, my parents didn't want me to become a dancer or actor. I mean they wanted—but not all the time. Not *professionally*, thank you, that's the right word. They wanted I should go to college and get good education. They are both educated themselves. Mom is a journalist and Dad was a maths teacher before he began drinking. But there was no money for my college. And then one very bad thing happened. Oh it was very bad—Oh God, oh God, why did you punish me?'

Clasping her hands, she let them fall to her lap, and stared straight ahead of her, while gradually becoming teary-eyed. With a sad smile, she continued:

'I got admission to college in America. It was for acting course in the New York Film Academy! They were giving scholarship also. But my visa was rejected. I don't know why. Maybe because not enough money in the bank. They thought I will run away! I don't know... I was very disappointed; it would have changed my whole life. Then suddenly many things happened—and I came to India!'

She looked, in the same moment, joyful and shy, and seemed to be waiting for encouragement. Suddenly Sasha could not restrain a certain thought:

---

[10]Yes Sir

'You're a child!' he cried. 'You can't be older than sixteen.'

'I will be seventeen in May,' she admitted. 'But don't tell anyone. Then people don't take me seriously! That's why I don't like to talk about my age.'

Her cheeks were apple-red and her eyes were whole skies of innocence, across which, like flashing storms or gentle rain, her various moods appeared and then were gone again. Her lips drooped and unconsciously parted, as she looked Sasha full in the face, with that grave attentiveness that fitted her most naturally. *She was only sixteen! He had guessed so already—but now to think of it!*

'How did you come to India?' he asked. 'And how has it been here? How have *you* been here?'

'How have I been!' she exclaimed. 'I don't know! Here I am! With no work! Ha ha!' She play-acted a look of mourning and then laughed again in self-reproach of her theatrics, forgetting what he had asked. Sasha repeated the question.

'Oh, India happened because of my Indian Uncle!' said Elena. 'It was his idea. He was a friend of my mother, working in the Embassy in Kiev. They were friends; he used to come home sometimes. Meet me too. He already knew me from my dance shows. But after the visa got rejected, he got this idea that I should come to India with him, because he had to go back anyway and he could help me with Indian visa. So that I could study more in India and he was gonna pay and all that. Mom was happy actually... Actually first she was happy, then later she was not happy. But I grabbed the chance! India was also a dream to me! So like that, I came. On the plane to Delhi.'

Full of memories, she smiled dreamily at Sasha, but then, although he had said nothing, her smile crept away of its own accord. All the while, a breeze had been blowing in from the windows. It was not cold, but she shivered and once again began to look tensely about the room. Sitting not far from her feet, Sasha noticed her toes digging into the rug spread on the floor. He put aside his curiosity and turned his head away, so that she could be free from all scrutiny.

'Accha, what about your friends?' asked Elena. She had sat up straight in the chair, and was frowning. 'You said you have friends who have work?'

'Yes, I have some.'

'Like who? Film directors? I'm interested in doing films or ads, rather than modelling.'

'I know some people,' said Sasha evenly. 'There's one friend of mine—Malik. He's not made a film yet, but he's a writer and director. And I know Ahishor Frances, if you've heard of him.'

'Ahishor Frances!' She gaped. 'Man, of course I've heard; he is my favourite! *Schrodinger's Cat*, I loved that film. I even blogged about it, and then the same day—can you imagine—I saw him at a mall in Saket! Ahishor! I thought it's like a sign from God!'

'I don't know him very closely,' Sasha said. 'Also, as you would know, he's decided to stop making films.'

'Gosh, I read that, but is that really true?' Her excitement was untrammelled; she was laughing and blushing. 'Maybe he needs to find the right heroine? Haha! I'm just joking! But how to meet him? I don't want to be simply another girl who wants a role! Also don't tell him anything about my age!'

'We'll see what's best,' said Sasha, a trifle curtly. 'Anyway, you're saying he's in Delhi now.'

'I don't know if he's still there. I had spotted him about two weeks ago. Gosh, that was amazing!'

Sasha was silent, distracted for the first time since the meeting at the beach. The news of Ahishor's being in Delhi was playing on his mind, clamouring for his attention. There had come upon him a desire (familiar and compelling) to be alone, to think over all that was happening, in a bath of darkness and solitude.

Elena was staring expectantly. She was fresh-faced and strangely calm, as though her bout of excitement had washed her worries clean away.

'So then, who else?' she demanded. 'We can meet someone else?'

She was gazing down at him, with her arms folded. Her feet were now tapping on the floor. A moment later, when he continued to be silent, the girl raised an eyebrow and a smile broke out on Sasha's face, clearing his mind joyously.

'Come with me now,' he said, getting up. 'We'll go meet Malik right away!'

A Stormy Evening

Even as Sasha was walking down Versova beach in Mumbai, to where Elena stood crying, Ahishor was stepping out of a barsaati[11] in Jangpura, New Delhi, into an evening of impending rain and thunder. He had been working all afternoon. His laptop now rested on the bed; newspapers and magazines lay in thick piles on the floor. A television set (which he switched on every day for the nine o'clock news and the heated debates that ensued) was the only other item that occupied the little room on the roof.

Only two doorways away was Mihir's well-furnished apartment, but Ahishor had insisted, against all pleading, on inhabiting the place that had been built for servants.

He was smoking as he strolled over to the parapet. He looked somewhat sloppy, as always, but also relaxed, in loose red shorts and a faded black T-shirt. He had put on some weight, which looked well on him. No one, merely by looking at him, could have guessed what lay within.

For he was in an extraordinary state, thinking hard and

---

[11]a small rooftop room

deep, and writing down exactly as he thought, holding back nothing. He felt (almost) as though he could not stop the process, but could only sit tight on a giddying mental ride that was leading him from revelation to revelation, like milestones on a marvellous road. In any case, he had no desire to stop it. There was a picture forming in his head, which was growing brighter and sharper with every news headline he read, with all the freshly revived convictions of his own experience, and even the things he sighted as he looked down now, over the battery of grimy white walls and barren rooftops.

It was a dying and doomed city. The buildings were petty; there was no inspiration in them. The paint was peeling wherever one looked. The terraces were marred with heavy lines of shapeless laundry. The criss-crossing lanes were hemming each other in. There was the usual scurrying and scampering going on in the marketplaces. Within their stifling rooms, people were breathing heavy sighs, burping and scratching themselves. Their eyes were vacant with inertia and an endless learned monotony, interrupted now and then (though in truth, only continued) by outbreaks of barbaric passion, as when they burst crackers, or beat their wives. And it was the same everywhere.

The crawl of the right wing all over the country, was, he knew, only one of those low passions, writ large. And it too was doomed, for it was the very father of doom. Then Ahishor's heart quickened mysteriously, as he heard the wail of the muezzin, calling over the rooftops, like a dirge for them all. A smile came to his lips. It was the twilight hour—the time of day when, often in the past, he had laid down on his bed, steeped in melancholy and inarticulate fears. But now, he was coursing with energy, all in readiness for an unthinkable victory. His fists were clenched by his sides and irritation flooded through him, taking, in its sweep, various fragmented thoughts of people he knew and had known, and things that had been said and done and prophesized. He set his gaze on the dark clouds on the horizon. It pleased him to listen to the thunder. Soon there would be rain.

Presently, he turned and saw that he was not alone. Mihir was coming quickly towards him, in his inexorable, rolling gait, and there was a girl keeping pace beside him. She was square-built and short-haired. With a strange jolt, he recognized Anamika.

'Are you free now?' asked Mihir. 'Come inside.' Though his voice was eager as he approached Ahishor, there was also a note of deference.

'Hey, you've changed,' said Anamika. 'You look different.' She too spoke with a marvelling sincerity.

'It's been a while,' he said to her. 'I *hope* I have changed.'

'Come inside,' beckoned Mihir. 'Anyway, it's going to rain. We ordered kebabs and I'm opening the wine. Oh by the way—your mother called on your phone about an hour ago. I told her you were busy—like you asked me to.'

'That's fine.'

As they crossed to the terrace door, Mihir added casually: 'The police have filed an FIR against Pande. He's going to be arrested anytime now.'

'And then will he get bail?' asked Ahishor sharply.

'Not for a while. Too much outrage has built up already.' Saying so, Mihir jutted out his lower lip, lifted his bushy eyebrows and cast a doleful look towards Ahishor, who smiled and continued to smile as they made their way indoors. Then, however, he became grave, quietly helping to carry the wine and kebabs to the drawing room, while Mihir, with a bright face and gleaming eyes, chattered on.

'I don't think he expected that anything would actually happen to him. Don't you think he would never have expected it? I would like to see his face when the cops come calling! He must have thought it would blow over just on Twitter and Facebook. These people are so pompous, Anamika, I tell you. They're used to getting away with everything. Everyone accuses me of loving that generation too much. But if that were true, I wouldn't have done this to Pankaj Pande. I only love the good people. I love good people of all generations...'

They had sat down around a table in his drawing room, with plates and glasses atop it. 'If you're not at the table, you're on the menu! Hahaha! Isn't that a nice saying? I want to say it every time I sit down to eat. It'll be like a prayer. Better than saying grace, *hai na*[12]? More appropriate!'

'Shush,' said Anamika, smiling. 'Why can't you ever be serious?'

'I am always serious about serious matters! Ask Ahishor if I'm not serious!'

Ahishor smirked and bit into a kebab. Chewing, he looked steadily from Anamika to Mihir, who was now breathing indignantly.

'I hate Pankaj Pande!' Mihir cried. 'I detest such people! Bloody rapist! Crook! He struts about like a king, airing his views like a lord. What has he ever achieved? He's not a great artist. He's not even rich. Do you know how he really makes a living? He makes ads for underwear and fruit juice brands. It's a fact. He is no great artist. Has he ever won anything at Cannes? Or anywhere important? He never deserved his reputation.'

'Mihir is a wonder,' said Ahishor, smirking again. 'He is less

[12]isn't it

angry that Pande is a rapist—or a sexual harasser, one should say, to be fair. He is more angry that he was overrated as a film-maker.'

'No! I'm not more angry about that—but that is criminal too!' said Mihir. 'I value meritocracy! I may not know anything about Bollywood, but I do respect the parallel cinema movement of that era. Because it had integrity. And I think Pande just piggy-backed on it. I don't think I'm wrong in thinking that...'

'Why are you both laughing?' he asked, for both Anamika and Ahishor had started chuckling.

'You look like an apple,' said Anamika. 'You're *that* red. You're redder than a red velvet cupcake. Uff, now don't get more angry—you *are* a cupcake!'

Silenced thus, Mihir took a gulp of wine, and proceeded to eat. But his good spirits were evident in his appetite.

It had begun to rain. Soon the sound of the storm filled the air. Ahishor leaned back on the sofa and locked eyes with Anamika.

'How do you find India,' he asked, 'now that you're back?'

'It's not like it's the first time—' she started to say, and then broke off. She turned her head to one side. Her eyes had narrowed with disgust. 'I sure picked a good time to return.' Her voice was shrill. Then she turned again with a painful smile.

'The guard downstairs,' she said, 'every time I come and go from here, he looks at me like I'm this fallen woman. I know everyone isn't like that. But when you asked me that question just now—that's what I thought of!'

'People like us can no longer sit quietly.' Ahishor now looked from her to Mihir, who was eating with satisfaction, and back to Anamika.

'It's a historic moment. The right wing has every advantage

on its side. Patriarchy is in the seat of power. Conservatism has popular support. It also has the support of our traditions and our majority religion.'

'On a narrow interpretation,' suggested Mihir, between loving bites of meat.

Ahishor made a gesture of dismissiveness. 'Who are we kidding?' he spoke with distaste. 'The argumentative Indian—so says Amartya Sen—our great culture of debate was permitted only to those so authorized. The others—the lower castes—they had boiling oil poured into their ears for daring to listen in. So, fundamentally, it was not a culture of argument; it was a culture of authority.'

'That's not what you used to say,' Mihir pointed out absently. His eyes were still on his food.

'I know that. I used to extol the many-sidedness of Hindu traditions. Well, I've learnt better. We won't find any answers in our past, so let's stop trying. We have to understand very clearly that a new word must be spoken—a brand new word. And we are the ones who must speak it, because we are the only ones who've got it.'

'We?' asked Anamika.

'You and me and him. And all the liberals of India, of every generation. Though we are a tiny minority, we are perhaps not so powerless. (He raised his voice above the downpour outside.) We are indeed the cultural elite of India, and we must be the vanguard of cultural change. But we have always been cowardly. We have never flexed our muscles; we've let our strength atrophy. That's why we're now sitting around, wringing our hands, while even our traditional strongholds are simply taken from us. Look! Art and academia are plunging into an abyss. Science too. The country is sinking into an intellectual darkness, which will change it forever. Unless we act. We absolutely have to act!'

'I agree,' said Anamika, her eyes widening. 'I agree completely!' A series of emotions were passing over her face. She was first savouring Ahishor's words, then her own visions of the future, and then, in her rising excitement, growing anxious.

'But what can we do? Do you really think we can change anything?'

'Let each person do his or her bit,' said Ahishor. 'We will soon find out what is possible—and plenty is possible. Many things are on our side—the Constitution of India is on our side. The trouble is, we are not a unit. We, ourselves, are a house divided. How many liberals, who are now moaning and groaning on the Internet, voted for the right wing in the election? How many?'

His eyes were shining. He was sipping from his glass, his body at repose, but a tremor of pure emotion was travelling through him continually, which was discernible in the twitching of his mouth and hands.

'At that time, they only wanted to get rich. Now they realize the values they sacrificed—without getting any richer either, of course. But our real riches are our values. How many of us truly believe in them? Not Pankaj Pande! And he's only the latest dirty old hypocrite. There's been Tejpal. There's been Pachauri.'

'Yeah! What's with these men?' cried Anamika. 'It's so disappointing!'

'They grew smug,' said Ahishor, 'with their sense of modernity and progressiveness. They saw it as an accomplishment, rather than a responsibility. Whoever feels accomplished looks around for rewards. I'm sure Pande truly believed that no woman could say "no" to him. Especially not a younger woman of his own social class; surely she must admire him! He's been praised as a feminist, you know—by foolish people. They puffed up his pride even more. But that pride took him full circle—from chanting about freedom and consent, to violating it.'

'I am not as harsh as Mihir,' he continued. 'I believe Pande was a force for good—at some point. ('I liked some of his movies!' exclaimed Anamika) Yes, that's what makes this a pity. But like many of that generation, he atrophied—as I was saying before. After a point, he simply felt entitled to have a good time... Nobody should feel entitled,' he finished quietly.

But Anamika continued to look at him. She was nodding silently, moved by strange and unruly emotions. With darting eyes, she looked him over, and suddenly found herself fixated by Ahishor's bright red shorts. She was still smiling to herself, while he raised his eyebrows askance and brought his glass to his lips. Then suddenly, as if from nowhere, a thought came to her, plaguing and disturbing her. It was unremitting.

'So,' she asked hurriedly, 'have you been in touch with Maithili?'

Ahishor frowned. Anamika knew she was reopening old wounds, yet an uncontrollable sadness was coming over her. 'She's not been in touch with any of us. Not even her parents!'

He looked expressionlessly towards Mihir, who seemed, in turn, to be studying him closely.

'I don't know why I thought of her suddenly,' Anamika cried. 'I guess I just feel bad about the whole thing. Here we all are—and it's so good being together! I still don't know why she had to disappear.'

'I don't know why you bother,' said Ahishor, with his gaze still fixed on Mihir. 'Maithili was a bore. She was interested in nothing, because she herself was uninteresting in every way. Time is short and one has to move on. I'm sure you have more relevant people to talk about.'

'I know, you're right. I shouldn't think about her. I just—I want her to suffer! You shouldn't do this to people! Especially not to someone who did so much for you! I guess you understand; I know, I should forget about her. But I want her to learn a lesson! She's gone and joined a god-man, you know?'

Ahishor turned sharply. 'What do you mean?'

'Yes. She's back in India! She's in a god-man's ashram in Mahabalipuram.'

'What god-man?'

'Sadhguru-something… Narayanan… Sadhguru Narayanan is what he calls himself. My dad figured it out. She had a letter sent to her parents.'

The amazement was plain on Ahishor's face, but he beat it back with a look of scorn.

'Yes, I've heard of him,' he said. 'He's got a growing following, I believe—among fools. Well, I'm surprised she's back in India. I thought she would have stayed safely away. But I'm not surprised she's come back to something ridiculous like that.' He exhaled firmly. 'Anyway, as I said before, it's an irrelevant subject.'

The rain was falling steadily and long rumbles of thunder were still rolling across the night. It fell to Mihir to break the silence. He (who had never stopped eating throughout) now licked his fingers, while a smile crept onto his lips.

'I met somebody,' he said, dramatically.

'What do you mean?' asked Ahishor, with a meaningful look.

Mihir was momentarily horrified. 'I mean I met a great man. Fantastic man. Anamika knows! I met him via Uncle and Aunty. I want you to meet him too, Ahishor. I told him all about you. His name is Satish Dhawan! You haven't heard of him, right? He used to be with the UN long ago. Now he runs a strategy-slash-policy-slash-business consultancy. I mean, he's not well known to the aam janta[13], but he's a big, big shot. He's everywhere. And so full of life! Full of ideas; optimistic about the future! He's someone who genuinely believes that everything we take for granted about India right now, can change—and he knows how to get it done too! You must meet him.'

'Sounds very interesting,' said Ahishor. 'Sounds just like what we need.'

'Oh, he is! Trust me.'

A phone rang out, in insistent peals, from a far corner of the room. 'That's yours,' said Mihir. 'I had put it for charging. It'll be your mother calling again.'

With a grunt of annoyance, Ahishor got up. He returned soon to the centre of the room, holding the instrument to his ear. But there was something in his expression that made the other two alert.

'Yes, I'm listening,' were the only words he spoke between long periods of quiet (except for the rain without, whose cadence was unaltered). Finally, he said, 'I'll call you back.' Then he turned around with a strange, arresting fluency, like a dancer slowly pirouetting.

'That was Sushant.' He was staring at the wall above their heads, with unfathomable eyes. 'He says that Ruhi Khanna is dead.'

---

[13]common people

In the Pews

As Sasha arrived at Malik's apartment building, he started to experience pangs of doubt. Zohra Aghadi was a squat block of black window grills and stained outer walls, hemmed in by a narrow, dusty courtyard. Rubble and garbage lay in piles near the stairwells. When they approached the entrance, a huge rat came running out from the dirt, and disappeared into the caged cavern by the stairs where the electricity meters sat in sinister rows. But Elena showed little reaction and no horror, only nodding seriously when Sasha, trying to joke with her, suggested: 'Bloody India!'

'Malik is a truly nice person,' he had told her while coming. 'In a way, he embodies the best qualities of this place—Versova. He accepts new people with respect. Instead of being proud and judging them, he tries to learn from them. He watches and listens. He has a real talent for scriptwriting. And he works very hard. He is suffering in the film industry but that is no shame. I think he will help you. I want to surprise him; we shall drop in unannounced! I don't think he'll mind.'

Inside, Malik was sitting cross-legged on his mattress, in a vest and cargo shorts, banging away at his laptop, from which emanated loud strains of Hindustani classical music. Around him were two plastic chairs, a dusty shelf of old, plastic-bound scripts, and (incongruously) a gleaming mantelpiece with elaborate bric-a-brac (a brass Buddha, an ebony horse), which belonged to the owner of the house and had been left untouched by Malik. A ceiling fan was spinning at a brisk pace.

'Elena what?' he asked energetically, after Sasha had introduced them. 'What's your surname?'

'Hamolka.' She turned shyly towards Sasha as she spoke. 'Hamolka. It's our family name.'

'Very pleased to meet you Elena *Hamolka*!' said Malik, emphasizing the name and shaking her hand in a way that made her laugh.

'So, the question is,' asked Sasha, 'what kind of work should Elena look for? You know, about auditions and how and when they happen. Do advise her.'

'If you don't mind my asking,' Malik paused, thoughtfully, 'how old are you exactly?'

Elena glanced at Sasha, and then answered firmly, 'Seventeen.'

'Ok, so then a little bit more paper-work will be there, since you're not yet eighteen. But anyway, fuck that—I'm sorry, do excuse my language!—ehehehe!—actually, I'm a bit—ehehehe!—lost! I was inside this script *ki duniya*—the world of my script. Oh, do you speak Hindi? Very good! Wow! At your age, I was… I was doing nothing! I'll tell you what—I'll give you a few numbers of coordinators, who get jobs specially for foreign actors. And you should add yourself on some Facebook groups. You're on Facebook obviously? … Good good, I'll also add you—I'll do it now only!'

He sat himself back on the mattress, while they took the chairs. From the floor, he began to direct a further set of curious questions at Elena. She answered gamely, though somewhat guardedly, and in general terms. In between, she looked many times at Sasha, who smiled and nodded with reassurance.

'What about workshops?' asked Sasha. 'Elena can do some acting workshops too.'

'I want to,' she nodded at once.

'Wohkay!' Malik agreed. 'I will forward a Facebook message about workshops also.'

'Thank you very much!' Her hands lay crossed on her lap, while she gazed down at the large figure of Malik, half-dressed, typing and clicking and humming along to his music. She was beaming, full of secret smiles and very excited.

'Done!' said Malik. 'Sasha, *ek minute andar aa*[14].'

'What happened?'

'*Andar aa re!*[15] I want to show you something.'

In the kitchen, he turned and placed his hands on Sasha's shoulders. A grin had appeared on Malik's face, which, beneath the bright white tube light, appeared unshaven and lined from a lack of sleep.

'Tell me properly now,' he asked softly, 'what's going on?'

'Nothing,' explained Sasha. 'I met her just a little while ago today, on the beach. She was crying all by herself—because a coordinator cheated her. She's only a child. I don't know how long she'll be in Mumbai—but I want to help her.'

'Really?' Malik scrutinized him a moment longer, and then grunted roughly, breaking away. He opened the fridge and pulled out a bottle of Coke. 'That's very noble of you! Ask her to go back to her country; that will be best for her.'

---

[14] come inside for a minute

[15] Oh, just come in!

'Why do you say that?'

'Because she's a foreigner re.[16] What will she do here?'

'Don't foreigners find work in this industry?'

'She can do item numbers.' Malik took a swig of Coke. 'I don't know re! I can't even figure out *mera kya ho raha hai*[17]... No, nothing happened—that's the problem. I'm just writing and that's it. I've got like five scripts hanging with producers, not getting sold. Even when they get sold, people don't pay. I'm owed four lakh by two different producers. My girlfriend is coming back to India in June. She's got a job already in IIT Mumbai. So we are most likely getting married this year. I mean, it's not a big deal; her parents are very cool. My parents are also cool. But we will basically be living off her income... Khair, anyway, it's fine, fuck it! Ehehe! You tell me. What are you doing besides rescuing damsels in distress?'

'Did you read my script?' asked Sasha, but he felt strangely troubled and barely heard Malik saying, 'No re. Not had the time.' Instead, he looked at Malik afresh, studying his visage. They were narrowed eyes that slid about the kitchen. It was a bored gaze that yet flared with ugly, flickering enthusiasm. Malik put the Coke bottle back in the fridge, then filled a glass straight from the tap above the kitchen sink and drank it down noisily. Suddenly raising his voice in song, he waddled back to the room where they had left Elena.

She was on her feet, with her hands clasped, staring at the door. As they entered the room, she swivelled, as though in terror.

'What happened?' cried Sasha.

---

[16]An exclamation used for emphasis.

[17]what is happening with me

Her hair hung loosely all over her face. She shook her head. 'I need to go.'

'Wait re!' Malik loped back to the mattress and landed on it with a grunt. Sasha tried to see if Elena was smiling (for it had been a funny sight) but the tension that had come upon her, remained. Her nose was wrinkled as she glanced about the room.

He realized that it was stifling inside; not merely because there were no windows, and despite the ceiling fan's ostentatious speed.

'I have one more contact to mail you, my dear Elena Hamolka!'

'Malik knows Ahishor too,' Sasha said suddenly. Then she did look up.

'Elena would like to meet Ahishor,' Sasha continued, with a smile. She opened her mouth wide in protest, but her face (so distressed a moment ago) was bright with excitement. 'Maybe we will all meet sometime,' said Sasha.

He looked at Malik, willing him not to make any sardonic or dampening comment on the matter. But Malik appeared entirely absorbed in what was on his screen. He was leaning forward, his eyes bulging and his mouth parted. He scratched his stomach and his side and, with all eagerness, shifted his body closer to the computer. Then, as a crazed grin appeared onto his lips, he cried out: 'Fuck! What the fuck! Ruhi Khanna has committed suicide!'

Sasha moved forward in a daze. But he stopped short of the laptop, from where Malik was reading incredulously.

'Ruhi Khanna, a thirty-three-year-old actress hailing from New Delhi, was found dead at her Sewri flat today morning! The cause of death is alleged to be suicide. Fuck! I'm seeing the link on Facebook. The *kaam waali bai*[18] found her. It says she had hanged herself from the living room fan!'

He turned to Elena. Her face had become ghastly white. The corners of her mouth were trembling.

'Come, see,' said Malik. 'Apparently she left a suicide note... Hmm, but it doesn't say what she wrote. Fuck! I wonder what she would have written! I know she was not normal but this is too much re! Come see!'

Sasha dropped to his knees onto the mattress, and Malik partly turned the laptop towards him. There was a series of 'RIP' messages on Facebook—and then, in the same series, somebody's holiday photos. In another tab was open a tabloid's brief report on the incident, which came with the promise that more details were to follow.

'Let me check her Twitter,' Malik said suddenly, pulling the computer back onto his lap. 'I'm sure she would have tweeted something about it!' He began to hum afresh to the classical music that was still filling the room. 'Ahh! She has been tweeting against men! "A Nobel for whoever can explain why Indian men are so disgusting!" Ehehe! Nothing directly about suicide though.'

There was a scuffling noise in the room. Elena had grabbed her handbag; her eyes were wet and swollen.

'Hey, what happened Elena?' Malik called out. 'Did you know her too?'

She shook her head mutely and turned quickly to the door, her heels clicking. At the door, she stopped and fixed them both with an odd, half-accusatory look, which was, at the same time, full of expectation. 'I need fresh air,' she said. Her voice was

---

[18]'maid.

giving way, turning her strong accent into something essential and affecting.

'Wait, I'm coming,' said Sasha. 'Malik, are you coming?'

'*Nai re*,'[19] said Malik, from the mattress. He sounded bored. '*Tu ja*.'[20] I have to finish my script.'

There shot through Sasha a seething rage. It was all the more vivid for the suddenness of its coming. He stared at Malik, still scrolling and reading, with his large head swaying to the music, like a wind chime tossing about in the breeze. Terrible words of condemnation resounded in his head, but he held them back. Yet, he felt glad to say in words that came pouring out—'You do nothing but work, Malik! What's wrong with you! You are better than this; why do you just sit here?'

'What are you talking about?' Malik was astonished. 'What can I do about it? I have to work re!' he continued, with rising irritation. 'Fuck all this, fuck it, fuck it!' He began to click shut the various tabs he had opened.

Sasha closed the door behind him.

Darkness had fallen at last. The street lights threw white pools on the tarmac. Close by, there beckoned the colourful displays of Yari Road. But Elena was walking away quickly, up the long road they had come down together. A bus was bearing down on it now, groaning hideously. She shrank to one side, where an iron railing bordered the narrow pavement. He half ran to catch up with her.

Her cheeks were stained with tears. Sasha touched her shoulder and came around beside her. 'She died!' gasped Elena. 'She was on Facebook!'

---

[19]No, man
[20]You go.

'I know, it's awful—did you know her?'

She turned her head to the sky, where a full moon was sailing amongst the clouds. The grief on her face was so profound and her expression so stricken with hopelessness that Sasha asked again: 'Did you know her?'

Elena shook her head briefly and cried: 'You both knew her—and she's dead! She was on Facebook!'

This latter fact, for some reason, seemed to have particularly shaken her.

'We only have little time.' A queer determination was coming over her face, 'Whatever we have to achieve, we have to do it now. But why did she—' The words would not emerge. She broke out into an uninhibited shudder.

'I knew Ruhi,' said Sasha. 'She was a friend of mine. She was upset about many things in this city. Work—and other things. I used to try to help her.'

He was staring at Elena as he spoke, his heart overwhelmed with inexplicable pangs. She was listening, perhaps, though without any outward sign of it. She was walking hard, still blinking back her tears. Then she stopped, started to walk again, flung a look about at the traffic and came to another halt beside an empty auto.

'I want to pray,' she said. 'I'm going to Bandra.'

'Why to Bandra?'

'There is a church there I heard about.'

'Which church? There are many. The most famous one is Mount Mary. But won't it be shut now?' Sasha wondered aloud.

'Let's go quickly,' she pleaded. 'I want to go. Are you coming?'

'Yes,' he found himself saying, a tide of emotion burgeoning in his breast.

They climbed into the auto, its little engine revving furiously.

Shops, buildings and people passed by in a hurry, yielding only one distinct sight, which, however, Sasha would not soon forget. At a popular coffee shop milling with people, Ahishor's old confidante, Bharat Mishra sat alone at a table. His fingers were steepled in front of him, long and thin, like his face, which was unnaturally calm.

Then, while they were still on J.P. Road, the voice of a Muslim preacher pierced through the air. He was shrieking the sermons via a loudspeaker from a room above a kebab stall. A beautiful green wrought iron staircase led up to the madrasa. Sasha understood nothing of the words, but there was something in the man's urgency, his desperation in the middle of the street, which felt right to him. Yet he was glad to leave it behind.

For most of the journey, Elena looked out of the vehicle. The breeze dried her tears and calmed her to a degree. Sasha's thoughts too were muted. The auto seemed to go blessedly fast; red lights turning to green as they sped towards their destination and the traffic snaking down the other lane. It was around eight o'clock when, having negotiated Bandra's bustling lanes, they rode up a hillock to where the church stood.

Elena sped ahead while Sasha was still waiting for the driver to return the change. She was guided, as though by instinct, through a lit courtyard, past branching pathways and the faces of strangers, into the cool, rearing darkness of the church hall.

That was where Sasha found her. She was the lone figure in the empty pews, bent down on her knees before the icon of Mary. She was surrounded by all that was ornate and magnificent, but it was she, herself, whom he looked at most of all. She was wholly free of self-consciousness. As she knelt, in her faded flower-patterned dress, she seemed transfigured. Her eyes were sealed shut by her long lashes. Her hands were clasped, her lips moved quietly; there were the signs of grace on her sweet face.

Kneeling beside Elena that night, it was not only Ruhi whom he remembered. All those about whom he had been worrying for weeks paraded before him. Their faces were wilder, their prospects more fearsome than ever before; but now, for the first time (as he felt his strength breaking and stinging tears rushing to his eyes) he gave over his worries to God.

Out of the Woodwork

At the beginning of the next week, I found myself in Jangpura, climbing the steps to Mihir's flat, on an acrid, wintery Sunday morning. He had called me out of the blue—but calmly, in a reassuring way. It was as though he had never forgotten about me, and was simply calling on a predetermined schedule, which I merely happened not to be privy to.

Yet, even before I heard his voice, the very moment I saw his name flashing on my phone, I had felt something catch inside me. Hope, like a delicious memory, was let loose within me. I realized that Mihir was the one person whose judgment I trusted, the one person who would not judge me for staying away from Ahishor in the time of his trouble. He would understand how dearly I wanted to build my career, with someone whom I could look up to. Versova was full of cranks and oddballs, people revelling in failure and people bound for ruination. I had worked with Jatin—that was enough! I wanted to be safe now, and in safe and wholesome company. Nobody knew how disillusioned I had been with Ahishor, and though I was acutely aware of my presumption in feeling that way—of my cowardice and my snobbishness—nonetheless, that was how I felt. Small wonder that I had come back home, to my mother's morning tea, to the warm blankets of winter, to wander in familiar places and search (futilely, I was aware) for my lost sanctuary—my childhood.

Mihir, however, understood. For he had said to me, with perfect candour:

'I'll tell you the truth, Dhruv—I too had given up on him. But I was mistaken. It happens. There's no shame in that. Now we are back and these are very exciting times, Dhruv. I don't want you to miss out on this. Nobody holds anything against you. Ahishor knows your potential. We both want you to be a part of this.'

'What is it exactly?' I managed to control my excitement enough to ask. 'Is it a start-up?'

'It's much bigger than that,' he said. 'You could call it that, but it's much bigger than that. But don't worry!' he chortled suddenly (I was not sure why). 'Come to my house on Sunday and we'll talk.'

When I arrived as instructed, in the late morning, I was surprised to discover a full house. (A jumble of voices had been audible from the street, and all the way up the stairs). Inside, I was disoriented. The atmosphere was festive and inattentive, full of sunshine and snacks and a running chatter. There were people reclining on sofas, springing up in occasional bursts of (probably) alcohol-fuelled excitement, then falling back, full of giggles. They never ceased talking, however. They were articulate throughout. I only recognized Mihir and Anamika and I looked, in vain, for Ahishor. But Mihir immediately began to introduce me to the strangers.

There were three of them, though they had seemed to me more in number, from the commotion they made. The one who had caught my eye from the outset was a small, sharp-faced girl in a blue kurta, with bright, black eyes that seemed to scrutinize without apology whatever they rested on. She was Alisha, a lawyer, who (Mihir explained) had just started her own practice and was 'killing it already.' Hovering near her was a tall, extremely handsome young man, with leonine locks and a groomed stubble. This was Gaurav, a freelance journalist, who (I was informed) was the author of a dashing new book on India's economic reforms, and had a much-acclaimed column in a leading business and lifestyle magazine. I pretended I had heard of the book, and knew the magazine well, but being neither well-read, nor up on current affairs, I was already feeling out of place. Alisha was terribly pretty (the word 'foxy' passed my mind) but under her gaze, I not only felt that she was out of my league, but I also felt discomfited and troubled for reasons that I could not explain at all.

The third stranger was a young man named Prabhat, who seemed to enjoy a special status in the group. He was teased by everyone about various little things, and listened to with a smile when he spoke, but, though indulged, he was not patronized. I gathered he was a sort of eccentric genius, who had written a novel before calculating there was no money in that business, and now played Internet poker for a living and was rarely seen in the daytime when he slept. He looked sleepy to me that morning too, though it was difficult to tell. His eyes, in any case, were half-shut and his straggly hair uncombed. His shirt was half unbuttoned and he reclined in his jeans, with a placid smile on his thin face.

'Which college did you go to, Dhruv?' asked Gaurav, casually. All of them, along with Mihir, had been to the same college in Delhi, and then abroad. But theirs were elite institutions, and mine decidedly not. I was perhaps too conscious of this as I answered, for Gaurav proceeded to grin and slap me on the back.

'Calm down,' he said. 'Nobody's judging you, man.'

For some reason, I did not feel reassured. He had on a lopsided smile. From the sofa, Alisha was smiling too, her lips quivering with superior irony. I heard Anamika click her tongue and exclaim delightedly: 'Poor thing!' Then, as I stood there, Mihir put his arm around me.

'Dhruv is a wonderful film-maker. Versova's finest! He's going to make waves. He was Ahishor's right-hand man in Versova. You don't mind me saying that, do you? ... What do you mean it's not true? He's modest! Oh he's great; I love Dhruv. Everyone loves him. He was also a good friend of Ruhi Khanna's.'

Mihir suddenly turned grave. In the eyes that now turned to me, I spied (for the first time) a real curiosity. I was about to protest that this wasn't really true either, that I only knew Ruhi in passing, but I stayed silent.

'What about the perpetrator?' came a sharp voice from the sofa. 'Did you know him personally too?'

'You mean Pankaj Pande?' I asked. A frisson was speeding through me as Alisha stared. 'I mean I knew him, but not well. Actually my ex-boss was a really good friend of his... *Is* a good friend, I guess. I don't know at the moment.'

'And what was your opinion of Pankaj Pande?' she continued steadily.

'I mean, he seemed nice,' I extemporized. 'He was thoughtful, very intelligent—obviously. I'm a fan of his work. A generous person; he took a lot of interest in me, for example, as a young guy starting out in films... I definitely didn't expect such behaviour from him!'

'Where have I heard that line before?' A fixed smile had

appeared on her face. She kept staring at me, while I wondered if more questions were coming.

'Did they find out why she did it?' I asked at last, whirling around, addressing nobody in particular. 'Ruhi, I mean. Did she leave a note or something?'

In the silence that followed, I felt I had misspoken. 'We'll talk about that later,' said Mihir. 'It's a bit disturbing.'

'Who is your ex-boss?' asked Alisha suddenly. 'The one you said was Pande's friend.' I told her at once, but Jatin's name did not seem to register, and she frowned and turned to Gaurav instead.

'Did you read the mail I sent you? The forward from Mihir?'

'Yeah, yeah,' he nodded, pursing his lips.

'But actually—this is what I love about Twitter!' said Alisha fervently. 'It reveals people's true colours!'

'What are you talking about?' I blurted out. My voice, even to my ears, was sounding louder than usual.

Her eyes flashed in my direction. 'Are you on Twitter, Dhruv?'

'No,' I shook my head.

'Do get onto Twitter. You'll understand more of what's going on all around you. This is free advice, I know. But you will benefit.'

'Oh, *thanks*,' I nodded. My impertinence was quite spontaneous, for I had little control of my reactions. Alisha looked daggers at me, while I found myself concentrating on how pretty she was. But elsewhere in the room, Anamika was smiling. Soon I heard her calling my name, in a kindly way.

'Mihir made a compilation,' she explained, 'of the worst abuses that Ruhi had to face on Twitter, when she came out with her allegations. It was really disgusting. It wasn't just the bhakts[21] talking this crap. I mean, there were lots of those obviously. But even other people who're always acting all modern and pro-women and liberal.'

'Self-styled liberals,' said Gaurav, with a graceful laugh.

'That's just what Ahishor is saying na,' she nodded. 'Until liberals stop betraying each other, we can't do anything to improve the rest of the country.'

'Where is Ahishor?' I asked at last. 'Isn't he here—in Delhi?'

'He's missing him,' Mihir grinned delightedly. 'See! It's very touching. Yes, Dhruv. Ahishor is very much in Delhi. He's gone to Ozymandias right now, to meet somebody extremely important… Oh! You don't know Ozymandias? I'll tell you about it later.'

That was the first time I had heard the name 'Ozymandias'— the name that is now burned in my memory. It is difficult to believe, because I never visited the place, but even to the day that I write these words, I feel transported there without warning. I smell the rich leather and the wood-polish and the scent of the swimming pool, the chlorinated waters lapping in the dark, amidst the rumblings of conversation and the high, gay, girlish laughter that I can never get out of my head.

I had started to wonder what precisely Mihir had called me for, and why in the presence of these other people, when the discussion took another turn. It began with Alisha saying in a loud voice (I realized that it was her ordinary tone, though it was much louder than most people's) that the Twitter trolls who had maligned Ruhi ought to be prosecuted for hate speech. Suddenly, I became aware of some movement out of the corner of my eye. Prabhat was disentangling himself.

---

[21]In this case, 'bhakts' refers to right-wing supporters

'This is rather inconsistent,' he spoke in a wheezing, sibilant voice. 'If one is a liberal and one professes free speech, then this is all a part of it. Misogynistic speech—even granted that this is misogynistic speech, and I think that term gets bandied about too freely; but alright, even granted that—misogynistic speech cannot simply be equated to hate speech. Free speech means permitting the truly odious, not just what is agreeable. If we want the right to speak out against established systems—religion, for example—then we cannot deny the same right to the other side.'

The look on Alisha's face had gone from mere attentiveness when Prabhat had started to speak, to stormy indignation.

'Oh alright!' she yelled. 'So calling a rape victim "a lying bitch" and a "publicity-seeking slut" isn't hate speech? Shaming her isn't hateful? And that's nothing!—I don't even want to repeat the things that were said about her; the things they said they would do to her!'

'No,' said Prabhat, contemplatively. He looked sleepy. 'It may be hateful, but it's not hate speech. Hate speech is that which encourages imminent violence. If we treat all abusive language as hate speech, then we may was well give up on free speech.'

She turned to face him, but he was so abstracted that he did not seem to feel her concentrated glare upon him.

'What about when speech itself has a chilling effect? Are you familiar with that situation, Prabhat? Research has shown that misogynistic speech creates an environment where women are unable to speak; they are stifled. It's the same sort of reason we have speech laws for abusive language against Scheduled Castes and Scheduled Tribes. If you don't realize this, I think you may need to check your privilege—and do some reading.'

I spied Anamika shooting a look at Mihir, who seemed

to sigh. Prabhat frowned and (having briefly considered his interlocutor) looked at the ceiling.

'I'm referring to the principles of liberalism,' he said, in a tired, fair-minded tone. 'The SC, ST laws violate free speech too. I have no hesitation in saying so. The point is, once you make the claim that a particular group is simply too traumatized to handle abusive speech, you have embarked on a very slippery slope. I am not, for a minute, endorsing abuse, but as always, in liberalism, a speech is to be countered with a speech, not with force. If you take the stand that we are so traumatized that we cannot speak and so we are entitled to use force—I mean the force of the criminal law—well then, the religious right wing does exactly the same. They say their sentiments are so hurt by what they call "blasphemy" that blasphemers must be thrown in jail. Is that alright? No, the solution is for every offended group to find a way to speak, or to find advocates to speak for them. Isn't that what advocates are for?'

'Prabhat, you talk in the air,' she continued to shout. 'You are always theorizing, but there is a limit to theory. This kind of armchair theorizing is itself the most egregious example of male privilege. Ruhi committed suicide! What she faced on Twitter drove her to suicide!'

'I haven't forgotten—'

'But it's just not important to you.'

'It *is* important to me!' A flush had come over the young man's cheeks. For the first time, his composure was dislodging, and also for the first time, he sounded insincere. 'If anyone goaded her to commit suicide, they are liable, of course. But if they just doubted her word and questioned her character—I mean, however reprehensibly—that is not abetment to suicide. You know that! They *can't* be prosecuted.'

'They can be,' she said, with suppressed triumph. 'They can be and ought to be. And the same goes for everyone who talks their language. As for Pankaj Pande—he should be booked for murder now. But thanks for arguing, Prabhat. You've given me a preview of what I'm sure I'm going to face tonight. I'm on NDTV at nine o'clock.' She swivelled suddenly and looked straight at me. 'It's a discussion on online misogyny and what measures can be taken to counter it.'

'Oh, damn good!' The words tumbled out of me. 'I'll watch it for sure!'

I hardly dared to look at Prabhat. He seemed to me reduced to a wounded thing, licking its wounds. The truth was that I was shaken by the argument. It was less the words and more the way they had been spoken; and the looks—merciless and irreconcilable—that had been cast on one another. I had thought there was an atmosphere of ease in the room. But it had been savaged in seconds. Then I saw the handsome young journalist looking drolly at Prabhat, and saying, 'Prabhat, you better watch it too.'

'Oh definitely,' he answered brightly. I watched him take a breath. 'Congrats Alisha! Nine o'clock news is damn good!'

'Thank you!' she was smiling most prettily.

I was still tense. Involuntarily, I looked at Mihir, who, at that moment, was stifling a yawn.

'Mihir's getting bored,' said Gaurav, continuing to smirk.

'I am,' he replied. 'I actually am. Because this is not a conference room.'

There was silence—then the doorbell rang. 'Ah, good,' said Mihir, moving leisurely to the door. 'Giri Joseph is here.'

Everybody straightened or sat up in attention. Our combined

gaze followed Mihir with a kind of awe, as he ushered in the famous writer, and immediately engulfed him in a bear hug that was reciprocated only clumsily and with some consternation. However, the man was grinning when he emerged into view again. He was wearing a still crisp kurta-shirt, with a jhola[22] slung across it. He moved to embrace Anamika with enthusiasm. Then, running a hand through the little hair he had, Giri looked about the room, and (as I filled with pride) greeted me by name. I felt the others staring in amazement.

'Great stuff,' said Giri, turning passionately towards Mihir. 'Cracking stuff!'

'You read it, eh?'

'At one go. I couldn't sleep last night. I kept turning over all the meanings and ramifications and... and... what it all means! How it ties in with everything else, you see? It's fascinating! Not that I don't have some rather *deep* disagreements about—'

'No doubt,' interrupted Mihir. 'No doubt you do. But that's not the point, of course.'

He nodded eventually towards the waiting trio. 'Have you met Gaurav Kapoor? He's one of our best young writers of narrative non-fiction.'

'Delighted to finally meet you!' said Giri. 'We missed each other at Jaipur.'

'And Alisha—brilliant criminal lawyer, LLM from Columbia; you will hear a lot about her. And Prabhat, who's an international poker champion. He gave up writing for poker.'

'Wise man!' exclaimed Giri.

'And you already know Dhruv.'

This time I received only a perfunctory smile. While my old

---

[22] a cloth bag

insecurities came flaming up again, Giri pulled a slim pamphlet with a dark blue cover from his jhola and handed it to Mihir, who passed a hand over it lovingly.

'Is that the printed Manifesto?' Anamika asked, peering.

'That's the one,' answered Giri. 'Mihir very kindly lent it to me, for my book.' Suddenly, he turned and addressed us all, in rambling, increasingly cryptic words. 'I mean my new book, which I am writing now. I am writing, broadly speaking, about the future of India. I am prophesying, to be perfectly frank, and I'm afraid my prognosis is dire! I see a great struggle in the offing. Nothing short of a civil war. It's begun already, really. Ahishor has said some brilliant things in there—and I do believe that if there is any hope to be had, it's along the lines he suggests. I would dearly love for him to succeed. I don't see it happening though, I'm afraid. Or perhaps I just lack the courage to actually involve myself.'

'Oh, you *are* involved,' said Mihir. 'Make sure you write about the Manifesto, in your *Guardian* piece. That's the only reason why I lent it to you. I'm not kidding. Haha! Well, I know I can rely on you, Giri. But Dhruv has not even read the Manifesto. Dhruv, come here. I think all of us have read it now except you. We are all in this together, Dhruv. And many others, who are not here today. Now take this! Don't worry, there are more copies being printed as we speak. Take it and read it—and then come back and we'll talk!'

So I did. I began to read the little booklet in an empty bedroom in Mihir's house, while the others talked in the other rooms. On the cover page were inscribed the words:

Freedom Unleashed: An Art that Moves
The New Culture Manifesto

I turned the page and started reading, and as I read, there rose up around me, gradually, the special atmosphere of a place both familiar and miraculously altered. It was Ahishor's voice, unmistakably. I recognized, in many spots, old thoughts that I had heard him speak. But I had only heard them as fragments, and now the fragments had acquired a body, and the body had come to life.

The Manifesto

1. The Death of Death

'Apathy is one of the characteristic responses of any living
organism when it is subjected to stimuli too intense or
too complicated to cope with. The cure for apathy
is comprehension.'

–JOHN DOS PASSOS

*When living things die, they disintegrate. But it does not follow
that disintegration is deadly, or that integrity, or stability, is a sign
of life. On the contrary, properly understood, integrity is the essence
of deadness, which we perceive in things that are dead and always
have been—like solid rock and statues. In the living world too,
integrity serves, not as a proof of life, but as a carrier of death.
The fossils of plants and animals transport death across centuries,
as do the mummies of human bodies. Meanwhile, that which is
alive is always changing, falling apart—even unto death. Therefore,
disintegration neither carries death, nor foretells it, nor even (properly
understood) causes it. Disintegration's relation to death is to banish*

it from sight. If anything, it is the death of death, that which clears a space for new life and makes death the soil of life.

For centuries, India has been a byword for the spirit of survival. What Mark Twain said of Varanasi is true of every part of this country. It 'is older than history, older than tradition, older even than legend—and looks twice as old as all of them put together.' Commentator after commentator has remarked on the miracle that is India. That, with its enormous human diversity of every kind, its continual shocks to the system from within and without; it has survived essentially intact through millennia, while all around it, nations disintegrate into war and terrorism. And so we congratulate ourselves on our everlasting life, and give thanks that we are not Afghanistan, nor Pakistan…

We, who hold to what is written here, have said enough already to suggest a different explanation—one that will disturb many but invigorate the few who understand that only the truth gives life and freedom. For the signs are not of life. The Indian phenomenon is indeed extraordinary—as extraordinary as it is ghastly. But even before we have spoken, there shall be an outcry: 'What about our spirit of tolerance and assimilation, which has been taught to us since childhood?' 'What about our ancient Hindu philosophy, which lives not for one short life but many incarnations?'

We say again, it is time to stop denying what we already know in our hearts. Everybody does feel that something is greatly amiss in this land, and everybody, privately, mourns it. When we shake our heads and aver that 'it happens only in India', when we remark, with a shrug that 'this is India', we are acknowledging this strange characteristic. We are gesturing, euphemistically, at the reality that is both too simple and too horrible to confront. For the reality is that we are lifeless; that our enduring longevity, our astonishing integrity, bears all the marks of death. That no lifeblood energizes us, but only a fossil mould preserves us. And the name of that mould is: apathy.

Apathy imprisons the land; we hold this, now, to be self-evident. From the rural farmer who, having no hope from the government, is content with suicide; to the man of the city, who looks over his degraded fellows with the hollowed-out gaze of the walking dead; to the barbaric revelry of our festivals that destroy the environment in every way—apathy is the cornerstone of the entire Indian edifice.

There are some who wish to dilute this truth. They fall, in general, into two categories. The first consists of those who are steeped in the very traditions (like the caste system) that have fossilized the country. These are the old and the rheumy-eyed among us, brainwashed from birth, who will fade away of their own. But the second category of naysayers are both more dangerous and (to us) more contemptible. They consist of those who, while knowing better and feeling the aching burdens of India's false self-congratulatory behaviour, shrink from taking steps. Selfishly, they desire, instead, to find safe havens of their own, whether in gated colonies or foreign shores. They desire that the boat not be rocked, lest their own, well-appointed cabins be disturbed. Their concern is not the nation, but their own peace of mind. In this category fall many of our intellectuals, many of our mature and well-regarded men and women of the world. Thus, they pay lip service to what they hardly believe, extol as 'tolerance' what is merely indifference and sing the praises of 'democracy,' while studiously abjuring the actual fruits of our system of governance, and, from their ivory towers, make a great show of their common touch, making much, for example, of the essential goodness of the man on the street.

Now, it is not our concern to meet the objections of those who *disguise their cowardice with comforting theories, for we are here to act, not to persuade. But let it be understood that such optimism is a crime that is committed most of all against the ordinary people whom it purportedly hails. For even a man in jail will laugh occasionally; it does not mean he is happy in jail. A man who is starving will eat crumbs; it does not mean he is content with crumbs. The flicker of life in the midst of a wasteland does not make it any less a desert. The only thing thus implied—and this, indeed, is significant—is that all is not lost. But this realization does not (like the false optimism) bring an end to thought and action. It begins it.*

India, then, lies dead from apathy. How long has it been so? No one can say. Even during the flowering period of our earliest epics, the canker of caste was present. No doubt, the terminal decline began as this canker, instead of falling away, intensified, killing the possibilities of life and growth across the social spectrum. Babur, in the sixteenth century, lamented over us. We were invalids when the British came, and though the genius of one man spurred us into activity, it is now trite that we have forgotten his legacy and settled ever deeper into our embalming liquids.

But we do not wish to be more morbid than necessary, though the subject is necessarily morbid. For we write, not to lament, but to bring good news. If India were hopelessly dead, it would not even know it, because the dead cannot tell they are dead. Yet, there are some of us present in this land, who are coming alive, whether by historical accident, or the merits of our thinking. We, who are coming alive, hereby commit to a new way. It begins with an end of stability, an end of meaningless outward integrity, an end of apathy. It begins with the destruction—of death.

2. The Child and the Monster

'But he doesn't have anything on.'

−HANS ANDERSEN

It is late in the day. Others have sized up the state of affairs, and have found in it an opportunity. They come with the promise of change, they come with clout and fanfare; therefore, they are tasting success. Yet, what is their promise? They say they wish to take us back to a time before our deadening began. But this is impossible in every sense. It is impossible to truly identify such a past. It is impossible, therefore, to take hold of it, without being poisoned by it afresh. It is impossible, in any case, to turn back the clock. What these men really wish to do is to usher us into a fresh state of denial. For an old and ugly man cannot become young and beautiful again—and he knows it. All that he may really do is insist that if only seen in the proper light, his sores and boils are really beauty spots. The old man, greedy for the energies of youth, will not be able to recover his youth. He will become a dirty old man, a predator and a monster.

His greatest enemy will be the one who sees honestly, who terms as 'ugly' what is ugly, and is not swayed by the swayable multitudes. The eyes of the child, which, as in Andersen's fairy tale, saw that the emperor has no clothes, see also that the new Hindutva is but a corpse in fancy dress. For saying this, the child is whipped. His clear-eyed vision is hated with a passion, because it is the only thing thwarting the monstrous entity from being accepted everywhere as king. Yet, just as the real grace of the old lies in surrendering to the new, so the grace of the young child is his power to evade and prevail over all oppressors.

Two roads out of apathy lie before the country. Yet one of them—the one we are rushing down rapidly—is an awful illusion. The way of the monster leads not to life, but to another spasm of death. There remains only the way of the child, and the patter of a few, determined footsteps, treading it, step by step.

3. Freedom Unleashed

'All good things which exist are the
fruits of originality.'

−JOHN STUART MILL

We are talking about liberalism. But liberalism is an old word, grown tarnished with bad practices, and we, who hold to what is written here, are not interested in walking the old ways. Liberalism in India has flourished for many decades—but only in theory; only as an 'ism'. In practice, it has been an imitation, a self-conscious farce, an apology. For true liberalism is not a proficiency in the English language; it is not a knowledge of names and theories; it is not the school or the college one went to; it is not the preserve of any class. Above all, it is not a compromise.

The worst of it is that these counterfeits are not even all of our own fashioning. We have fallen into them from our mimicry of the West, although the West, married to money, is no more married to freedom. The West—holier-than-thou from its Judeo-Christian foundations, shot through with racism and patriarchy, an engine of wage-slavery—also denies the quality of freedom, both within its borders and beyond. Yet, because of the worship of those like us, it continues to lead, blind to its failings. Truly, then, the blind are leading the blind. Not only has our mimicry misled us, it has robbed us of our own original strength and closed us to the realization of our own, unique opportunity, our chance to lead the world. For where else, but in India, does such apathy exist, which, by being destroyed, will reveal the power of freedom?

The lovers of money see India as a great market for goods. But we are really the greatest market for freedom. Every ancient oppression of our land, and every modern riff on it, is a fresh avenue for the assertion of individual choice. Our energies, longer frustrated here and in more myriad ways than anywhere in the world, will release with greater force and variety than anywhere in the world. That no one exalts us, will keep us humble, and that we dictate no doctrine to the world, will enable us to perfect it for ourselves—in practice. Certainly, we will not forget our core ideal, which is: the right to freedom of every individual, to be expressed in an environment of freedom, while always respectful of it. Nor do we deem it unimportant to state our beliefs in black and white. But we do not wish to get lost in words, and never shall we make them an end in itself. Our revolution is not of words, but of practice. Indeed, one of the most terrible compromises that Indian liberalism has struck, to date, is to be content with mere words, to rob them of their natural power to change. No wonder, that having been timid for so long, our journalism and academia have fallen so swiftly into the hands of the new Hindutva. Only a little better is the fate of our art. It, too, is striking deals with the devil—frittering itself away, or hiding in little corners and gaping vainly at the mirror. Yet, it is here that we may make a beginning. Art—and especially cinema—shall be freedom's most powerful ally.

4. An Art that Moves

'And why should not men of art serve the people? [...]
How came it to pass that these two things, which were
as much made for one another as a key for a lock, were
separated, and why are they so separated that we cannot
imagine how to reunite them?'

−LEO TOLSTOY

The world over, art proliferates. Perhaps never before in human
history has so much art abounded, in every type and form. We
have witnessed a worldwide democratization of the means of artistic
production. And this has rightly been hailed. Yet, there has been a
corresponding concern as to the trivialization of such productions.
It is well that all can make art; but it is not well that none of
it should matter. However, we are not concerned with the general
phenomenon. A society that boasts a vivid, contemporary history of
deep artistic engagement may suffer no harm, and indeed benefit
from a period of frivolity, just as a teacher in a classroom may do
well to joke, provided he has also taught.

This, however, is not the case in India. Those who tom-tom an
ancient Golden Age of Indian art, do so insincerely, for (as we have
noted above) very little about our ideological past is either certain
or certainly good. In any case, these are matters lost in the mists
of time; the contemporary—even the historical—situation is clear.
Our classical art has remained the preserve of particular sects and
castes, our regional art is confined to localities and languages; but
spanning the massive mainstream, there is practically no reading,
no music, no painting, no serious theatre, and no philosophy of
any consequence. There is only one art that dominates our people,
as a unity, and dominates to such a degree that serious academics

write in all seriousness that it furnishes part of the very fabric of Indianness. We speak, of course, of cinema (and, in general, of the visual medium).

At its finest, cinema is an art like no other, where huge sums of money are made to serve truth and beauty. At its gaudiest, it is the only art where money serves the ends of more money, in gargantuan ugliness. It is not difficult to say at which end of the spectrum our pan-Indian cinema, our unifying force of Bollywood, resides. So devoted is this industry to lucre that it has deified the lowest common denominators of our society—our regressiveness, our unfreedoms, our dead apathies. The fate of Bollywood, as an artistic entity, is abundant proof of the death—indeed the ever-deepening death—of our country.

But more interesting for our purposes is the fate of those voices within this industry, which claim to be different—to be liberal. For they are well placed to act. Many of them fill the executive positions at our biggest production houses, yet nothing of liberalism is evident in the movies they commandeer. A smaller number are stuck in a compromise. They attempt to 'seed' mainstream entertainment with liberal ideas. Their subtle attempts, unfortunately, produce movies that neither entertain the crowds, nor sufficiently propagate the values of freedom. Nevertheless, these attempts are smoke signals of distress, which we have read and understood.

Meanwhile, on the fringes of Bollywood, the liberal voices of our independent cinema are caught in existential crises. Not understanding how to make themselves viable, they collapse into the artistic equivalent of frustrated shrieks, while sinking into personal despair. As for those who have been luckier, and for those who delight in repeatedly hailing a 'new dawn' for Indian cinema, we may add that any number of foreign accolades cannot justify an art that cannot take hold of—and move—the hearts and minds of its countrymen. If we are charged with bitterness for saying so, let it be understood that I, Ahishor Frances, who am writing these words, have tasted more such accolades than any other in recent times, and that I count my own past work in this category—that of trinkets and baubles.

But we propose a way forward, which is both a way out for those voices that are stifled and a way back to the essentials of art and cinema. For the essential purpose of art—most essential when a society is tottering, whether in the pangs of infancy or the pangs of death—is to help it stand on the solid ground of values and ideals. In such circumstances, to place a premium on entertainment—or indeed on the aesthetic—is to fail miserably as an artist. Those who still insist that cinema may not be used as an ideological tool, are like men under fire, refusing to shoot back because of their belief that guns are made for hanging on walls. But the enemy does not believe this—and here the enemy is right. All who know the history of art, and especially the history of cinema, know this. Even the wretched masses that worship and mimic evil on the screen, acknowledge, by this very fact, the power of the screen.

Let our liberal-minded artists understand, therefore, why they are in confusion. It is because they have failed to put first things first. They have whispered and signalled the things they ought to roar about. They have used the immensely powerful medium of movies, not to put forth what is in their hearts, but to gesticulate in failure.

It is time to stop wringing our hands, or justifying our cowardice and our slavish greed. Before we are forcibly and finally overwhelmed, it is time to act. The art of moving pictures must become an art that moves the nation. Our film-makers must man the front lines. We impose on them the greatest responsibility, because their medium of communication has the greatest reach and the most direct influence.

Yet, not only cinema artists, but all artists are called—and not only artists, but all people. All lovers of liberty must use what resources they can to preach liberty to India.

5. The Good Fight

'Freedom is never voluntarily given by the oppressor; it must be demanded by the oppressed.'

–Martin Luther King, Jr.

In a country ridden with minorities of caste, class and religion, we, the liberals of India, are the most fraught minority of all. For those minorities who have little access to power, and therefore no opportunity to assert themselves, are yet fundamentally healthier than us, who have held, and still hold (though perhaps not for long) positions of influence in the country, yet have failed to be ourselves due to sheer self-doubt and perversity. Our very existence has been denied. Our identity has been regarded as no identity, neither of the East nor of the West. So successful has this internal oppression been, that we have accepted it too. The term in vogue, by which we describe ourselves—'people like us'—reflects the faltering nature of our sense of self. Its connotations of soft mockery lay bare our self-loathing.

Our first priority, therefore, is to assert our identity as liberals, paramount over all others. We, the liberals of India, are an autonomous cultural group, cutting across all lines of caste, class, region, language and ethnicity, united solely by our commitment to the values of freedom. We reject all other monikers and all attempts, in the name of 'Indianness,' to pin upon us any other identities whatsoever. Indeed, it is our virtue that we cannot be tied down thus—that (though we are conscious of our urban-centredness) we can, in principle, be found anywhere, popping up like fresh flowers, scattered through the land. For we are like children in this slumbering land, and our free, unfettered activity is now its only hope of wakening.

We must raise our voices. We have called upon artists to lead the way, but all must raise their voices, from every part and corner. For we are too few in number, not to each pull our weight; nor is this a time for pious and fastidious doubts about preachiness, or selfish retreats into one's own pleasures, or hesitations about imposing one's views on others. It is obvious that as liberals, we cannot ever use vigilante force to propagate freedom, even if we had the capability, for this would be a plain contradiction in terms. But the word has the power that the sword does not. The force of conscience is available to us—and in this we must trust. Let us never forget that freedom is the natural leaning of the human being. The young person in the little town, who may rabidly support the right wing today, does so only from his repression. He has developed a taste for economic freedom alone. But if he only extended his appetite towards personal freedoms of every kind, if he realized all that liberty, in an environment of liberty, can bring him, he would never turn back.

We cannot emphasize enough the importance of our unity. Because we have been loath to embrace our identities as liberals, and, in our timidity, anxious to make peace with the enemies of freedom, so there has grown within many of us a perverse irritation, as witnessed in frequent outbreaks of self-flagellation and infighting. Too often Indian liberals tear each other down, for causes too petty to be worth mentioning, not realizing that the cause of their frustration is their failure to be proud and unite to fight their common enemy and spread their common message. A house divided cannot stand. We condemn such betrayals and resolve to put an end to them.

We are at an epochal moment in the history of both our nation and the world. Wherever one looks, one sees forces of selfishness and greed, or, at best, of petty aims. Ideologically, hatred and bigotry have found new votaries and religions continue to oppress, but the great dream of individual liberty as the foundation of human civilization has been reduced to a cliché and leached of life, least present there, where it is assumed to reign. Let the light then come, from the corner least expected. Let the Indian liberal go further and deeper than any of his or her predecessors or contemporaries. Let us proclaim freedom as never before, in the face of that bigotry, which, for us, is not the face of a distant, dangerous land, but of our very neighbours. We do not hesitate to call our task a fight, for though our means can never be crudely violent, it is a certainty that our fate is to struggle, by all possible means. But the fight for freedom is the one and only good fight.

An Unmasking Is Begun

When I had finished reading the Manifesto, I sat where I was, with the pamphlet open on my lap. My eye went back over particular sentences and passages that seemed, to me, especially impressive. A peculiar sensation was coming over me. Though there was no one with me in the bedroom—only the fan twirling and the curtains gently billowing by the balcony doors—I was adjusting my expression to an imaginary audience. I nodded and grinned heartily. I shook my head in disbelief. My eyes were opened wide throughout, and I was still grinning, as one overwhelmed, when eventually I stood up and began to make my way back to the drawing room.

In the corridor, I was met by Mihir, who was hurrying in the opposite direction.

'Hi Dhruv!' he cried theatrically. 'Read it?'

'It's really *something*. It's powerful, man. I love—'

'Yes, yes, yes. I know. Get back in now—there's an important discussion happening; I want you to be there.'

'Ok!' I said, after a moment's uncertainty over which way I was being asked to turn.

When I entered the drawing room (it was much quieter

than before), Anamika at once gestured that I should sit. From a corner, I stared in silence. The composition of the room had altered. Alisha had left and I could not spot Prabhat either. In Alisha's absence, the young journalist, Gaurav, was at centre stage. He was nodding his handsome head attentively, face-to-face with a man in a Nehru jacket whom I recognized as Maithili's father, Suraj Krishna. Ira Joshi, Anamika's mother, was sitting beside him, with her hand resting lightly on his arm, though her head was turned the other way, while she talked softly with Giri Joseph. She looked comfortable and at as much ease in this bachelor pad as she had been when I had last seen her at the literature festival in Mumbai. It was obvious that her presence had calmed the excitable writer, and was doing the best it could to soothe Mr Krishna, who was visibly on edge.

'I haven't gone there myself,' Mr Krishna was saying. 'Though I have a good mind to. To tell you the truth, I am just not terribly keen to be further disrespected by that loony bunch.'

'But you haven't been able to speak to her,' said Gaurav, in a deep and quiet voice.

'No. They don't deny she's at the ashram. But they say she's doing some sort of programme, where she can't be disturbed and that she's opted not to be disturbed. Apparently it doesn't matter if it's me, her father, calling. I told them, "What if there's an emergency; something's happened in the family? I absolutely need to talk to her!" They said, "Sorry, it makes no difference"—actually, they didn't even say sorry!'

Gaurav clicked his tongue in sympathy. 'They are like this. Ashram inmates even include fugitives. Literally—people who are wanted in court. They run such a tight ship that even the law can't get inside. This is known to happen in many ashrams, though not Narayanan's—so far. But Narayanan's outfit has a certain reputation for money laundering. Like I said, I've been researching all these guys for a while.'

'Ira told me,' said Mr Krishna. 'After that, I read your piece about Asaram—very fine piece. And the other one too—about the Samjhauta Express blast. Very fine; it was very good. I guess what I'm wondering is, what we can do about *my* problem!'

'Why don't you write a piece about the money laundering, Gaurav?' asked Ira, breaking away from Giri. 'I was telling Suraj that while Maithili can't be forced to come out of some place if she's decided to go there, she might make the right decision if the true facts about this guy are made known. Right now, he only seems to get the most *gushing* coverage.'

'He has a pretty clean image,' nodded the young man. 'You'd be surprised, but even in my own circles, I have friends who follow him on Facebook.'

'Oh, I know!' Ira said in a sing-song voice. 'I've heard him talk; he's very smooth. There's no doubt he has intelligent ideas about various things. But that doesn't justify him being crooked and hoodwinking people with false promises, and, of course, he is doing that! I mean, that is the heart of the baba business, if I can call it that!'

'Well, the Manifesto says it all,' Gaurav shrugged. 'If liberals don't step up against these guys, nobody will. Instead, we're falling for them ourselves. But we do have a plan for Narayanan.'

There came a noise from the door. The latch turned and the door opened soundlessly. Ahishor stepped into the room. He was wearing a felt jacket and cargo trousers. He did not enter at once, but held the door open until a fat man, sweating gently, had followed him inside. I took no time to recognize Dipankar Joshi, especially since mine was the first face his eyes lighted upon. Then, looking about the room, he grinned and observed: 'Durbar is in session!'

I started to get up because I couldn't spot any chair or sofa for him to sit on, but he waved me down and went, with a grunt, to join his daughter on the mattress. Anamika whispered something in his ear as he settled down.

I was feeling light-headed as I watched Ahishor extending his hand towards Mr Krishna. It passed my mind that they might know each other from the days when Ahishor had dated Maithili. How much had changed since then! And how strange the room had become, with the older people showing up, squeezing in amongst the young, not seeming to mind the messy surroundings. In the disorder, I felt a sanctity that was intimidating; as though I was witnessing a ceremony too compellingly significant to stand on ceremony.

When at last he turned in my direction, my heart was hammering. My palms were clammy; I moved them away from the Manifesto.

Blessed joy, he was smiling! His eyes were burning gloriously, his chest rising and falling with triumphant breathing. Then as his smile vanished (mine did too), and as his face became drawn and concentrated, I too sat up and stared hard at him, until he had gone behind Gaurav and leaned against the wall, folding his arms. Afterwards, I simply followed Ahishor's gaze.

'Now that we're doing this systematically,' Gaurav was saying to Mr Krishna, 'we're going to plan our moves carefully. Yes, I could go to press with some hard questions about him, but they would only be questions, at the end of the day.'

'But at least if the word gets out—if people get some idea! You said he's a money launderer?'

'It would only put him on guard. Look, I'd love to nail

the guy. I want to break the story that nails him, but I have to make sure I time it right. We've just got to be a little wise about this. Narayanan is complacent right now. And he's getting more complacent by the day. Let's keep him like this for a while—and then strike.'

'Strike how?'

'We're planning that. For starters, Ahishor is planning—that is to say, we are planning—to do a sting.'

'What sting?'

Mr Krishna's eyes were bulging. He was straining forward from his seat. In his excitement, the youthfulness of his features showed all the more sharply. But he had lost his self-assurance.

'What sting?' he demanded again. In the World Bank, Suraj Krishna had possessed a reputation for impatience with subordinates who failed to come quickly to the point. They would have recognized his tone now. 'You say a "sting". A sting is no joke. When are you planning this for?'

'Well, there's an arts festival happening in Mumbai in April. Narayanan's been invited. We might move then, but it's not really—'

'Which arts festival?' cried Mr Krishna, as Gaurav trailed off, and turning, looked askance at Ahishor, who was stepping forward. 'I think these questions can wait,' said Ahishor.

He stood in the middle of the room, his gaze moving from one person to another, till it came to rest on Mr Krishna.

'I want to make sure we're all on the same page. I know you're concerned about Maithili. So are we. I'm personally quite shocked that she is where she is. She always had such high ambitions, such grand aims... But Maithili is not the reason we're doing this. We would be attacking the god-man class regardless. Why? As liberal Indians; for the sake of our values. So, there are some principles here. I don't know if Ira or Dipankar showed you the Manifesto... Nobody did? ... Well, I would like everybody here to read the Manifesto! Then they can decide if they are really with us!'

His voice rose sharply and he wheeled around, his sleeves flapping. The rebuke was felt by all of us, including the older people. I saw Dipankar staring at Ahishor, with (albeit amused) admiration, while Ira exchanged a strange little smile with Giri Joseph. But Ahishor turned back on Mr Krishna and called him by name.

'Suraj, I do want to help you, and we will expose this god-man and others like him. I have just met a very enlightened and capable individual, who will partner us and help us in all that we do. But whatever we do, it will not be with gentleness, tact or diplomacy. Yes, I said it will *not* be. There will be an 'us' and there will be a 'them'. The lines will be clear and the sides will be polarized. Do you follow my meaning?'

Mr Krishna was frowning, but then, as he leaned back in his chair, understanding dawned upon him. And then he frowned again, only hesitantly.

'Look...' he said. Ahishor was standing with arms crossed, not far from him. 'I take it you're referring to the little essay I published in *The Telegraph*, some time ago. Well, that essay was written in solidarity with you, Ahishor, after that unfortunate incident—the attack you suffered. My only point was that we have to be careful how we frame this debate. We don't want to show such blanket aggression that we incite a backlash and alienate people whom we could otherwise work with. That was my point then, and I'm sure I stand by it now as well.'

'Then you must read the Manifesto,' said Ahishor, 'and we must not talk more until you choose to change your mind. Your attitude of compromise is doing nothing but emboldening the other side; your intellectual pride is blinding you and weakening us all. When I was hurt, your words hurt me more—and they strengthened my brother's cowardice. So I know which side you are actually helping. When I heard about Maithili's situation and then was told that you are coming here, I hoped I would find you of a different mind. But it is not just Maithili whom you are damaging. She is less of a victim to begin with, having made her own choices. You are damaging all the other women, whom the patriarchy is crushing. And I have to think of them too.'

He had turned and started to walk away, but then stopped and tossed his head sideways.

'The one thing we can't afford is liberals who let down other liberals. It's gone on too long in this country.'

I felt a hand on my shoulder, and turned to see Gaurav looking down expectantly. I handed the Manifesto to him. He passed it to Giri, who gave it to Ira Joshi. Mr Krishna took it from her, and began, with knitted brows, to read.

As Ahishor once again slumped gracefully against the wall, I noticed Mihir, further behind him. He had appeared in the corridor, but he had not come into the room. He only stood there, perfectly still; yet, it seemed to me that he was bursting with anticipation, peering at everyone with burning eyes, like one who is waiting for his moment.

Falling through the Cracks

Tara Krishna had remained in Mumbai. She was aware of her husband's appointment with Mihir and Ahishor, for he was meeting them at the Joshis's suggestion—a suggestion that had been made in her presence. But to her surprise, she had demurred, though not outwardly. She had not dissuaded him, but had sworn off the trip herself, truthfully citing a pressing headache that drained her of the strength to leave her Malabar Hills apartment. The sea breeze, she hoped, would soon restore her. It had failed to, thus far. Nevertheless, she was grateful to be alone.

The following afternoon, on Tara's invitation, Jatin came to visit. He found her in a dressing gown—tired, hollow-cheeked and wraith-like, yet also with a strange radiance in her cheeks and eyes. They sat together in the living room. The house was resplendent, winking in the streaming sunlight, but also poignant in its emptiness.

'Any news?' inquired Jatin huskily.

'None,' said Tara, staring out at the sea. 'She's cut us off completely.'

After a brief pause, he burst out, 'You know what? If I

were you guys, I would just go down there—and let's see who stops me from meeting my daughter! I would break my way in if I had to!'

Tara took a breath; her mood was altered already. She could no longer be attentive to the calming sea.

'Suraj says that he doesn't want to go all the way for nothing. Because we can't insist on seeing her; legally we can't.'

'Legally!' Jatin snorted. He was crouching forward already, with his hands poised tensely on his knees. 'Sometimes I absolutely fail to understand Suraj. I don't want to use the word—but this is cowardice! Essentially, this is cowardice.'

'He's not a coward,' Tara winced. 'In fact he's gone to Delhi just for this purpose. Ahishor is doing a campaign against god-men. I mean to say, he's picking up the pace of whatever he was doing before. So Suraj is trying to make sure that Sadhguru is targeted too. So that Maithili leaves him.'

'What do you mean "Sadhguru"?' asked Jatin, frowning at once.

But Tara only put her fingers to her temples and closed her eyes.

'Well, if I were you,' Jatin continued, 'I would not have anything to do with Ahishor. There's some serious lack of stability there. I know I have said the exact opposite in the past. Everyone knows I've been his biggest supporter. But I can see that something has gone terribly wrong. Maybe he's been influenced by somebody, or maybe—I really don't know what it is. But he's lost his moorings—badly!'

'Just because of Pankaj Pande?' said Tara. Her eyes were still closed while her fingers moved over her pounding forehead.

'That is a very good indicator! They've thrown him in jail, Tara. They've denied him bail. It's a direct consequence of the smear campaign by Ahishor and his Twitter mob. I mean, I can say this much for Pankaj—he is not a rapist! He has his faults—but he is not *that*!'

'So Ruhi was lying? The poor girl…' Tara spoke faintly.

'I know, it's a tragedy! But what has she said in her suicide note? I know they haven't told us—but she hasn't blamed Pankaj, has she? And doesn't suicide also prove emotional instability? It isn't, by itself, a judgment on Pankaj. But that's the only way it's being interpreted—thanks again to the smear campaign! There is a bloodlust here, Tara, I swear to you!'

She opened her eyes, which were red and glassy. 'I don't care about Pankaj Pande, Jatin. Can we not talk about him?'

'I only brought up the subject because you mentioned Suraj going to Ahishor.'

'Yes, and I do have reservations about that. But my reservations have nothing to do with Pankaj or what happened to Pankaj. I think he is getting exactly what he deserves—and shame on anyone who maligns the poor girl! Can you listen to me now for a moment, and not raise your voice?'

Her heart was sinking as she spoke, for she hated to lose her temper; it filled her with a sense of defeat. She looked at Jatin—his face was mottled red with the effort of restraint; his body, dwarfing her sofa chair, riveted by injured pride.

It was a beautiful afternoon. The sea looked so splendid from her window. The house was airy, clean and sparkling. *Why had she spoiled it all by calling such a man? … But this was supposed to be one of her oldest friends. What had happened over the years? Had she filled her life with all the wrong people?*

Doubts flooded her, which would later flare up into questions, and then, of their own steam, would hand her her decisions.

For the moment, she quelled them all, in a rush of trust.

'I've been thinking...' She clasped her hands and searched Jatin's gaze. 'I don't want to be my own daughter's enemy. If Maithili has made up her mind, I want to understand her first. Because she knows what she is doing; she is headstrong, but she is intelligent. She is nobody's fool! And Sadhguru is not just any quack; he has a name. A lot of people admire him. I was watching some videos on YouTube—and I liked the way he spoke, I really did! Why should I attack a man whom my daughter respects?'

Her face was aflame with emotion; she looked decades younger, if also unbelievably naive. Jatin frowned slowly, conscious of Tara's beauty.

Suddenly, fearing what he might say, she rose quickly and took a few steps towards the balcony, throwing out her arms as the sea filled her view.

'I am not a disbeliever!' she cried. 'I have never thought that this—all this! (she swung around to face the rich interior)—that all this—is all there is to life! I do believe in something beyond the material world.'

'But you don't believe in God.' Jatin continued to frown.

'Well, I believe in—a force! I believe in a life force that unites everything in the universe!' Her face was contorted, while her arms waved in front of her; it seemed they were moved by strings pulled from elsewhere. 'I think that's the foundation of all belief systems. Reiki, for example! And do you know what? Sadhguru doesn't believe in any god either. He says we should be seekers, not believers. That makes sense to me. I think of myself as a seeker too.'

Jatin raised his eyebrows and sighed. His gaze wandered about the room before it settled again on Tara, standing defiantly by the balcony.

'Look, I'm an agnostic myself,' he said, 'as you know. But

what I do believe in, is honesty. In fact, I couldn't care less what a person believes in, if he is honest, but if he is a liar and a crook, then that's what he is. Now of course, I haven't researched this guy as much as you seem to have. But I saw that letter—that letter you got. That was the work of a lunatic, Tara.'

'But that wasn't from him,' Tara shook her head energetically. 'That was from his follower, Shonar!'

'Whoever it was from! She is the one who has converted Maithili, right? And she was doing it on the authority of her guru.'

'You can't judge a person by his followers,' exclaimed Tara. But even as she spoke, a tiredness swept over her. She looked at the sofa, though she stayed on her feet. She wished Jatin would stop speaking, but he did not.

'I can still understand,' he said, 'what Suraj is doing. He is going to the wrong people—that's his mistake. But at least he is trying to take the guy down. You, on the other hand, are exhibiting a kind of Stockholm syndrome. Just because this baba has fooled your daughter doesn't make him a great man after all! Sometimes you have to fight, Tara; you can't avoid it.'

'Yes, you would say that,' she said, with a sudden sneer. 'You never can avoid it!'

'What does that mean?' he retorted hotly. 'I'm trying to help you, you know that.'

She opened her mouth in a silent cry and then rushed forward, falling onto the sofa. But she sat up again immediately, cradling her head in her hands.

Jatin stared, nonplussed. With an effort, he dropped his voice to (what he imagined was) a gentle murmur.

'You know I'm on your side, Tara. I care deeply about Maithili. And heck! Most of all, I care about you and how you're feeling! You know that I always have! I just don't want you to lose your head over this. Look, I didn't want to just come down, tell you a few consoling words—and leave. Because how would that help you? I want to help you! I'll go down there myself. I'll go down to the ashram and find her, alright? I'm serious! I'll do anything it takes, I don't give a damn! What do you say? I'm absolutely serious!'

But she had no words any longer. The burning sensation in her hands and feet, which had never fully ceased since the day it began (three weeks after Maithili had left home), was flaming up once more. She felt encased in fatigue, with energy only enough to form sentences in her head, but not to withstand the futility of speaking them. She could tell him that words of consolation were all she really wanted, that she had hoped to be encouraged by him, strengthened to follow her own inclination—which was to support and not oppose her daughter. But now she knew it was a forlorn hope—and she blamed herself for ever entertaining it. He would only argue—and argue. It was his nature.

She looked up groggily. He was speaking again, demanding to know why she was silent, repeating his offer with passionate sincerity. He expected praise for it. He was hurt because she had not praised and thanked him. He was pouting, his lower lip was trembling and his eyes were unnaturally wide and shining, in the way she knew well—it was the same every time she had broken his heart.

'I'm sorry, I have a terrible headache,' said Tara.

She sat back and stared at the ceiling. It was indescribably irritating to look at him. Something in her heart, which was more than resentment, was hardening every moment, while she waited, now with her eyes closed, for the meeting to be over.

*　　*　　*

Jatin left Malabar Hills in a state of discontent. Down by the roadside, he looked at his watch and cursed under his breath, because all the passing taxis were occupied. He had another meeting at the other end of the city; he was going to have to rush to not be late. None of this, it seemed to him, had been taken into account by Tara, when she clammed up the way she did, and made his having come all the way utterly pointless.

Why did people invariably disappoint? Even Tara, on whom he had lavished so much of himself for so many years, always making sure to put his best foot forward. But it seemed she had fought his influence every step of the way. It saddened him more than anything, though sometimes—yes, sometimes—it was offensive.

'Everyone's a fanatic,' he exclaimed loudly, startling a passer-by upon whom he bestowed a furious look. But he completed the rest of the thought in his head. *On the one hand, a smug coward like Suraj, and on the other hand, Tara, openly worrying herself into weakness; and then there was the younger generation, either wholly shallow or frivolous, or full of strange bloodlust. He could not understand it! He was not a cynic, no matter what people said about him. He knew that he always looked and hoped for soul and honesty. But what was to be done? Who was to do it?*

The sun was strong; Jatin was perspiring when he finally stopped a taxi (almost leaping into its path) and yanked open the door and gruffly mentioned his destination. The driver made no objection, because a trip to Andheri meant a good fare. He was also not bothered when, later, they slowed to a crawl in the traffic, somewhere between Dadar and Bandra.

There were grey and ugly buildings on both sides of the bridge, which was choked with cars and two monstrous buses. Entering through the open windows of their taxi, to the tune of a horrible palpitating rhythm, were the exhaust fumes of the one nearest them. A moment later, Jatin rose up from his slumped position and ordered the driver to roll up every window.

'It will be very hot!' the man objected.

'Do what I am telling you!' he exclaimed. 'Isn't it better to sweat a little than to die of pollution? Or you may not care about that! You may be fine living like an animal—but I am not—and I'm paying you! If you were so concerned about heat (he added, after a moment) you should have installed an AC! But *that* you won't do!'

As the driver reluctantly rolled up the windows, Jatin shifted his gaze towards the buildings, hive-like, sprouting like spores, and the pedestrians marching in a single file, like ants, along the side of the bridge. Intense hatred welled up in his heart. Not for the first time, a fantasy came to him, of the sea rising up over the city, of a gigantic tidal wave that would break to bits the highrises, sweep away the slums and drown the inhabitants of them all, like rats (then, at last, they would be screaming, as they ought to be screaming already). It would serve them right—because they lived like rats. A desperate smile came to Jatin's lips. But shortly it metamorphosed into a look of disgust.

'Switch it off!' he shouted at once.

Searching, perhaps, for succour, and still smarting from Jatin's tongue-lashing, the driver had switched on the radio. He seemed to have found what he was looking for in a Bollywood song full of pulsing beats. But Jatin felt that he had been plunged into hell—he was a connoisseur of good music.

'I said, *switch it off!* Do as I am telling you!'

'Don't shout,' grumbled the driver.

'I'm not shouting,' retorted Jatin. 'But because you are ignoring me, I have to repeat myself! Turn the radio off!'

In the silence, there was only the heat, the driver's muttered recriminations and the muted murmuring of tens of engines. Finally, Jatin breathed with relief, as the cars began to rev. At last, there was movement on the bridge! But as the bus eased ahead of them, the road opened up momentarily, and the cars behind honked and honked, the taxi was still idling.

When Jatin saw what was holding them up, he could hardly believe his eyes. The driver was making his gutkha. He had been patting down that vile powder at leisure. But even now, after gulping it down, he was dusting his hands instead of taking to the wheel. Bellowing an expletive, Jatin opened the car's door and almost fell out onto the bridge.

He was unmindful of the traffic. The honking was incessant all about him, but he paid it no heed and went marching between the vehicles. Then he began to climb the railings, beyond which a small group of people had stopped to look, thus also interrupting the stream of walkers. He was lifting himself up and was about to jump over, when he felt a rough hand pull him down. He cursed, dropping to his feet. Getting up, Jatin beheld the face of the taxi driver (a squat face, full of astonishment, the eyes flaring stupidly, the lips moving as though crazed).

'*Paise do!*[23]' the man cried. 'Two hundred and forty rupees! *Paise do!*'

He turned away in disgust, but there came another tug at his shoulder, and Jatin snapped. His arm moved like a whip and slapped the face that was filling his vision.

'Fuck off! Fuck off! First learn your job, then ask for money!'

Shaking off the man, he vaulted over the railing and broke into a brisk walk. He was expecting, any moment, to be stopped by the crowd, but was pleased to discover that nobody was getting

---

[23]Pay me the fare!

in his way. (Though a contempt for the onlookers also rose up in him.) However, footsteps were hurrying behind him and the same desperate voice was shouting the words '*Paise do! Paise do!*' Casting a glance over his shoulder, he saw that the driver, incredibly, was still giving chase. Meanwhile, on the bridge, the taxi stood abandoned and even the honking had diminished, as the traffic simply adjusted to the blockade.

He was ready when the driver came near. Lunging and bringing forward both arms like a pair of powerful pistons, he shoved the man to the ground. Then, as he lay there, he reached for his wallet and drew out three hundred-rupee notes.

'All you want is the money, right? Take it! Take three hundred! Take it, you're so pathetic!'

The notes fluttered towards the fallen man, who clutched at them with wide eyes. When he had caught every one, he got up and stumbled backwards hurriedly.

'Madman!' he shouted, from a distance.

'Pathetic!' roared Jatin.

Epochal Pictures Private Limited

Such were the events that preceded the meeting that evening. I was not present, for I was still in Delhi. But this is the truth: I seem to see myself there already—a ghostly presence in the office that I was very soon to join, perched on what would become my favourite seat (nearest the window, in the conference room). Turning my head, I glance down at the office buildings of the famous production houses, a swimming pool of an apartment complex and the malls along the main roads. It was always a wonder to me how Andheri, from that vantage point, looked so clean and organized. And I liked the office too, because it was spacious and colourful, with a modern look, many couches and windows, angled walls and sliding doors. There was a raffishness in the atmosphere, a sense of real fun and creativity—though I shiver now, when I remember to what end.

Together at the long table, with their smartphones placed in front of them, were Sushant and Bharat. They were exchanging looks and waiting. Meanwhile Jatin, seated opposite them, was pouring all his concentration onto the tea-things that our man Friday, Ram Prasad ji, had brought in a moment before.

'First things first,' explained Jatin, sipping deeply. 'Ahh! I needed that. Thank you, the tea is superb!

He bit into a biscuit and chewed purposefully. 'These are excellent too!'

'You're welcome, Sir,' said Bharat, with a smile.

'Jatin! For God's sake, call me Jatin!'

'Yes Jatin,' said Bharat, stealing another look at Sushant.

When I first beheld Sushant, in his fresh avatar as the co-founder of a company, I was both amazed and put off. I quickly realized, however, that he was as serious as he could possibly be about his new responsibility. To begin with, he was grooming himself—combing and shaving and dressing sharply. He had never been bad-looking, but now he looked his best. There was, in addition, a glow in his eyes and an ability to focus, where previously had been dullness and self-pity. No doubt it had helped enormously that he had cut down on the number of joints he smoked, had stopped drinking (except at parties) and begun to eat regular meals. He was quieter too, than before, and listened more.

Sushant, I understood, had too deep a sense of grandiosity to not crave power. It suited him, therefore, to be notionally in charge—but it suited him even better to be, in actuality, controlled by another; for (as I also quickly came to understand) the co-founders were not equal.

Bharat Mishra leaned forward and placed his elbows on the table. His eyes too were shining brightly—as they always did.

'Well, Jatin, let me give you a formal introduction, now that we are meeting face-to-face. I'm Bharat, and, of course, you already know Sushant very well. So, the two of us have been working in Mumbai for some time. Getting quite fed up with the film industry, like many young people. (He chuckled.) Recently, through some turn of events, and... ah... some common friends, we got in touch with each other. And we found a lot of similarity in our thinking. And now, an opportunity has opened up. That is to say, we have found an investor, who has been very generous.'

'I can see that,' said Jatin, looking about the room and nodding.

'Thank you. We are very happy about this space.'

'All the colours are not my taste, to be honest. I like an office to be spartan, so one can concentrate. But that's just me.'

Sushant laughed at once, and thus prompted, Bharat also smiled, though he was not pleased.

'So,' he continued, 'I should tell you at the outset, Epochal Pictures is not a *neutral* company. I mean, ideologically speaking, we are not neutral. Our purpose is to create content that combats the right wing, ok? Content that will promote libra—excuse me—liberalism. And modern values.'

'Sounds good!' said Jatin. 'I'm not interested in neutrality myself.'

'So, to begin with, we are looking at the online space. We're going to be producing feature films too, but we are starting online. We're looking at web series and documentaries in particular. We want to bring to light how ordinary liberals in India live, what they think and feel, the struggles they undergo in our society. Especially women—women liberals. Also we want to unmask the bigots who live among us… You had said one thing I really liked.'

'What was that?' asked Jatin at once.

'You had said in one of your interviews—I read somewhere— that the lives of ordinary people are actually wonderful material for documentaries. Because they tell us about our times. But we are not paying attention to them.'

'Absolutely,' nodded Jatin. 'Our storytelling is so obsessed with gangsters and glamour that we completely ignore the real people all around us. In fact, this is why I was planning to make—I still am planning to make—a documentary on Pankaj Pande. Exactly for this reason—as a conduit to make a point about a larger scene. In his case, the film industry, and Indian society in general.'

'It's a great idea,' smiled Bharat. 'That would have suited us really well, except for what has happened recently. *Khair, vo sab chhoddo*[24],' he continued smoothly, before Jatin could open his mouth. 'So, we really want to work with you, Jatin.'

'How do you know me anyway?' Jatin grumbled. 'Via Sushant, I know. But have you seen my work?'

'Not only via Sushant.'

'Dhruv also,' Sushant spoke up. 'Dhruv is going to be joining us too.'

'Really?' Jatin was amazed. 'But he never told me!'

As a matter of fact, it was only the previous evening in Delhi, that Mihir had given me the news of the new company. Yet, Sushant's presumption was justified. As quickly as I understood that the venture had the blessings of Ahishor and Mihir, it was understood that I would be a part of it.

'I guess we're growing quickly,' grinned Bharat. 'But we know about your work, obviously. Vaise[25], I also really enjoy reading your Facebook posts.'

'You do? You never like or comment.'

'I will now, I will,' Bharat promised, chuckling. 'I read all your film reviews, your political posts. We need a voice like

---

[24]Anyway, let's leave that

[25]By the way

yours, Jatin. Kyonki[26], you are not afraid to speak up.'

Sitting back, Jatin took a deep breath. After the day he had had, such words of praise were like rain on parched earth. But they were also the swelling up of a rankled ego.

'I'll tell you what...' He moved forward, in a burst of energy. 'Let's start with Friends of Freedom. My videos—our videos [he corrected himself earnestly, nodding at Sushant]. As you know, they were made in support of the liberal cause, against right-wing hooliganism, after the attack on Ahishor. They fit your objectives perfectly. They are relevant even now. You can relaunch them on your official channel, promote them properly—I was never able to do that; you see, I didn't have the bandwidth! And let's see what kind of response you get. Alright? How does that sound?'

Sushant, whom he was trying to fix with a look, was staring up at the ceiling with his eyes popping. There was nothing to see there; he was merely tense. Suddenly, Bharat frowned.

'While we liked the videos,' said Bharat, 'they were not good enough for us to use. We're looking for fresh content from you. Something along the lines—'

'What do you mean "they weren't good enough"?'

Bharat hesitated. 'I'll be honest.'

'Please!' demanded Jatin. 'Please be honest!'

'They were too boring. Not exciting for the viewer. The message itself was fine, but it has to be made more exciting. Just plain text on a black screen! Even with Sushant's music, the whole thing was not good enough.'

'I see,' said Jatin. 'So that's what you think?'

'If you see the number of views the videos got, I guess it's

---

[26]Because

what *most* people think.'

Jatin was beginning to breathe heavily. But there was a smile about his lips and his voice was already becoming composed and thoughtful. Bharat, therefore, did not see what was coming. And Sushant, who knew better, was not yet cured of his fondness for self-destruction. That he said nothing to save the situation, and was secretly eager to watch, was the proof of it.

'Let's say you're right,' said Jatin, in a contemplative tone. 'Let's assume that most people didn't like the videos. What that means is that most people would prefer to be distracted from a core intellectual message by irrelevant frills. And what that means, is something which we already know—or ought to know—which is that most people—'

He half rose from his chair, leaning over the table.

'—are *choots*!'

Then he sat down again. Across the table, Bharat's expression altered slowly. For Bharat was not urbane; he took no pride in bearing insults with sophistication. Every muscle in his lean face seemed to seize up.

'Kindly mind your language, Jatin. There's no need to abuse us.'

'Abuse you? When did I abuse you? I said *most people* are choots. When did I abuse you?'

He was mimicking a vast bewilderment, while Bharat held his gaze with narrowed eyes. Finally, Bharat relaxed—and at once, stinging and raging all over, Jatin spoke up.

'I said *most people* are choots… people like *you*!'

'Hey, hey!' Sushant could be heard, but as though from a distance. 'Enough, guys, enough.' He was waving his hands in a vague gesture, presumably of peace-making. But his words died away as quickly as they had been uttered

'I'm sorry,' said Bharat, picking up his phone from the table. 'Kindly apologize. *Nahi toh*[27], this meeting is over.'

'Apologize?' roared Jatin. 'Apologize for speaking the plain truth? You *are* a choot, if you don't understand the meaning of honesty in communication. If you're into gimmicks, you are a choot! What's more—you're a snob and an upstart! I have actually *done* things in my life! How dare you dismiss my work? You have done nothing; you have just got yourself this office because somebody's thrown money at you. And it's gone to your empty head!'

Bharat got up. 'We were just trying to give you a chance,' he shrugged.

'Give *me* a chance? You still don't understand! I was giving *you* a chance. You need me; I don't need you! Get that straight!'

'I knew of your mental problems,' continued Bharat, patting down his pockets and glancing about distractedly. 'Ahishor had warned me.'

'Ahishor? Is Ahishor your investor?'

'You don't bother about our investor. The point is, we were giving you a chance, despite your support for a sexual harasser. Khair…' Muttering in Hindi under his breath, Bharat turned to the door.

'Where are you going?' cried Jatin. 'Sit down! *I'm* leaving! *I* came and *I'm* leaving! And Sushant—I'm disappointed in you! If you ever want to achieve anything in life, stay away from this guy! Nothing you do with him will ever be a success! … Thanks for the tea!' Pausing to gulp it down, Jatin stormed out of the room, and down the passage outside, and through the main doors of the office, and out onto the landing.

---

[27]Otherwise

He was in such a state that he barely registered the young East European girl, who hopped out of the lift as he barged in, or the glow of hope and excitement that lay about her, like a halo.

*   *   *

For amidst all the passions and ambitions that were shooting up to the skies at the time, Elena and Sasha had found happiness in nurturing the homeliest of bonds. Just as the day of their first meeting had felt weighted with months-worth of experience, so were all the subsequent days they spent together, full of a stillness, stealing ever within. Two nights previously, after Sasha had served her roti, dal and sabzi (which she ate hungrily, not leaving anything on her plate), she had curled up most comfortably on the mattress in his hall. Beyond the windows, on either side of his rooms, there raged the sea and the street, but she slept till the morning, and was secure. The next day, she brought in her suitcase from Malad.

'You must stay with me as long as you are here,' Sasha had said. She had nodded with a look that took in its sweep both him and his house, before coming up to him and pronouncing with an all-knowing gravity: 'You are good.'

It was then that he knew what was meant in the saying: 'To be trusted is a greater compliment than to be loved'.

For me, however, it is painful to write richly of this relationship. For not long after, I was one of the sceptics and leering scoffers. To be sure, Sasha himself went through moments wherein he questioned his motives in taking in Elena. When she ate, sitting up on a chair, he would be by her feet, gazing at her openly. When her eyes welled up at this or that memory of her home, his own heart both melted and (at the same time) shouted for joy. He noticed her body—her frailness, her thin hair, her eyes and her beauty. But he found himself acting and speaking with surety and compassion; all else dissipating in the face of his tenderness and the instinctive certainty that he had been entrusted her, solely to look after her. He was discovering, with gladness, that he was better than he had imagined. He could indeed be good—as she had declared him to be good.

That night (the night that Jatin went raging into), Elena arrived home in a flurry of movement. She pressed the doorbell many times before bursting in, brushing by Sasha to quickly remove her shoes, her head held down in concentration, as he stood aside.

'How was the meeting?' he asked.

'Was fine.'

From the entrance, she made a beeline to the nearest wall socket and began setting up her phone to charge.

But this was not unusual; she was always darting from task to task. When she had finished at the plug point, she rose and went directly to the bathroom, closing the door firmly behind her. Meanwhile, Sasha sat down on a chair and waited for her to come out. Elena's abruptness, the fact that she seemed to take him for granted, did not offend him. As he sat down, he found himself smiling. The things he had been thinking of fell away from him and his heart filled with a simple gladness at her arrival. His very surroundings, the rooms of his apartment, felt renewed with purpose and expectancy. By the same token, he was a little tense.

As soon as she re-emerged, she looked straight at him (as though remembering to make amends) and asked: 'How are you?'

She had washed her face and tied up her hair into a bun. In the soft light of the living room, her cheeks were rosy fresh.

But even as she strained to regard him with all attentiveness, he could see that there was trouble pricking at her eyes.

'I'm alright,' he said, carefully. 'Not feeling very good actually.'

'Why?' She was still on her feet, lingering near the bathroom door.

'Come, sit,' said Sasha. 'Well, no particular reason. I've just been reading… and thinking.'

'Reading what?' She sat down, though not on the mattress he had indicated, but on a stool, which, owing to its extremely small size, was usually used as a foot rest. 'Thinking what?'

'Reading a Christian writer. His name is George Macdonald. He is very wise, very good… He says a good thing about death. He asks why we are afraid of death, when we are never afraid of a sunset. And another thing about work and busyness… about being busy all the time. He says it's such a mistake that there is such a thing as sacred idleness. That's a nice expression, isn't it? Sacred idleness! [The tension was growing in him, as he spoke.] It fits Mumbai, I guess—and Versova. All this bustle; everybody scrabbling; never a moment's pause to question what it's for!'

'I am liking it,' said Elena decisively. 'It's free here—it's not like Delhi.'

Sasha hesitated, and then laughed, shrugging. 'I guess that's true too.'

'Is that all you were thinking about?' she asked.

'No. Not all… And then I was thinking about Ruhi… Ruhi, yes… I was thinking that I should have—I could have done something, perhaps, to save her.'

'What you saying?' Elena exclaimed with disapproval. 'What you could have done? That girl was depressed about the producer guy, because he did something bad with her! Nobody should take any blame.'

'What producer guy?'

'You don't know? I heard about it from one coordinator, Akash; he keeps texting all kinds of things. I don't know if it's true or not.'

'What name did he say?'

'It's Ritesh Azad, of Elevate. They are saying she had written his name in her—in her note.'

'In her suicide note!' cried Sasha, thinking aloud. 'No, I hadn't heard that. As far as I had heard, there was no name at all.'

Then he noticed Elena, flinching miserably. He stopped and turned his gaze away. He looked at the window nearest the street. When he strained to listen, the traffic noises were audible, but they only highlighted the rare quiet of the room. He knew well that all of Versova, teeming with people, things and a thousand encounters every hour of the day and night, was pressing up against them. He could imagine it; if he walked over to the window, he would see it under the lowering skies. Yet, this silence too was real.

'It's not blame exactly,' said Sasha softly. 'I don't blame myself directly. But Ruhi used to call me. She did need me—for advice; or just to tell her something that would give her strength. And sometimes one person can stop another person from falling. I believe that. People have that power, and that dependency. I could have done better than I did... So I do blame myself.'

He took a long breath. Elena glanced at her phone, but looked quickly back. She was listening.

'I don't know why I'm telling you this,' he confessed, 'but I want to. The thing is, I didn't *only* want to help Ruhi. I was also tempted to take advantage of her. You understand? Because I was conscious of my power over her. I knew I had influence over her. So I was tempted. I did imagine seducing her—under the pretence of helping her. I didn't do it! Thank God I didn't! But the thought was in my head. Perhaps it was there too much. And that must have prevented me—made me less able—to actually help her... Elena! Elena, I'm sorry! I didn't mean to upset you! I shouldn't have said anything... don't know why I did!'

Her mouth had parted in a silent cry. Her eyes had welled up and her whole face was etched with pain. But she shook her head and tried to speak.

'It's not you.' Her voice was surprisingly clear and strong. 'Not you, not you! You are a good person!'

'Then what is it?' he asked softly. 'Was it the meeting? Tell me about the meeting. You haven't told me yet.'

Before answering, Elena composed herself with long breaths and dabbed at her eyes with a hanky.

'I left early. I told them I will not do it.'

'Do what?'

'Their video. They wanted to make viral video with bunch of girls talking about their bad experiences in India. I thought it could be fun, because of all the silly coordinators and what things they text me! But they kept asking more things. They wanted to know only... only private things, even from the time I came to India. Whatever I said, they wanted more! "What was the first bad time? What was first bad time?," they kept asking—and—'

With a sudden gasp, she ceased speaking. Sasha looked at her, alert.

'This is that new company, right? Epochal Pictures?'

She nodded. Her mouth was twisting all over again, her

fist clenching over her crumpled handkerchief. Sasha found himself staring at the pink and blue embroidery. He remained quiet, while she turned to her phone and swiped and tapped the screen. Then she handed it to him, saying: 'This was their mail.'

On the screen was the following text:

Dear Elena,

Epochal Pictures is a dynamic new production house, working for nothing less than social and intellectual revolution. As one of our debut projects, we wish to present eye-opening, personal accounts of ordinary women living in India, regarding the abuse and harassment they face in society. The objective of this video is to shock the viewer into awareness and action, while also providing a cathartic release to the women involved.

All of Epochal Pictures's productions, including this project, will be presented by Ahishor Frances, director of Schrodinger's Cat, and promoted by a committed publicity team.

Auditions are on the dates mentioned below. We look forward to seeing you.

With best wishes,

Bharat Kumar
Sushant Anand
For Epochal Pictures Pvt. Ltd.

'Bharat and Sushant!' exclaimed Sasha. 'I know them! Were they there when you went?'

'Yes,' Elena nodded. 'I didn't know you knew them! But did you see? Company has tie-up with Ahishor! Ahishor Frances is gonna present this video! And now I have lost my chance!'

'The video sounds terrible,' said Sasha, with unexpected vehemence. 'It sounds sensationalist and exploitative! The bit about Ahishor doesn't matter—it's good you turned it down.'

'I am a street-person,' wailed Elena. 'I have no home. And I throw away all my chances!'

An extraordinary rapidity had infected them both, in speech, thought and emotion, for many things had suddenly become clear to Sasha, without needing to be told, and she too had sensed his knowledge in her bones. In the same charged vein, he continued:

'Don't say that, Elena! You have a home—with God! I mean it! I'm telling you the truth—God looks after you always! I'm the same as you—that's how I know! I'm a street dog too!'

'I didn't say I am a dog!'

'Yes, alright—a street-person! I am too!'

A little while later, they were both smiling and trembling. Sasha rose to his feet, shakily.

'I'll make tea. I'll put extra milk and sugar—the way you like it.'

When they were together again, nursing the warm cups between their palms, Elena told him in detail, what he had already understood in essence. It was the story that Bharat and Sushant had craved to get out of her, as they leaned forward with unblinking eyes and bared teeth—until Elena, seized with a sense of foreboding, had rushed out of the room, overcome with nausea. It was not a new story, as these things go. A middle-aged man had taken up and betrayed the trust of a young girl.

The one whom she had looked upon as her mother's best friend, and called by the name 'Uncle', had seen fit to abuse her. But beyond the banal and sickening horrors, there were details in the story that Sasha could scarcely believe when, later, in the privacy of his thoughts, he joined them like little dots and traced a face he knew.

Mihir Returns to Town

The news about Ritesh Azad, which young Elena had heard, was spreading rapidly. Nobody was fully certain of its veracity—the police were denying it even while journalists were reporting it, but there was an equivocation in the official denial that made it less than convincing. As to where the story had come from, it was assumed that one of the investigating officers had leaked the information to the media. Only later was it generally realized that the rumour had originated via a tweet—from an anonymous handle to boot. 'The Spirit of Sartre', an account that had been lying dormant for months, with only forty odd followers, had put out the following message: 'First Pankaj, now Ritesh. Ruhi's suicide note blames Ritesh Azad. Damn the Mafia!' This was followed by another message that read simply: 'He messed with her!' And from there the thing had spread, and refused to die down.

Finally, ten days after everyone started talking about it, a press conference was held by the police to clarify two things: one, that Ruhi's suicide note (which they insisted would not be made public, to prevent speculation, and out of respect for the wishes of her family) mentioned no names, and two, that it did contains a reference to 'a person connected with film production,' whose identity was still being investigated. Simultaneously, the investigating officer admitted that unrequited love was being looked into as a cause for the suicide. All this only fanned the flames of the rumour; indeed, in the general understanding, it practically settled it as fact. The reference in the note could not be to Pankaj Pande—he was a director, not a producer. 'Sartre's Spirit' was, therefore, right—gaggles of powerful men were behind Ruhi's sordid demise. Nor had the aforementioned 'Spirit' gone quiet—far from it. In a series of explosive tweets, it indicted the police for attempting a 'cover-up' to protect Ritesh, whose general character it also cast aspersions upon (suggesting a propensity for violence); hinted that the undisclosed suicide note cast guilt on other eminent men of Bollywood too; reminded everyone of the rot in Bollywood, and the grossly exploitative relations between young struggling actors and the money bags; declared that more revelations were forthcoming; and that it would not allow the wrongdoers to get away.

Meanwhile, the paparazzi, which had been waiting for an opportunity, descended in droves upon Ritesh's home, office, father's and stepmother's apartment, in-laws, maid and driver—indeed, wherever inspiration struck. So it was, that on the cheerful March afternoon when Mihir arrived at the house of Karim and Nalini Frances, a fracas was in progress, involving three security guards and one particularly pesky member of the media. It was disturbing the leafy quiet for some distance all around.

The journalist was proclaiming his rights and duties at the top of his voice, when Mihir stepped into the compound and declared that he too had come to see the Azads. But when the beleaguered guards turned wildly, he put his hands together and bowed.

'I am a friend of the family. Please call Naliniji and tell her that Mihir Malhotra has come. She is waiting to meet me. And I have come all the way from Delhi to meet her, because it is important.'

This last sentence was a half-truth, because he had plenty of other business in Mumbai too. But Nalini really was on tenterhooks. She was anxious to see Mihir, because he had met Ahishor, and she was in a storm of anxiety over her son.

For even as Ritesh found himself dragged unwillingly into the headlines, Ahishor was making a triumphant return to the limelight. With the online release of The New Culture Manifesto (a print launch was proposed for later, along with multiple translations, so that all of India could read it), he was once again a sensation everywhere, almost as he had been when *Schrodinger's Cat* had released. Then, of course, he had received universal praise. Now, while tending in that direction, the reactions also showed caution and confusion, and in no one did the ambivalence rise to such a fever pitch as in Ahishor's mother. For she had never seen this coming. *Though all the signs had been there in front of her, though she knew her son intimately, she had somehow failed to read them—or him. And what had he gone and said about Ritesh?*

She almost pulled Mihir indoors, before slamming the door shut.

'The place is surrounded! We're living like captives!'

She was plainly beside herself. Her hair fell wildly over a loose, patterned tunic. It was unnerving to see Nalini Frances so bereft of composure—with no concealing make-up. But Mihir smiled blandly.

'Your guards are doing a most efficient job. Erring on the side of zealousness, perhaps, but that's understandable.'

'Ohh, don't talk about it!' she said dramatically. 'One of these guys even got into the house. He was pretending to sell bedcovers of all things! Only I know how I'm managing!' Suddenly she looked him straight in the eye. 'Now you tell me—how is Ahishor, and what is he doing?'

'I came to share all my thoughts,' Mihir smiled again. 'But it might be easier sitting down, Nalini.'

Saying so, he reached out his hand and let it rest on her shoulder. She was momentarily surprised at his audacity and then felt a spurt of irritation; an angry crease formed over her brow, but she checked herself in time. He was, after all, a guest—and a decent boy.

'Sit please… You'll have tea?'

'Tea would be great! With milk and sugar please. And something to eat if you have it.'

'I can ask the maid to make pakoras,' offered Nalini dully.

'Wonderful.'

Grinning to himself, Mihir walked towards the sofas, from where he let his gaze wander about the room. He was wearing a look of contentment and amusement, though his foot kept tapping the carpet.

'Karim's not home?' he inquired, when Nalini returned from the kitchen.

'No, he's with Ritesh.' She stared into space and took long, deep breaths. Slowly, her face became composed, though there remained a telltale twitch in her right eye. 'They are all very angry with Ahishor.' As she spoke, her hands slid down to the pockets of her tunic.

'Why should they be angry with Ahishor?'

'Oh hush, darling!' She paused to light a cigarette. 'He's not exactly been supportive.'

Mihir watched her carefully. She was squinting and grimacing as she exhaled. He felt momentarily overmatched, sensing that his instinct towards clowning would run aground before Nalini's superior dramatic presence. He quickly became sincere.

'He is supporting his cause,' he said gravely. 'You have read the Manifesto. He wrote it all himself.'

'I *have* read it,' she exclaimed. 'And I agree with it! But I'm also not sure about it!'

'If you agree with it,' smiled Mihir, 'what is there to be unsure about?'

'Why didn't he defend Ritesh? It's not like him! Just because he backed out of the documentary? And I always knew that documentary was a bad idea! It was you all—you all who insisted on doing it! But I know Ahishor doesn't hold grudges. He's not like that.'

Mihir smiled again, this time at the thought of how much a mother could fail to see what was obvious to everyone else. He began to feel sure of himself.

'It's not about grudges. Look... I remember when we all sat here and talked about that documentary. You were worried then, and it looks like your worries have come true. We didn't want it to happen this way; we wanted Ahishor to be diplomatic, neutral. But he surprised everyone! I think he even surprised himself. And now he has taken the view that everything that happened was for the best. See, we were all looking to avoid trouble—but Ahishor decided to court it.'

He sat up straight and was terribly grave.

'And I, for one, have realized that he is right. At first, I thought like you—if you'll pardon my saying so. But I was wrong—he is right. And I'm standing by him... As for Ritesh, you know very well how (he gestured towards the window) these people pester for quotes. They got to Ahishor in Jangpura too. He spoke off the cuff, but what did he say that was wrong? All he said was, "*a*", that anyone who mistreats anyone should be punished and "*b*", that we must judge people by how they behave, not by the positions of power or privilege that they occupy.'

'But what does it sound like?' she pleaded, full of distress. 'It sounds like he is saying, "Yes, Ritesh is guilty of this girl's suicide"! That's how everyone's interpreting it! And Ritesh is family; they are brothers! Oh, these vultures are having a field day! Haven't you seen those gleeful headlines?'

'Never mind the headlines; nobody takes tabloids seriously.'

'But they do! Karim says we have become a reality-show society. Everyone's performing before the media, and the media decides everybody's fate!'

'Well, that's certainly bad. I'm sure nobody wants that... Ah!' Mihir looked gleefully at the tray of tea and pakoras as it arrived. Waving away the help, he poured out the cups himself. Then, as he held out Nalini's cup for her, he caught her eye meaningfully.

'You have to understand that family is irrelevant here. This is not about family. Ahishor has a cause. He cannot be—he is not a nepotist. Blood may be thicker than water, but it's not thicker than spirit—not thicker than the spirit of right and wrong!'

He felt extremely pleased at this turn of phrase (a laugh caught in his throat), because he was usually not eloquent.

'Well it's not a blood relation,' said Nalini quickly, which amused Mihir further. Then she sat back, staring at the window, smoking, thinking and biting her lower lip rather prettily.

'But it's dangerous!' she said suddenly, as though snatching at the words. 'To make things into movements and manifestos— when does that go well?'

'When *have* things gone well?' Now Mihir was certainly in the grip of inspiration; his mind was racing with all the right words. 'Should things just keep going on as they are? We are heading to a dark age. Should we keep going? But Ahishor—your son—Ahishor has sounded a bugle of resistance. And some of us have heard it! ... Besides, movements and manifestos do end well. They did during our freedom struggle; they have, all over the world—whenever right-thinking people decide to do right!'

He was getting through to her. He could see she felt a flicker of attraction; that she had sensed the possibility, though never expecting to. She put out her unfinished cigarette and licked her lips.

'It isn't right that he forgets about family. He hasn't even been talking to me! He answers me in monosyllables. I call, and he says he has to go, and he puts down the phone. It's never been like this!'

Now she was working herself up to tears.

'That's why I'm here,' Mihir said, leaning forward. 'I know it's been difficult. But Ahishor has been aloof from everyone—he needed that space to do this work. Heck, he's barely talked to me either, and he's been living on my terrace! But of course he wants to be close to you; he needs your support, it goes without saying. He needs your support.'

'Of course it goes without saying!' She produced a handkerchief and held it close to her face as though to ward off the tears. 'But I want what's best for him! If he's going to antagonize everyone, even his own family—I'm not talking about myself; I mean Ritesh and Karim—how will this work then?'

'Good question,' nodded Mihir. 'I'll tell you the truth—I thought exactly the same thing at first. But that's just it. I was wrong. I didn't realize what a groundswell of support he has. With this Manifesto, he has put his finger on the pulse of our people! *Our* people! You know the writer Giri Joseph? Of course, you do. He's probably the greatest literary star we have right now. He is championing Ahishor; he is going to praise him in *The Guardian* this Sunday. You know Ira Joshi and Dipankar Joshi? The socialite—yes, the socialite—and the civil servant. They are right behind him too. Oh, many many people are! Indian liberals are standing up; it's amazing, but it's happening. Now the only question for all of us is, which side are we going to be on?'

'What do you mean?' Nalini uttered a laugh, but she was looking at him with wide eyes.

'He says it in the Manifesto too. It's a critical time. Whoever is not helping at this moment is hindering. All the more when they are being counted on to help.'

Suddenly, Mihir got up and stepped around the table to where Nalini was sitting. He lowered himself down beside her. He was grinning now, beatifically, as she stared at him, amazed.

'Ahishor is a genius!' he declared.

Her face lit up, as though a switch had been pressed. She inhaled deeply and began, almost in spite of herself, to smile. As she continued to stare, now with trembling and enchanted looks, Mihir judged that she was quite won over. Though she checked herself and opened her mouth to voice a doubt, he was quicker.

'We are on the winning side,' he said, dropping his voice for sheer pleasure. 'Believe me, something amazing is happening. And I haven't even told you the best part. The owner of Ozymandias is with us. You haven't heard of Ozymandias, but you will soon. It's a new club that's started in Delhi. It's very private, but every great Indian liberal is going to be a part of it. Ahishor—'

Nalini's phone rang once. She glanced at it. 'Karim's back,' she said.

She looked about hurriedly and then got to her feet, even as two loud knocks were heard on the door. As she went to open it, she darted a backward glance at the ashtray where she had stubbed out her cigarette, at her handbag resting on the table, and then at Mihir, right behind them both. She meant, in some inarticulate way, to disapprove of the proximity these told of, but he, in the meantime, had settled down deeper into the sofa, and, indeed, thrown his arm about the backrest. He was thus seated, when Karim Azad entered the room.

He came in with heavy steps. The kurta was flowing as ever, his presence was still arresting, but the great man was plainly not himself. He looked, with pursed lips, at Nalini; then, as he noticed the visitor, he simply stared. Mihir smiled brightly. Inwardly, however, he was surprised to see Karim so strangely slowed (he had been prepared for outbursts of indignation). Only in a certain lingering of his gaze was the man's displeasure showing. But an overriding confusion was writ upon his face.

'It's me,' said Mihir. 'I came from Delhi today.'

Karim nodded imperceptibly and raised his head towards the window. He stood awhile and gazed. All of Versova was in that view—the quiet lanes, the tops of trees, the shops and buildings by the main road, and the sea twinkling in the afternoon sun. In the crush of the city, that blurred conglomeration of desperate villages, Versova stood out. It was a village too, but somehow distinct, with bright lines and a definition that drew his approval. He was glad, just then, to find something to approve of.

'I came to say there is no need to worry,' Mihir continued.

'Ahishor is doing good work and getting good support. We all must pull in the same direction, that's all. Then there is no need to worry.'

Mihir felt a deep joy in being cryptic and getting away with it, all the more so in the face of someone as generally scathing and fastidious as Karim. But the latter, it seemed, was too troubled to take stock. Nalini stood by the carpet, clasping her hands unconsciously, while he continued to stare fixedly at the window. Eventually, he moved to sit down on the spot Mihir had recently vacated. For some moments, he remained quiet, wrestling a deep frown. Only when that had cleared did his eyes, at last, narrow in a familiar way.

'You are a journalist, aren't you?'

'By training, yes. But critics argue that I am a politician in journalist's clothing.' He laughed gleefully. There was a long pause.

'Since you are, at least formally, a journalist,' said Karim afresh, 'I am curious to know what you think of the way in which the media is behaving these days.'

His voice too was slow with fatigue. But his eyes, become small, and appearing smaller still in the large face, were fastened on Mihir.

Another exulting frisson passed through the young man.

'I think I know what you're referring to,' said Mihir innocently. 'Well, as someone who knows the principles of good journalism, I know that sensationalism isn't one of them. But I think something interesting is happening in this country. I mean, the sensationalism in our media has started to centre on issues that actually do matter—rather than which film star wore what and when. It's quite a unique phenomenon, even if you look around the world. We're finally getting really passionate about our behaviour: I mean, what kind of people, we modern-day Indians are, what kind of qualities we possess as human beings and citizens. I would say, this is not a bad thing.'

Karim said nothing, but the darkness was stealing over his face again, making dull even his gaze. Unconsciously, he turned again to the window, but Mihir got up and went over to stand in front of it, blocking off the light.

'Is it bad,' asked Mihir, in a musing tone, 'that the media has become a judge of people? Ordinarily, yes. But these are not ordinary times. Besides, you are forgetting something. (Here, he ignored Karim's look of affront.) With social media, we are all the media now. So today, when the media judges, it is really a democratic judgment, unlike ever before. And then there is another thing.'

They were both staring at him. Once again, he felt unusually gifted. Mihir was used to befriending people, especially artistic and philosophically minded folk, but he did not know that he himself could preach abstractions so easily. He glanced upwards, in a motion of gratitude, but suddenly he was seized with laughter and he had to spend a moment grinning at the floor, until this mood of risibility was gone.

'In the past too,' he pressed on, raising his voice, 'our society has had its darlings and its whipping boys. But these categories have been based on entrenched privilege. What we are seeing now is a churning of the old order. It is a noisy business of course, this democratic judgment, but at least it is an open marketplace and the currency here is not your identity or your bank balance or who your father is. (Here he waved a hand in Karim's direction—though he was gesticulating generally.) The currency is simply the quality of your behaviour. I don't even know how we reached this place where behaviour has started to matter. I'm just happy we are here. This is the one marketplace where liberals have, at least, a chance to score. That's why all the real liberals are flocking to it.'

'And who decides…' Karim was speaking more forcefully than before. 'Who decides who is a "real liberal"?'

'Why, the marketplace of course,' said Mihir. 'But I think Nalini understands. We were talking before you came.'

They threw sharp looks at each other.

'I have to go now,' said Mihir, darting forward. 'I'll be in touch though. I'm in town now!'

A New Recruit

From Nalini's, it was only a short walk to his next stop. But having set out briskly, Mihir gradually slowed his stride, inhaled and exhaled deeply, and smiled to himself in part-admonition. There was no need to rush. It was important to congratulate oneself on negotiating tricky terrain. So, first he did that.

It was also a beautiful day for a stroll. It occurred to him that he had never really noticed this part of Versova. He began to look about keenly, for it was pretty and green, and the apartment buildings were posh. He remembered the wonderful view from Nalini's window. It would be nice, he considered, to own such an apartment. Or better still, a whole tower! But for that he would need to make a lot of money. Unfortunately, he was never going to be a Salman Khan. Journalists never did get rich—did they?

This thought made him frown; it did not amuse him and he made a silent vow that he would one day own a tower twice as grand as any there—only not in Mumbai. For in Mumbai, the stink surrounded everything. It was certainly, in many ways, a microcosm of India, and that was Anamika's point about India.

As if on cue, he spotted a man in rags, lying face down behind a bus stop, invisible to the passers-by who were oblivious to him. Mihir came to a halt, his eyes trained on the prone figure. What, he wondered, compelled the destitute to continue living? Why did they all not simply commit suicide? One thing he knew—if they were to trade places, and he were to find himself thus situated, homeless, with no money, no prospects, no one to admire or respect him, he would kill himself straightaway.

Suddenly he bristled and wished he had not walked this way. He very rarely philosophized about existential things. All he knew was that if it was not full of success, life was truly horrible, no matter what anyone said—a hideous thing, unbearable to contemplate.

He was still standing and frowning to himself, when he heard a voice at his back.

'Hi, hi, young man.'

A strange-looking woman was staring at him. Her clothes were plentiful, old and shabby. She spoke good English in a booming voice. 'Do you live nearby?'

Mihir shook his head, 'I don't live in Mumbai.'

There was no change in her expression. 'I live in Bandra,' she said. 'I have to go home, but I forgot my purse.'

'That's a pity,' said Mihir, beginning to smile.

'Please lend me two hundred rupees, young man. You might be in my shoes tomorrow.'

'Don't curse me, Ma'am,' he laughed.

She frowned and inclined her head. Her mind was visibly working behind her beady eyes.

'You can give me your address and I will return the money to you.'

'But I live in San Francisco,' said Mihir innocently.

This seemed to make no difference to her. 'Write down your address and give it to me.' She threw a quick glance down the road. 'I need to get home urgently. Please give me the money quickly.'

'I'll give you the money,' said Mihir. 'And you don't have to return it to me either.'

Nodding impatiently, she held out her hand.

'But you have to do something for me too,' he continued. 'That's only fair. Now, what I want you to do is: you see this bus stop? I want you to walk around this bus stop one time and come back here, and then I'll give you the money. Ok? Yes, just go around it and come back, that's all... Here is the money. (Mihir showed her the two notes.) See, I have the money here; just go and come, as a favour to me... And be careful to avoid that man lying at the back... Oh, and do it on one leg please. On *one* leg. Like this. (He hopped a little distance to show her.) Just like that, it's easy. You must do it on one leg.'

The woman, who had taken a step towards the bus stop, now stood and stared. Then, like a dark wave, her face was swept with anger. To Mihir's immense astonishment, she lunged towards him. Uttering a frantic cry, he struck out blindly. His eyes were shut, but he felt his fists making contact with her face and heard a cry of pain. When he regained his footing, he saw that the woman had fallen down. She was squirming and groaning on the pavement, clutching her face.

He stamped his foot, threw a last look at her and hurried away. Nobody on the street stopped him, for either the incident had not been noticed, or he had been reckoned without blame.

* * *

At the gate of Zohra Aghadi, he felt that he could walk no more. It was sweltering outside, but the outdoors were still preferable to the meagreness of Malik's apartment. How, he wondered, could anyone create anything in such cramped conditions? Pulling out his phone, he asked Malik to come out instead—he was waiting at the gate. Then he walked up and down, crunching gravel viciously, until he spotted the large figure ambling out towards him.

Malik, however, was not alone. Following him, with a jumpy stride, was the hunchbacked young man whom Mihir recalled from the previous year at Nalini's house—the one who had made such a spectacle of himself, talking about God. And he had kept hearing about Sasha, ever since. He was supposed to have been madly in love with Maithili and had incurred Anamika's wrath for his galling perseverance. *There was indeed something leech-like about the fellow*, he thought. *Rather pathetic and pious.*

As the two men approached, Mihir felt an instinctive sense of warning, a sixth sense that here was one to be avoided. Ordinarily, he paid attention to his instincts, but just then (he was fatigued and annoyed) he dismissed it. *No doubt, Sasha was a little unhinged—frustrated in work and love—but so was practically everyone in Versova. Was that not, paradoxically, what made them so useful?*

'I'm sorry,' he called out cheerfully. 'I just need fresh air!'

'Cool, cool,' Malik chuckled. 'Let's walk to the panwaadi[28], I need a cigarette. What? Ah, you said fresh air! Ehehehe! Oh, I don't know if you two know each other. This is Sasha, he's also a writer. And this is Mihir—'

---

[28]paan shop

'We've met,' said Sasha.

They walked in silence for a short distance. At the corner of the road, there was a paan shop that sold cigarettes, and a tea stall beside it. Mihir and Sasha both refused Malik's offer of a cigarette, who instead ordered tea for them all.

When he had taken a few restoring drags, Malik asked casually: 'Are you moving to Versova?'

Mihir started.

'No! Of course not! Where did you get that idea?'

'Ehehe, ok! You don't have to look so shocked!'

'Well…' Mihir studied his glass of tea and then looked about the street with an unpleasant smile that eventually turned on Malik.

'I'm not moving to Versova. I've come to bring change to Versova.'

Assisted by his bushy eyebrows, his smile became questioning, and Malik's face, which had been beatific in a cloud of cigarette smoke, darkened a shade.

'I read the Manifesto,' said Malik. 'I mean, I liked it. I had some issues with it, but I liked it.'

'What kind of issues?'

'Like, it's very true; everything he says.' Malik began to speak with great sincerity. 'But what will happen in terms of practical steps? It can go viral on Facebook, but *uske baad kya*[29]? See, at the end of the day, people have to work and chalao their ghars[30], I really don't know who has time for… *revolution*. Hahaha!'

He let go of his tension with a big, open-mouthed laugh. But Mihir sighed wearily.

---

[29]'uske baad kya' means 'what after that'

[30]'chalao their ghars' means 'earn their living'

'What have we been talking about, if not practical steps? What is Epochal Pictures? It's not an illusion.'

'But you haven't told me anything about it,' protested Malik.

'You've been told all about it. You've been told about the April project too.'

The carefulness of his speech was the only nod Mihir gave to Sasha's presence. But his attention remained focussed on Malik, who was casting about guilty looks and taking several quick puffs of his cigarette.

'You said that wasn't finalized.'

'So what? It's in process. You need to realize that everything happening here is very serious. More serious than the writing jobs you've been doing for random producers. How many scripts have you written, Malik? Many, right? Many many. And how many releases do you have?'

'Those jobs chalao my ghar,' said Malik sullenly. But Mihir turned on him with sudden fury.

'Are you worried about money? Epochal will pay you two lakh a month! Every month! Two lakh on the first of every month! Now are you listening?'

He did not stop for an answer, but continued passionately, in between restraining sips of his tea.

'We have money because good people have invested in us. These are people who are very comfortable; they are living very well; they don't need to get involved with something new. But they are doing it because they believe in us... And then there's you guys! You guys really disappoint me. It's classic crab mentality. None of you is achieving anything, despite your supposed love for cinema, despite your talent, despite the hard work you're constantly putting in... You're all trapped in this place. It's not just that your scripts don't get made into movies, but the ones that do, are mediocre. They are timepass. Half of them are plagiarized… It's the truth, don't deny it.'

Malik, as one convicted, hung his head.

'Now, here arises one among you, who is doing things differently. He is showing you the way out. And instead of following him, you want to drag him down!'

'I don't want to drag him down re!' Malik tried to laugh. 'Sasha, you tell him; I have the utmost respect for Ahishor.'

'He doesn't want to drag him down,' Sasha assented. 'But he may not want to join him.'

'I'm not even saying that,' put in Malik hastily, remembering the figure recently mentioned. 'I'm not saying I don't want to join.'

Mihir gave him a withering look—then he turned to Sasha. 'Have you read the Manifesto?'

'Yes, it is a remarkable document.'

Rushing to a judgment, Mihir continued, 'I'll bring you up to speed. Epochal Pictures is a new production house, aimed at producing content that fulfils the goals of the Manifesto. Web series, movies—all kinds of audiovisual stuff. If you're a writer, you should come down to the office and have a chat yourself. If you fit—who knows! We're hiring.'

Sasha smiled apologetically.

'The Manifesto is remarkable and laudable in many ways, but I'm sorry, I don't support what has been happening ever since. And even before.'

'What?' Mihir was astonished. 'Ever since *what*?'

Sasha looked around, at the blackened kettle on the flaming ring and the wooden bench where workmen sat with their glasses of cutting chai. The tea shack was a little oasis of shade and solace, for the heat was terrible a few paces away. A new customer came along, working the phlegm in his throat. He then turned and spat it out. It seemed strange to speak out in such a setting. But then it came to Sasha that the street was quite the best place for it.

'You want to change India, but you first want to tear it down. Now, you may not even realize this but you are enjoying the tearing down, not the building up. We can all feel that happening. It's there—that energy of destruction… it's in the air.'

'What energy? I don't know what you're talking about,' said Mihir.

'Really? Stop to think. I think you do; you know very well… And it's because you have started with a fixed ideal of your own making. Instead of letting the destination come to you, letting change happen faithfully, you are trying to use your strength to push through your own purposes. However noble it may seem to you, what you are doing is destructive. I know about Epochal Pictures. As far as I can see, they are rejoicing in destruction.'

'Don't join them, Malik,' he added suddenly. 'Don't stay as you are, but don't join them.'

Then his heart sank to see Malik drawing level with Mihir, looking at him with mirth. He felt the pangs of doubt. *Had he spoken wrongly, or too much?* However, he soldiered on.

'Yes, you are trapped in a bad system. Going on the same way, working the same way, is not helpful. That much is true. So you must dig deep and really do your best work—and keep backing yourself. Malik, you are a truly creative person; you're a warm person. Remember Afroza, the girl in Hyderabad? You lost your nerve with her. But you also cared for her, because you are full of caring. That's why she trusted you. So create better now, tap into your warmth. Don't let despair get the better of you—but don't destroy!'

Malik stood open-mouthed, with the cigarette in one hand and the glass of tea in the other, till he burst out laughing.

'Ehehehe! I am not despairing re! You think too much! You're too dramatic re!' He continued talking, laughing and protesting, finishing his tea and slapping Sasha on the back.

But Mihir had taken a step back. There was revulsion leaping from his eyes. They were fastened on Sasha, just as though he was a snake that had come slithering out from the undergrowth. He himself could not have explained what filled him with such intense hatred. But he was shuddering with the emotion, furious with himself as well, for having deliberately ignored his instincts. The mood of the moment had taken him in—as well as Sasha's appearance of docility, the tea stall and the sunny day—though he had known from the very beginning that here was an enemy as deceitful as the snake that would strike at every opportunity.

He opened his mouth; there emerged an angry, gnashing voice, quite unlike his own: 'Bye, Malik! I don't have time for this.'

Simultaneously, he put out an arm to stop one of the autos that were passing by continually. Before the two men could react, he had jumped into a vehicle and barked out his destination. He turned back, however, to glare at Malik, who was lumbering forward in astonishment. He kept staring at Malik for several moments, before speeding away with finality.

*   *   *

Before the red light at Juhu circle and en route to Andheri station, Mihir tapped the auto driver on the shoulder.

'Take a U-turn from here. I need to go back to Yari road.'

The driver grumbled, but back they went. As they returned

to the vicinity of the tea stall, Mihir put out his head and peered. It did not take him long to spot what he was looking for. There was Malik, alone, trudging towards the gate of his building. Mihir directed the auto right up to him; indeed, headed Malik off as the vehicle halted. Then he got out casually, as though performing routine business, paying the driver but not acknowledging his recent company, who was already exclaiming in surprise.

'Bro! I'm really sorry, I told Sasha he shouldn't have talked like that. He is a sweet guy, but he is like that sometimes; just ignore him. *Accha sun*[31], I was going to call you. I want to work with Epochal re. It sounds really interesting.'

'Do you have five rupees change?' Mihir asked after a pause. 'Give it to him please. Thanks... If you want to work for us, you can't be mingling with riff-raff. I'm not kidding. Being part of Epochal is a mission, alright? It's not just a job.'

'I get it,' said Malik anxiously. 'I want to try it... I want to work for you.'

The auto wheeled away; the engine noises faded into the afternoon. It was still and quiet all about. A watchman was slumped in his chair in the distance. The two men stood looking at each other, in the shade of the old building.

Mihir stepped forward. On his chubby face was a ferocious grimace.

'How did he know about Epochal already?'

'I don't know... He must have heard from someone... Oh ya!'

'What?'

'He heard from Elena. He told me she went for an audition.

---

[31]Okay, listen

For the sexual harassment viral video. He didn't like that concept, that's what he—'

'Who is Elena?'

'Elena…' Malik smiled and then started explaining. Mihir listened with no expression at all, until, as the seconds wore on, a look of sheer amazement spread over his face.

'You're telling me,' he said, with every appearance of shock, 'that he is currently living with an underage Russian girl?'

'Ya… I guess… Not Russian, she's from Ukraine.'

'I should have known already!' cried Mihir. 'I knew from the beginning. A pervert!' He spun on his heel, his face half raised to the sky and his mouth hanging open in a way that was comic. Yet, Malik, who was always quick to see a joke, was suddenly seized with the feeling that nothing was more impossible than to laugh, nothing at all.

The Currents and the Tides

I, however, was in a heady state. I felt as though I had emerged out of lengthy, dreary languishing (just how lengthy, I saw in retrospect!), into that state of life for which I had been made, but which I had lost touch with, somewhere along the way. Now it was finally here, and the best proof of it was that I had begun to remember vividly the sure ambitions of my college days, realizing with a kind of breathless delight that they had been prophetic after all. For I had been a star in film school, one of those for whom great things were predicted by all. And though I was (not insincerely) ambivalent towards conventional markers of success, I had been confident of one thing: my life would be bursting with meaning and significance. Then had come the first pangs of fear, the job with Jatin, and before I knew it, the rabbit hole that led to the opposite of Wonderland. But sitting in Epochal's office, surfing the net with my headphones plugged in, I could celebrate the old songs of love and glory once again.

It was part of my work to monitor public discourse. We had technology to track trending topics and the most shared articles and videos, but above and beyond the analysis, was apparent the writing on the wall. In my first week at Epochal came two bits of news, both terribly exciting, in contrasting ways.

The first was an announcement from the Ministry of Culture. The government would be beginning a programme of 'cultural cleansing' to restore 'Indian values and respect for Indian heritage' in all government-run cultural institutions that had been 'corrupted by Western encroachment.' That it was an upper-caste Hindu, a known proponent of the 'Hindutva nation', who was delivering this glad news, only made it the more *comforting* for all of us Westernized and corrupt. We, who believed in such abominations as individual liberty... You see, I am lapsing into sarcasm even now.

But then this report was almost bracing. It put to the fire that deceitful doubt, which, I am ashamed to say, crept up on me in every period of lull—the thought that the grand old moderates were right after all, that everything was more or less okay, and there was no lasting trouble afoot in the country. That Ahishor was simply *overreacting*. That is what my parents would have said, had they known the real mission of Epochal Pictures. Now I was convinced again, more strongly than ever, that to keep them in the dark was justified.

And then came Giri Joseph's *Guardian* essay. As a piece of writing, it was mediocre. Giri had adopted a 'tough', though distanced, style, which, in my opinion, spoiled his stated support for the Manifesto. He gave off the impression of being situated at the very zenith of empowered liberalism, from where he condescended to cheer on the Indian hopefuls. I suppose he merely intended (with a Western audience in mind) to provide a bird's eye picture of what was happening in India and why Ahishor's movement mattered. He did, however, include a link to the original text of the Manifesto—and in a matter of days (such was the novelist's pedigree and the influence of the foreign press), our readership had shot up by tens of thousands, across continents. The title too was catchy, though Ahishor himself didn't care for it. It was called: 'A Young Artist Works a Revolution'.

Although there was little said in the essay that was not said more powerfully in the Manifesto, Giri did illuminate for me one aspect of what was going on, with the following passage:

> *The Constitution of India is decisively liberal. Various progressive legislations also exist on paper. Albeit, with many missteps, the one organ of the State that has shown an inclination towards building a culture of individual choice is the Supreme Court. Interestingly, therefore (if somewhat ironically), the young revolutionaries are soliciting law enforcement to aid them in their fight. This ensures that their outrage does not merely expend itself in a social media echo-chamber. Instead, the moral force of social media is joining hands with the blunt force of the law.*

Then I remembered that Pankaj Pande, the alleged rapist, was already in jail and that Ritesh Azad would go in too, if he had done Ruhi wrong. It was not, in fact, a bad start!

* * *

One morning, before anyone else had come in, Bharat and I were alone in the office. He was sitting on one of our bar stools in the central hall, drinking coffee and picking at his teeth. I was slouched on a couch, looking at a script that one of Mihir's contacts had sent us, and also checking Facebook.

'*Kya hua*, Dhruv? What happened?' From where he sat, Bharat must have seen my eyes widening.

'It's Jatin,' I said. 'He's gone berserk again.'

Previously, when Pankaj had been arrested, Jatin had gone on Facebook to fulminate against 'bloodlust', 'mob justice' and 'people one expects better from'. Now, once again on his preferred turf—the Facebook status—he had trained all his guns on Epochal Pictures. There were phrases that were familiar to me ('the pompous ignorance of the new generation of Indian yuppies') and there were flailing barbs ('half-baked upstarts with neither ability nor respect'). He was warning everyone on his Friends List to stay away from Epochal Pictures and all such 'trendy frauds', even if 'those who ought to know better are siding with these companies'. In this delicacy (by his standards), I perceived that his soft spot for Ahishor persisted. But simultaneously I realized, with a sinking heart (a troubling sensation for me), that he had not even spoken to me once, before publicly denouncing my new employer. No doubt that was my punishment for not consulting him before joining.

Bharat walked over, his teeth bared in a grimace. He softly uttered vile curses as he read Jatin's post. But when he looked away from the screen, he said: '*Pagal insaan!*[32] We will ignore him.'

'Yes, that's the best thing to do,' I agreed at once.

'On Facebook, we will ignore him. Because there is no need to give him any attention here. Anyway, no important person is liking the post... Even though he has everyone on his Friends List. Everyone will see this.' Bharat began to curse again and a brooding look came over his face.

'They won't,' I was eager to assure him. 'Most of his friends have unfollowed him. He's ranted against so many people on Facebook that everybody's learned to ignore him. Jatin has no impact anymore.'

---

[32]Madman

'*Maarunga saale ko!*[33],' said Bharat, clenching his jaw suddenly. 'I should have punched his face that day itself... By the way, please like and share the piece that I shared... I posted it just now. Did you see it?'

'*Kya ho gaya?*[34]' he asked. For I, having just then clicked on the page, was in a frenzy of excitement.

'I'm just seeing it,' I cried. 'But this is a mistake! He wasn't supposed to write this! We were supposed to do the sting first!'

Mr Krishna's piece had been published. In the middle pages of *The Times of India* was a gossipy, aggressive op-ed, certainly unlike anything this gentle thinker had ever put out before. Taking the Ministry of Culture's recent announcement as his point of departure, he had produced an athletic, freewheeling slam of all 'self-proclaimed guardians of Indian culture'—with special attention paid to Hindu god-men, and in particular, to Sadhguru Narayanan. Herein he had put down, with a wink and a nudge that did not mask the anger and the frustration, every unproven allegation of money laundering, land grabbing and criminal intimidation whose existence (I guessed) he had learned of from conversations in Delhi.

I was aghast.

'Mihir had specifically said not to publish anything against him, until after the sting happens! Now he'll be on his guard!'

'*Chup kar*[35], Dhruv!' Bharat snarled. I stopped in surprise.

He was bending over me, with his hands on his hips. I couldn't help noticing how slim and strongly built he was. It was a gift, but he was also disciplined about his fitness. Much

---

[33]I will beat that wretch!
[34]What happened?
[35]Shut up

had changed in my relations with Bharat. Of course, I had never liked him. I had felt that he was an inferior talent, clinging to Ahishor and acceptable only in the role of a sidekick. But ever since I joined Epochal, I had found him full of quiet authority. I also couldn't help noticing—and respecting—that he did not seem to hold any grudges against me.

'Mihir is not your boss. And he is definitely not my boss. *We* will decide what is good for us.'

'Yes, but—this is bad timing, isn't it? He should have waited. Gaurav; there's a journalist who is with Ahishor, Gaurav Kapoor—'

'*Pata hai*[36],' said Bharat.

'Ya. So, Gaurav was going to do a proper essay with facts and arguments. This piece just looks like a hatchet job!'

'Was it not a hatchet job when Sushant tweeted about Ritesh?' Suddenly his eyes were bulging ferociously out of a murderous visage. '*That* Mihir loved! But *this* he has a problem with? Arré, if we are going to expose this baba, what is wrong if someone else also wants to help? Why should we be doing it alone? Are all these journalists so cowardly that they cannot shoot the first arrow?'

'No, but—now he will be on his guard,' I protested.

'Arré Dhruv, he will anyway be on his guard. *Toh kya ho gaya?*[37] We are conducting a sting operation; we are not asking him for an interview!'

As I fell quiet, my mind seized on something. 'Sushant was the one who tweeted that?' I asked. '"Spirit of Sartre" is Sushant?'

Bharat nodded impatiently. 'And Mihir was thrilled about

---

[36]I know
[37]So what?

it. That's fine, I don't have a problem. But our goal is to fight these babas. See, boss, I am not going to take orders from Mihir before I share something. First, he was happy to let Ahishor fight these guys alone. Now when there is a movement, he is trying to control it? Let me explain something...'

He reached out and touched my shoulder, before sitting down next to me.

'You know the saying *"Behti Ganga main haath dhona"*[38]?'

'Yes, of course,' I said.

'That's all that Mihir is doing. He is not bothered. Mihir only wants to settle scores with successful people. Because he has that chip on his shoulder. He is playing games, he is getting kicks! He is not really bothered about Hindu fundamentalists. He doesn't know how dangerous they are. But I know that Ahishor is right; the country has to change, otherwise life here is shit and will remain shit!'

As I looked at him, I saw, with dawning surprise, that he was speaking from the heart.

'Yes, you have more experience,' I said suddenly. 'We all grew up in urban settings—we were sheltered—but you have seen how bad it actually is.'

Bharat's eyes widened further. There was something comical about his stare. Then he seemed to relax. 'Haan,' he said. He patted my shoulder again. 'Yaar, we need all possible help to fight these guys. I told you before—they can do bad things. Share that piece, ok?'

'Ok,' I said.

Though I had 'liked' it, I was still in two minds about

---

[38]This Hindi saying is closest in meaning to the English idiom 'Jump on the bandwagon'.

sharing it, when I was distracted by a message that had popped up in my browser. It was from Jatin.

I've been wanting to speak to you, Dhruv. But I have realized that any conversation between us, at this point, would be pointless. You may not be aware of how much you have changed in the past few months. I'm afraid it's not for the better. Perhaps in another six months we will be able to talk again. In that time, either you will have learned something about yourself, the choices you have made and the company you have chosen—or I will have egg on my face. Either way, it should be interesting. Good luck—J.

* * *

A thick shroud of silence had fallen over the Krishna home, and failed to dissipate, though it had been three days since Suraj's article had appeared. Tara had spent them all in her bedroom, citing a backache, poring over her laptop, appearing only at breakfast and dinner time (and once for an evening walk), and making no conversation save the absolutely necessary. Mr Krishna pretended not to notice; he did not attempt to draw her out. He himself was filled with a deep sense of injury, for he had expected praise and encouragement for his act of courage. It had not been an easy piece to write. He had felt—if he was honest—like a man taking a leap off a high cliff (though once he had taken the plunge, how the words had poured out!). It was with a special pride, therefore, that he had produced the newspaper at the breakfast table, only to be met with sharply drawn breaths and venomous looks—as though he had committed a crime!

Now it was the hour of dusk, on the third day. In the

gloaming, the city lights were twinkling and the cars and taxis were beginning to look like shining insects. If one stood on the balcony outside the living room, one could see the famous Queen's Necklace coming alive as Marine Drive lit up. There was nobody present to see it, however. Tara was ensconced in the master bedroom, with the curtains drawn and the air conditioner humming. Suraj was upstairs in his study, which happened to also be the farthest point from the bedroom.

He was reading through his correspondence, with a glass of whisky on the table. It had been three days and the messages were still pouring in. Almost all of them were messages of support. Both Ira and Dipankar Joshi had written at once, assuring him of the timeliness and importance of his words. Many old acquaintances had written, including those who were not even living in India, but were worried about the direction the country was going in. He was not on Twitter, but he gathered that the piece was getting a lot of traction there. When he logged on to see, he discovered a great battle underway between the liberals and the Hindutva trolls, with the latter calling him all kinds of names. He was surprised at how little it bothered him. He felt oddly insulated, almost as though they were addressing another person.

Lastly, he saw that his son Vishnu had shared the article on Facebook, as had Vishnu's fiancée Sukanya, and this made him especially proud. His thoughts turned to their imminent arrival in India. Very soon now, they would be married to fine celebrations, wherein he would meet several of those old friends, who had just now displayed such splendid solidarity. Life was not so bad! Draining his glass, he felt terribly happy—and had a sudden longing to go down to Tara and enfold her in his arms.

A strange noise came filtering through the walls. It was

high-pitched and drawn out, like the twittering of birds. He had only just placed it as the new doorbell that Tara had ordered (a poor choice!), when the noise came again, and this time seemed to be running up and down his spine. Mr Krishna got up, frowning.

From the staircase, he noticed that the living room was dark and empty and that the bell was ringing unheeded. His annoyance gripped him as he stepped down hurriedly, though he had to move carefully, for the shapes of objects were fading in the twilight. *Where was the maid? Where was Tara?*

He reached the door and opened it himself.

'Hello,' said the waiting figure, 'I am Shonar.'

Suraj gasped; he was steeped in intense disappointment at once. It was not Maithili, though she resembled this woman down to the quizzical eyes. Then he felt himself growing tense, as the woman in the white robes continued to stare.

'You have already received my message.' She spoke sharply.

He heard the sound of movement behind him, and then Tara's voice, raised in worry. A blustering energy overtook him.

'Shonar!' he exclaimed. 'So *you* are Shonar! How did you find this house?' He continued to exclaim in inarticulate ways, until the visitor interrupted him.

'Because of his grace, Sadhguru will not have you arrested for the lies you have published. But you must apologize for what you have written. That is what I have come to tell you. Otherwise the consequences will be great.'

'How is Maithili?' screamed Tara suddenly, rushing up alongside her husband. 'Come in please and tell us everything!'

As Suraj struggled to restrain her, the woman outside took a step back, her eyes flashing from one to the other.

'I have not come to talk of Thalia. If you want to speak

to her, come with your heads bowed, and follow Sadhguru. I have come to tell you that if you do not apologize for what you have written, then you will suffer. For your son, who is to be married—on him will the punishment fall! Goodbye.'

Tara was still crying hysterically. Fearing that the neighbours might emerge at any minute, Suraj pulled her indoors quickly, and slammed the door shut.

The Ruler of this World

It was the same hour of dusk, on one of those same days, when Sasha walked up and down the length of his apartment, waiting for the doorbell to ring.

His eyes fell on Elena's clothes and underclothes, scattered on the mattress and draped over a stand. He gathered them up and put them into the cupboard. One of her black hats was perched jauntily atop a cane lamp, where it looked amusing. He let that remain.

He had not wanted to meet Sushant in his own home, but when he had called him, saying he had important things to talk about and inquiring if they could meet that evening, Sushant (who was, on most days, persistently soliciting company) had uttered many non-committal noises. Finally, he had insisted on drinking only in Sasha's house—until this prospect alone looked to be the motive force of the plan.

It was well past the time he had said he would arrive. Sasha felt irritable and anxious, though he wanted most to be calm and in control. When his phone finally rang (Sushant had forgotten the number of the flat), there was desperation in Sasha's voice; he felt, while giving him the details, as though he was clamouring for a great favour.

'I really love your place,' grinned Sushant, as soon he entered. Then he moved, with loping strides, to the window. He began to smoke, with a faraway smile on his face, while Sasha set about pouring their drinks.

'Chill, chill,' said Sushant, when Sasha called from the sitting area. 'I'm enjoying the view. What's your rent, bhai? If you don't mind.'

'Twenty-five thousand.'

'Fack!' He was wracked with little laughs. 'For twenty-five, this is expensive yaar. It's just a studio.'

'It is too expensive, but I like it still. All the houses in this city are too expensive.'

'I am living with Ahishor now,' said Sushant, in a contemplative way. 'He is in Delhi a lot, so most of the time I have the whole place to myself. It's better than where I was before…'

'Come, sit, say cheers,' suggested Sasha.

'But I really want a big place, bhai. I want a big house—with a pool—and a ni-i-i-ce sea view… Haha! I am remembering the view from Maithili's balcony. Have you seen that view?'

'No,' said Sasha. There was a jolt in his voice, for he was startled at the mention of Maithili. Then the discomfort was swarming through him. He waited in apprehension, but a fresh thought seemed to have struck his visitor. Sushant turned, his head leaning forward from his lithe body.

'What you just said… is extremely true. All places here are too expensive. But what can you do if you still want the house?' He chortled and wheezed once more. 'I was reading an article a few days ago. You follow cricket, na[39]? It said that Chris Gayle

---

[39]In this case, 'na' is equivalent to 'isn't it?'

has a private strip club in his house. Now ain't that a fine idea! But money, bhai! Money is needed!'

'Well, you have a job now,' said Sasha. 'That's a good start.'

'Ya-a-a!' Sushant nodded, looking both astonished and impressed. 'The job is good. The job is definitely... Bhai, I have never made this much money in Mumbai! Or in my life! Hehehe! But still, you know, television is still the real deal. I was telling Bharat, whatever cool shit we do online, it will be good for views and for a certain kind of crowd, but there is no money there. I mean, our investor is a really nice guy; best fucking financier I have ever worked with. (Another spasm of laughter seized him.) But the big bucks are in TV. I want to focus on TV after some time... Khair, right now I'm having fun! This is just... fun, bhai! I'm getting things off my chest! Fucking these motherfuckers! They deserve it!'

He stepped forward, grinning; his eyes were shining and his body was silhouetted against the darkening sky.

'That's what I want to talk to you about,' said Sasha. 'Come, take your drink.'

He held it out. 'What you're doing is also dangerous,' he continued, as Sushant grasped the glass. 'The Spirit of Sartre is you, isn't it?'

'Hahaha!' Sushant leaned back with a delighted look. 'How did you figure that out?'

'I just guessed,' said Sasha. 'It's clearly someone who likes philosophy—and doesn't like Ritesh Azad.'

Sasha waited as another bout of laughter seized his visitor. 'But you're getting carried away,' said Sasha eventually. 'You're spreading false rumours. Because these are half-truths at best.'

'No no no!' To his surprise, Sushant was still mirthful and seemed to take no offence at the charge. 'Nothing is false, bhai,' he cried passionately. 'I'll tell you, I'll tell you… Yaar, can we go to your roof?'

'The roof? Oh—I don't know—I've never been.'

'You've never been to the roof?' cried Sushant. 'How long have you lived here? Chal[40], let's take our drinks; it will be awesome up there. I was thinking of it even when I was neeche[41].'

They ascended on the lift till the sixth floor, and then up a dark flight of stairs. The door to the roof was not locked, but it was stiff on its hinges, and it took a moment for Sasha to push it open. With a resounding shudder, it gave way. Sasha held his breath as he stepped into the night.

It seemed, at first, that the parapet was floating in the sky. As they moved forward, the clouds dropped away and met the waters of the sea, and as they moved further (with quickening strides) to the edge of the roof, there appeared the rushing waves, each massive one etched in white froth, crashing gently upon the sands. From that height, it was a tremendous panorama— from the slums on one side to the rocks on the other, with the small, scattered figures of people in between, and the lights of the city where the shoreline curved and of the distant ships on the water. But their gaze returned to the breakers, which were almost directly beneath them, and whose tumult too, struck their ears unobstructed.

'Well, fuck that!' said Sushant. 'Now, if that ain't a sight for sore eyes!'

'It is amazing!' exclaimed Sasha. 'This is magnificent… I can't believe I never came here before!'

---

[40]Come

[41]downstairs

'Mere[42] bhai, you are crazy!'

He smiled sheepishly, accepting Sushant's teasing jibe, for he was thrilled at the beauty of the discovery. And he was still staring, leaning over the parapet, with the wind whipping through his hair and his clothes, when Sushant turned away and took a pull at his drink, his face turning grim.

When Sasha shifted his gaze and beheld the other's expression, a chill suddenly fell upon his heart. But before he could speak, Sushant did.

'You were talking about Ritesh…' said Sushant, contemplatively. 'Now, the point here is… Ritesh is not an innocent guy.'

'But what exactly did Ruhi say in her note?' Sasha demanded desperately. 'And how did you read the note in the first place?'

'Arré we had gone to the police station; we read it. And we helped the police to interpret it. That doesn't matter, bhai… The point here is, ki[43] it was choots like Ritesh who made her suffer.'

'She was in love with him—she had decided she was in love with him. And it was unrequited love. That was all, wasn't it? That alone doesn't make him guilty of her suicide, Sushant!'

'I just expressed my opinion,' said Sushant, shrugging. 'If the police thought it was justified, that's their decision… Anyway, why do you think she did it?'

'Because she was ill,' said Sasha. 'And of course, she was unhappy. Pankaj Pande was certainly to blame for that. To what degree, I can't say immediately. But Ritesh—'

'*Na, na, na!*[44] Sushant turned his head, grinning with

---

[42]My
[43]In this context, 'ki' means 'that'
[44]No, no, no!

macabre delight. 'She was unhappy *because of such people*! They don't deserve to be where they are. They are throwing money at safe shit and stopping talent from coming through. That's what Ahishor is fighting against, na? That's what we all are fighting!'

'You used Ruhi's suicide to attack Ritesh, because of your own envy—yes, envy,' repeated Sasha quietly. 'You are not fighting for a cause, Sushant. Ahishor may care about how liberal our liberals really are, but you don't care. You are doing this because of your own lust for power and money.'

A silence fell between them. He knew Sushant's eyes were protruding, continuing to stare at him in the greedy way they had, but he turned his gaze away and looked down below at the beach. The darkness had overcome everything swiftly. The moving figures were vague and shadowy, and the sea itself was but an invisible presence, a stirring in the night, and a sound rushing upon the silence. Then suddenly, the waves seemed very close, and loud in his ears. The tide was strengthening. He looked carefully. The shining white foam came up through the dark, again and again. Suddenly Sasha fancied that the sea was exulting, bullying the beleaguered land with sheer wantonness. And then he found himself looking back at Sushant, and in his eyes perceived the same mad glory.

'You think I'm a shallow guy,' said his companion, with a smile. 'It's true I want to be powerful, but I ain't shallow. I *believe* in power. I have *faith* in it.'

'Power banishes faith,' said Sasha faintly. 'It frightens it away.'

Sushant grinned. 'No, bhai. Having power makes life beautiful. There ain't nothing nice about being weak and struggling.'

Gulping down his drink, he threw a glance at the waves and began to think aloud: 'Money makes you free to do what you want to, but you still need the balls to do it. That's power.

Even when I didn't have money, bhai, I've always had power. But they grow together; you need them both in life—'

Sasha interrupted with sudden sharpness, 'So, then, what exactly is your problem with Ritesh running his company? Or with Pankaj Pande molesting Ruhi? Or raping her? These people just exercised their power, didn't they? Why are you opposing them?'

'Haha!' said Sushant. 'Come on...'

'Why? I'm asking you seriously.'

'Forcing is not cool,' Sushant made a face. 'I never force a woman, physically...' Then, as though disturbed by this caveat, he quickly made his grimace ferocious. 'But you know something, Sasha? I believe in absolute freedom. Absolute freedom! I am not like other people, bhai—even Ahishor and the other guys. They may be feminists and all that—but I am not. Because I know my Zarathustra, hahaha! I know that pity is the worst form of insult. Dekh[45] bhai... nobody is to blame for Ruhi's suicide. That's the truth. Suicide was her *own* choice. And I toh[46] knew what she *was*... I'm not here to defend her. But these motherfuckers are getting in the way of all of us. They have been using their power to keep us down. The point here is—I'm going to use my power to set everybody free!'

'So you admit,' said Sasha, 'that you are only using Ruhi to take down Ritesh. Now if you also admit that you are doing this for your own pleasure—not for any larger good; if you admit that you have no actual conception of any larger good, but only of the pleasure and the high this is giving you—then you will be completely correct.'

---

[45]Look
[46]Here, 'toh' means 'obviously'.

'It gives me pleasure, of course!' exclaimed Sushant, with a leer. 'What's wrong with that? It's a good thing to enjoy what you're doing. Hahaha! Don't look so stressed bhai! Life is simple... you complicate it too much.'

'You are complicated, Sushant,' said Sasha, with a sigh. 'You are terribly complicated.' He breathed softly, and added, under his breath, 'Like all twisted things.'

'*You* need a woman,' said Sushant, licking his lips, which were soft and fleshy, unlike the rest of him. 'Oh hey! Where is that girl?' He was evidently delighted at suddenly remembering. 'She is staying with you na?'

Sasha answered tensely, 'Yes, but she is out today.' He had been expecting the question all along.

'Elena, right?' asked Sushant. 'I met her in the office. I remember her very well.'

The wind picked up and he began to smile. Dreading what Sushant would say next, Sasha spoke rapidly.

'Yes, her name is Elena Hamolka. She is new to Mumbai and I am giving her shelter. Until she can be on her own.'

'Hahaha! I believe that nobody can shelter anybody,' laughed Sushant, 'in this world. We all get swept away... So bhai, are you—'

'No,' said Sasha, angrily. 'I told you already—I am giving her shelter. But you can't understand a thing like that, because you yourself are full of violence. That's the only reason I wanted to meet you, Sushant—to tell you this. You should know that what you are doing is wrong. However much it may be catching on—it's wrong.'

'Oh really?' The lanky figure was laughing in his face. 'So what are you going to do about it?'

'I won't talk anymore today,' said Sasha. 'Give me your

glass—have you finished? (Sushant shook his head.) Never mind; then keep it. I am going now; I have to be alone. Goodbye. You can stay here and enjoy the view if you like.'

He turned and moved with slow steps towards the door, his shoulders hunched. As the last of the sea breeze rushed over him, he wondered briefly if Sushant too would come at him with abuses. At the door, he paused and turned to look.

The young man was standing with his arms outstretched, his face towards the night sky, and his head thrown back in some kind of rapture.

*   *   *

Sasha did not return to the flat, but went out instead to the street full of light and noise. There was a new cafe across the road, as there seemed to be every few months in this most attractive and unforgiving of markets. It had warm yellow lights and bright red seats, and a smattering of faces he didn't recognize. Finding a table by the window, he sent Elena a message, asking her to join him when she could. Then he was alone with his thoughts.

After a while, he found himself thinking how much simpler it would be if he really was in love with her. He could then take on her welfare as his own responsibility and set about building her life with authority. It would be better for her as well. In that sense, were not the insinuations of Sushant and the others quite reasonable? The thought occurred to him that he was being stubborn in not even considering the possibility. Moreover, he could set right the wrong his father had done to her. Would it not lend a beautiful symmetry to the whole affair?

His spirits grew dizzy with the prospect. But when the fancy began to sour (as it did), he broke his train of thought and closed his eyes. Remembering what she had told him, and what, afterwards, he had kept hidden from her, he focussed on the thrill of that astounding coincidence—too great, surely, not to have been somewhere ordained—while deep currents of feeling set up inside him, against the man whose shadow seemed to corrupt all that it touched. Yet that too, he realized, was hyperbole. The truth was strange and liberating. For he himself was not corrupt—and nor was Elena.

Later, when she came in, he was filled with gladness, in affirmation of their relation. Elena was bright with beauty, coursing with youthful energy, and ordering all she wanted to eat and drink. She was cheerful, though the news of the day was as usual. There had been more auditions, more things to hope for, but no calls. She was happy, she said, to be missing the bad work in Delhi, even though she was losing money. She felt excited in Mumbai. But he also read the tiredness in her face, the strain that showed in her distracted gaze and her sleepy, surrendering smiles.

Sasha glanced through the window at the busy streets blurred with traffic, the anonymous pavements, and the faces going in and out of the cafe. He felt infinitely close to her and so he reminded himself that he must pray for Elena, even if he could do no more for her.

*   *   *

Before I relive the dramatic events at the arts festival the following month, a final scene of significance swims into my mind. I was not present, having already been despatched to Mumbai, but I know of a gathering that took place in Delhi one night, in the club called Ozymandias. It was a small and informal dinner, barely a precursor to the many magnificent parties that were later to fill those rooms.

The club had not yet officially opened, nor was everyone present that night destined to be a member when it did open. Yet they all felt perfectly at home. Under the shining lights of a false ceiling, the two girls, Anamika and Alisha, were finishing their last laps of the indoor swimming pool. The rest were already at the bar alongside—Mihir on Ahishor's right, gazed steadfastly at him; and Giri Joseph watched dutifully, while scanning the club's environs, impressed. Indeed, though the bar was dark and spacious, there was intimacy in the air, for everyone's attention was more or less on Ahishor. Regarding him with pleased smiles were Ira and Dipankar Joshi, and facing him, looking curious, amused and vastly interested, was Satish Dhawan, the founder of Ozymandias and Epochal Pictures's angel investor.

It had already been remarked upon (by Mihir) that this gentleman looked literally like an angel, which (though not particularly funny, as Mihir seemed to find it) was not untrue. He was cherub-faced, with thick, light hair that grew all around like a halo. His lips were pouted, and it was perhaps owing to this expression that there was something endearing, rather than obscene, about his fleshy arms and paunch as well. In a half-sleeve batik-print shirt, chock-full of colours and patterns, he sat upon the armchair like a large and curious baby. It was almost a shock to hear his voice, which was a deep drawl.

'One of the things I liked most about the Manifesto,' he was saying, with his little eyes fixed on Ahishor's face and almost seeming to gaze right through it, 'was how accurately it characterized my generation. We are indeed a generation to be pitied. I knew it too, when I was your age. We were all talk—and no example. We were really just terribly timid in the face of this country, and at the same time, we were full of grand ideas about how to run it—a most suffocating combination. So I decided

I would be different. I decided I would have some fun with my life—out of doors—not just in the cloistered corridors of a Gymkhana Club… But I suppose I was really not so different from the rest. See, now I have built my own club.'

There came, from the pool, the sound of splashing and the full-throated laughter of the girls.

'Not a stuffy one, I hope,' he continued. 'But a club nonetheless… But not a stuffy one!' And he smiled in a sheepish way. 'I have to say, we did have fun. There were some of us, who certainly knew how to have fun.'

He flashed a quick look at Ira Joshi. She might have blushed, but it was too dark to tell. Dipankar, however, was grinning, baring his teeth.

'Travelled the world…' Satish Dhawan was continuing, contemplatively, 'lived richly… expressed oneself and explored oneself… Yet always, with a sense of hiding, you see… With a clandestine quality… that only made it sweeter at the beginning, mind you. But it was a trap, as we discovered later, when we wound our way back home. This is home, you see. But we had let the weeds grow all over it. And your generation is not going to forgive us for our terrible gardening. Nor should it. Only—I hope you will allow us—to help you make amends?'

'Of course. I am very grateful for your support,' said Ahishor. 'It's very welcome.'

He looked tired but relaxed, on the couch where he sat. Everyone was continuing to stare at him. Then Mihir reached out and patted his shoulder, and they exchanged brief smiles.

'I also think we understand each other very well,' said Ahishor.

'Do we?' chortled Dhawan. 'I suppose we do. I think we make a good team, because although it is you all who are fighting the good fight—as you put it so rightly, in the Manifesto—you do need a certain backing, if you are to succeed—to what degree, we shall see. Not only financial, of course, but—dare I say?—a backing of wisdom. We old liberals have a great deal of underutilized wisdom, I dare say…'

Ahishor was going to voice his assent, but he saw that Dhawan was looking towards the Joshis and they were all smiling in unison. At the same time, the door opened and Anamika and Alisha came in, holding hands.

Their relationship had blossomed, surprising them both. Anamika's initial resentment of the other girl's rather vocal presence had turned to attraction. It had 'just happened,' and she was happy. With all that was going on around her, she felt happier than she had ever been since the first months with Maithili—and then she had only been full of hope. But now, she thought, she would not mind, if she never saw Maithili again.

'But I must tell you one thing,' said the baby-faced man with a sudden fervour that spread in a faint flush over his smooth cheeks. 'I must tell you, Ahishor, that I believe in your cause and support what you are doing… even if I did *not*, I would do this much for you—I would place a bet on you.'

He bent forward in a friendly way, and unconsciously, the others drew closer too, renewing their attention on the young revolutionary.

'Because I cannot resist a good bet. It is so much fun to see what will happen… from the safety of my club! There—see—you must forgive me. I am still a product of my cloistered old generation.'

'You are forgiven,' said Ahishor, with a smile.

The Great Debate

Arts and literature festivals were proliferating in the city, just as they were all over the country. Yet this did not seem to diminish the excitement that surrounded every new jamboree. As on an assembly line, there came rolling out ebullient listings in the tabloids and magazines, eager chatter about the list of speakers and pleased announcements of attendance from the speakers themselves; in sum, a real anticipation, among a certain section, of a socially and intellectually fulfilling weekend.

It was all, more or less, a bubble (or so it seems to me now), but at the time it was still swelling. We were not complaining. I myself was active on social media, successfully working up everybody's enthusiasm, including my own. Although Epochal's secret and precious work was not going to be related to any happenings on the stage, I think we had found ourselves (in an overflow of feeling) genuinely excited about the festival itself.

It was the month of April. The city was humid and appeared more crowded than ever, but now I neither minded nor cared. I felt far removed from the hot struggles of everyday living. My old preoccupations—the next audition, the next pay cheque, my parents' phone calls—were meaningless to me. I was spending as long as possible in the office and the days were passing as though in a dream, flowing above all things and never stumbling.

The others, too, must have been in the grip of this sensation, for their behaviour was also marked by a reckless, visionary audacity. It was impossible to remember Bharat as a cloying sycophant, when his eyes burned with concentration and he showed himself to be on top of all our affairs, knowing the way past every problem. As for Sushant, he was striding about like he was 10-feet tall. He was still scoffing at whomsoever he wanted, but his attitude was no longer (so to speak) that of a drunk lying in the gutter, but of one empowered with confidence. For one thing, he had come out as the Spirit of Sartre, declaring his identity openly and tweeting under his own name. I had not known, at the time, that this was an act of defiance, a riposte to Sasha's rebukes. I was merely impressed and astonished, because I knew he had not sought the prior approval of either Bharat, Mihir or Ahishor. Yet whatever they thought privately, none of them objected, and with this tacit ratification, Sushant had a freer rein. Epochal too, as a consequence, was springing into controversy, but it seemed we were making more fans than foes.

Between Karim and Nalini however, the differences that had begun ever since the day Ritesh had abandoned Ahishor's documentary, had suddenly become a gaping divide. For Karim, it beggared belief that Ahishor's flatmate should lead a campaign against Ahishor's brother, and not be thrown out onto the street. But Nalini, torn and conflicted as she was, refused to hear words against her son, lest they harm him supernaturally, or worse, shake her faith. It seemed these two were not themselves either, in those days. Thus, Twitter users, whichever side they took, found wonderful pastime in the spectacle of Karim Azad, reduced to trading barbs with the erstwhile Spirit of Sartre. But even that ignoble pit of mud was nothing compared to the one the great poet would soon find himself mired in.

It happened in this way: Headlining the second day of the arts festival was an event the organizers had planned for, months previously—a debate on the subject of 'Faith and Reason in Modern India', featuring Karim, Sadhguru Narayanan and a moderator whose job was to say as little as possible. Left to themselves, these powerful speakers were fully expected to put up a terrific show. There was particular interest around Sadhguru as the more enigmatic and controversial personality. Many had read the serious allegations that had been levelled against him just recently.

I had arrived early and stayed put to make sure I got a seat. Many others had also done the same. One among them was Tara Krishna, who had come alone. If her husband had heard of the event (which she was sure he had), he had not spoken of it. Tara told herself it made no difference to her—though in truth she experienced a subtle disappointment. He had not even spotted an opportunity by his own lights, to accost the man who had taken their daughter. No doubt, if asked, he would have said he could not bear to see him celebrated on stage. It was such petty pride—masking his cowardice! He could write a furious article, but not confront the person! There was no question, however, of any pride on her part. She had come alone, though full of nerves and not knowing what to do or expect. She sat in the third row, her heart racing apprehensively and her hand running through her hair continually.

Two rows behind her sat Sasha. What had brought him to the venue, he couldn't quite say. For he did not know that Sadhguru was the one whom Maithili had gone to. She had told him nothing, though he had written to her many times.

He was interested, of course, in the subject of the debate, but he was not in the mood to witness one. He had intended to avoid the crowds—until the day itself had dawned, and he had found himself getting up and walking out of the house. At the time, he imagined it was only because of his idleness on a Saturday evening. In hindsight, he would see it differently.

Then I gasped—and I wonder how Tara did not cry out. For there, behind the long-haired, silver-bearded figure in white and gold robes, a figure who looked as though he had stepped out of another century—wearing ornate, curved shoes, bracelets and necklaces, and with a topknot like a crown, there, standing by the steps of the stage and tasked with assisting her guru to safely place his foot, was Maithili.

Afterwards, I was surprised at how I had recognized her. She was in brown ashram robes, with her hair draped in a headscarf. Her face was in full view; distinctively pale, among all the others. But without make-up and from that distance, it appeared quite featureless—like the white face of a ghost. Nevertheless, it took me only a second look.

I saw Maithili then, a blazing personality. Her eyes, slanting and filled with pride, and her lips pursed with self-satisfaction, even as she bowed before the god-man and never took her gaze off him. There was no longer that inchoateness in her expression, which one perceptive reviewer of her debut film had noticed and remarked upon; none of the lostness that had always hovered about her, as though she had wandered into an alien and savage world and was trying to understand it with quiet desperation. Despite her dress and demeanour, I saw her suddenly as more strikingly beautiful than ever before, because, with the superiority at last stamped on her face, it had come into its own.

So, certainly, it appeared. When Sadhguru had taken his seat on stage, she disappeared into the aisle and I lost sight of her just as the programme began.

The lady making the introductions (a sober journalist, by reputation) was already gushing over the remarkably dressed Sadhguru, leaning so far towards him that it seemed that only the weight of her armchair prevented it from toppling over. To the other side of her sat a poker-faced Karim Azad. His own stage presence was considerable, but just then, as the microphone was passed to the god-man and he let it dangle from his hand, continuing to smile to himself until the murmuring in the crowd settled down, Karim looked overmatched.

'I know why you all have come today, in such large numbers,' Narayanan spoke in a rich, soft, slow voice, which quietened at once those who were still chattering. 'I know it's not only because of the air conditioning. (There was laughter, rather lusher than the joke warranted.) It is because—as she was saying, in her own words, and as I will say in mine (here the moderator flashed a toothy grin, which I immediately found intrusive)—we are living in a place and at a time in which these concepts—faith... God... religion and spirituality... and not just those, but reason and intelligence too... are all in the hands of fools. Now, when I say this, it doesn't mean that the situation was totally different before. Oh no! The fools have defined these concepts for centuries—the fools of every country. But what is changing now... is awareness. We are becoming aware.'

Sadhguru cleared his throat discreetly. He was sitting in a coiled position, with his head bowed, looking as gentle and peaceful as his attire was splendid. An atmosphere of intimate attentiveness had fallen, like a blanket, over the hall.

His English was as good as anybody's, but his voice was

accented, with the bespoke, thoroughly native accent of one who has mimicked Western phonetics. As he continued, I had the same sense of being in the presence of an extraordinarily clever mind, as I had had in the one-bedroom flat of the Navy Baba—though, many times magnified.

'When people say, religion is dangerous, faith is dangerous— they are absolutely right... Anything useful is also dangerous, because you have to know how to use it correctly. For example, fire is the most useful discovery man ever made, but you cannot play with fire... Now, those people who run about saying, "*My* God is better than *your* God, *my* morality is better than *your* morality, I am a good person and you are a sinner, because I have faith and you do not" ... these are all merely playing with fire... This is not the true tradition of the Indian faith. I won't speak of Western faiths. I am speaking... of the Indian faith.'

'But there are many faiths in India,' said the moderator, in a squeaky voice.

Sadhguru smiled. 'I am aware of that. I did not say that I am speaking of the faith in India. I said, "the Indian faith". That is, the faith that was born and has grown in this land... which has its roots in this land. Now you must hear me first,' he protested gently, as the lady opened her mouth again. 'Thank you... In this Indian faith, which is known as the Hindu faith, because it comes from Hindustan... there is no God, there is no morality, there is no sin or punishment, or heaven or hell... you may be surprised to learn this... You have learned that there are 30 million gods... That is correct—and it would be even better if there were 1.2 billion... Each one customized for each person. But properly speaking, we are a godless people. Because our gods are not beings in the sky demanding allegiance... Our gods and idols are simply man-made mediums, to help every person concentrate. They draw you into a reality, they transmit an energy... that is their purpose; they are not essential in themselves. What is essential, is only this: the seeking, by the individual, of higher states of being. That, which is beyond the realm of the five senses.'

Here he paused. At once, the moderator began to speak cheerfully. I don't remember what she said. It felt like an inordinately long time before Karim Azad took the microphone, and I was all ears again.

'Firstly,' began Karim, 'I want to congratulate Shri Narayanan for having dismissed all other gods and the concept of God and all other faiths—apart from his own. I mean that in all sincerity. Our agreement is vast, our disagreement is really very minor. I only feel he has been a little timid; he has held himself back. I would just go one step further than him—and dismiss his own faith as well.'

A cry of 'Yeah!' went up from somewhere in the audience and a wave of excitement passed through us all. Karim was in form! The moderator beamed and looked bashful, like a satisfied but modest cook when the lids are taken off the dinner dishes. The smile of the Guruji had acquired a certain fixity, as Karim leaned forward in his chair, his voice hoarser than usual, his breathing heavy and audible, but the words flowing.

'The topic that has been prescribed to us for this discussion is "Faith and Reason in India today". But there can be no "and" in this matter. It is a straight choice of "either, or". Therefore, for the same reasons that the Guruji rejects other faiths, I reject his own. He says that we are to seek some higher state of being, and furthermore—although he did not say this, he certainly meant to imply it—that we are to do so by surrendering our minds—*our reason*—to him, and to people like him. He spoke of the world being full of fools, who do not understand these concepts of faith and reason. However, I would say that he should be grateful for the fools. But for them, he would be out of business… To be a good, intelligent, capable citizen, no spirituality is needed, no gods and no god-men either. Our five senses and our intellect are more than sufficient. Anybody who asks you to abandon them is a dangerous person. He is an enemy of reason!'

A rambling note had entered Karim's speech, but by the time he paused for breath, I was both persuaded and full of admiration. At the back of my mind, I had felt that he would be muted in his views that evening. Now I realized that he was the sort of person who could not help being honest; who, being a wordsmith, could not use words dully. Although, in a similar context, he may have supported the timidity of his son Ritesh, he could not himself be timid—not when asked to speak. There was something thrilling about watching him in action, like a train at full speed, with every bolt rattling and yet, the whole thing under control. But my empathy was limited; I was, more or less, a voyeur—else, I would have seen how much on edge he really was.

'It is nothing new in our country. It fits in very well with our ancient ethos. What is this *guru-shishya parampara*[47] anyway? What is this tradition? It is the tradition of the caste system. And it continues, even with these modern god-men! In olden times, god-men would only accept Brahmin disciples. Other castes may be their slaves, may work for them, but only Brahmins would receive the so-called spiritual enlightenment. Now, in modern times, these modern god-men will accept disciples

---

[47]The teacher-disciple tradition in many Indian religions

from other castes—especially if the person has money. But that egalitarianism is only on the surface. It is a lip service they have been forced into by the march of modernity. Under the surface, their real attention continues to be on the wealthy and privileged disciples. All disciples are not equal, please understand! The ones who will help them to continue living in luxury—and fly them down to events like this—they are the ones whom the Guruji will attend to!—For whatever that is worth!'

Sadhguru, who had been smirking and chuckling into his microphone, could hold his peace no longer.

'Alarming ignorance,' he said, in a deep voice. ' Alarming ignorance. Now… if you want to know the facts… more than 70 per cent of our inmates in every ashram are from rural areas. These are underprivileged people, not high caste or class or anything. More than 80 per cent of our yoga and spiritual training programmes are based in rural areas. You must understand this—I come and work with you all, so that I can use your money to pay for my work with the poor. It is a kind of Robin Hood model that we follow. As for this business of accepting and not accepting disciples… Yes, we don't accept everybody, even today. But it has nothing to do with caste. Whatever be their caste, we accept only those who need and are ready for spiritual growth. Mr Azad, for example—he needs it very badly, but he is far from ready for it. Therefore, we would have to reject him; we would not be swayed by his illustrious lineage.'

In the general laughter that followed, the moderator began to talk again and I did not notice how incensed Karim had become. When he resumed, his anger was apparent in his voice, which had become high and strained.

'Well, I thank the Universe for small mercies!' he shrieked.

'I would not join any kind of spiritual programme, even if I was invited a thousand times over. In the meantime, I would like to tell my friend not to be so proud if his ashrams are packed with people. These are desperate people—that is the reason they are there!'

Suddenly, as sometimes happens, an unaccountable quiet fell over the audience. Karim too dropped his voice. He sounded wiser and calmer as he continued: 'There is a book that I encourage you all to read... *Godmen of India*, by Peter Brent. It is an excellent study of such people. It is too charitable a book, but there is one point it makes marvellously. The point is, that in our country, our system is such that the ordinary person spends his or her whole life totally under the domination of their family. They decide everything, from the time one is an infant to the time one is to get married—I mean *everything*! So, these people enter as a means of escape. No doubt the god-men are part of the same system, but they market themselves as an escape! So then, the one who is suffering under the domination of his or her so-called near and dear ones can run to these fellows and start a new life. That new life will be under the domination of the god-man, no doubt, but you see, there is a saying: "*Kaante se kaanta nikal aata hai.*"[48] It is not rational, it is foolish behaviour, but it is understandable... I can understand the sense of achievement. And it is most understandable for the lower castes, the Scheduled Castes, who are oppressed not just by their families, but by the whole society. What I am going to say next will sound bad, but it's true, and I say it with all sympathy: the Scheduled Castes and the underprivileged of Indian society are the biggest fools when it comes to running

---

[48] A thorn can be used to remove a thorn.

to gurujis… But none of this is anything for people like you to be proud about, Mr Narayanan. You are just taking advantage.'

'We are not writers of film songs, Mr Azad,' replied the god-man, 'who take advantage of poor taste.'

'Now, now…' cut in the moderator firmly, 'let's not make this personal, please. Both of you—please!'

Here, in spite of myself, I was impressed by the lady, for she had showed no hesitation in intervening between the two speakers and they had responded to her authority. There followed a period of abashed conviviality—during which, Karim, still struggling with all the ire inside him, turned it elsewhere.

'Look, I have no wish to be a killjoy,' he smiled in a strained way. 'If spirituality makes people happy, so be it. So long as it is not imposed on me… I don't even blame these people. They are businessmen, who have found a wonderful market. Why should I complain? Let them become rich and build their empires! I am not jealous! That is why I also distance myself from many of our self-styled rationalists and so-called liberal thinkers… Because in their criticisms, I perceive a kind of petty hatred that stinks of jealousy. I have the feeling that, very often, their real objection to god-men is that god-men are successful and make money. It is the same thing as die-hard Leftists who are opposed to all industry. I would say to such people, leave aside for one moment what other people are doing—it may be good, it may be terrible—but what are *you* doing? You have not been appointed the conscience-keepers of society! How, then, are you serving society? First, serve society yourself and prove your commitment to it. Then you will have earned the right to complain about who is harming it. But social and moral causes are not meant to be an employment-generation scheme!'

Karim slumped back into his chair, the last words seeming

to be wrung out of him and a weariness already spreading over his features, but I, without realizing it, was laughing to myself defiantly. He was referring to *us*! He was calling us 'leftists'! And they—the old guard of every persuasion—would all call us names, because for the first time in modern India, the young were fighting for freedom. The word echoed in my head, I was consumed by my own triumphant thoughts, and it took me a moment to register that, on stage, in the calm that had settled after the stormy contretemps, Sadhguru was echoing them too.

'The goal is freedom—Mukti,' he was saying quietly. 'We have always, in our civilization, yearned for Mukti. You can ask yourself too... in your heart of hearts... if the material world is making you happy. Or if simply pleasing the five senses satisfies you... We live in a world thoroughly influenced by Western culture, which is more and more obsessed with *things*. The entire focus is on being greedy and covering oneself with things. Now, I like things too—but only up to a point. I use them; I do not let them use me... When you cover yourself with things, you think you are becoming splendid, but you have actually imprisoned yourself; you have put on a lot of chains... Many people are now realizing this—young people especially—even from our great cities and urban centres like Mumbai. They have stopped looking outwards; they have begun the inward quest. In this quest, the guru is merely the guiding device. The road goes to Mukti.'

As though lifted on the soft cloud of his words, I felt myself entering a space of relaxation. Unconsciously, I scanned the faces in the crowd, trying to find Maithili again. I was momentarily impressed by her, for the sheer gumption of the choice she had made. But I could not spot her, though I heard Karim wishing aloud for 'Mukti' to go get his dinner, and the hall, quite sated itself, burst into giggles. There followed many murmurs and movements as people began to leave their seats. I too got up, for my phone was ringing. Malik was calling, and I was seized by the urgency of our mission.

After I left the venue, there took place a scene, which I read about much later in Sasha's diary. I reproduce the entry, sketchy as it is, below.

28 April 20__

It is 1 a.m. and Elena is still unreachable. I have prayed that she be safe.

Today I met Maithili again. Or should I say, I saw her? It was worse than I had ever imagined it would be.

She has joined a god-man. The things he said, I can hear her saying. He is not just anyone. He has power; whether from above or below—or how much from where—I do not know. It disturbed me even as I heard him speak. It is so sure of itself; its roots are so deep in the soil of this country. I felt a strange pull myself. But a shameful pull. As towards something unbeatable.

The talk was finished and he was going towards the parking lot when I saw her with him.

I did not call out but began to follow them along with the many others who were doing the same. I must have moved quickly. I was almost at the front of the crowd, when a woman pushed her way past me. It was Mrs Krishna. She was crying out Maithili's name aloud.

I saw Maithili swivel and stop. Her mother was rushing towards her. She had noticed, and she was waiting. I was only watching. Perhaps I was still moving. Yet, in the next moment, she had raised her head and turned it, and was looking directly at me.

What hatred was blazing in her eyes! It was as though I was a thing accursed! How her face had transformed! I averted my gaze and when I looked again, she was retreating towards the Guru's entourage. She was moving quickly, with gliding strides, though her mother was still calling her and stumbling in pursuit. In her haste, Mrs Krishna fell. People gathered around to help. I joined them. She was not hurt, but she did not get up. She was broken and weeping. I spoke to her—I don't know what good I did; I was burning with a kind of guilt.

Now I cannot erase from my mind the memory of that face. My desire is dead, I am sure of that. But what relation still lies between us? I have only wished her well—as one obliged to. I cannot do less! Lord, give me the strength to withstand her hatred and that of others.

I shall only write more when Elena returns.

After the Sting

But Elena was with us. At 1 a.m., when Sasha was writing his diary, she was finishing her second glass of wine—only her second, because the first had been the very first of her young life. Gemini's was closing and we were about to leave, a drunk and joyous group, celebrating, in full public view, the most secret triumph. Even now when I think back to it, my heart races a little, for it was a rare feeling—a delicious, dangerous pleasure. But happiest of all, having carried the day, was Elena.

Young and sweet Elena, in her flower-patterned dress! The toast of our table that magnanimous night! What a charming child she was! How sincerely she had performed! We did enjoy the novelty of her company—and how her face flushed each time she cast her eyes on Ahishor!

He leaned forward and spoke to her: 'Now, you must understand that what we have done today is very significant. When this video is released, we will be the talk of the town. And *you* most of all—because you are the daughter of the Russian countess.'

She burst into laughter, almost falling backwards, holding her hand to her frail chest and shutting her eyes in surrender.

We gathered around, smiling.

'We'll be prepared for everything that happens,' said Ahishor. 'Many people will call us bad names; even threaten us. But the right people will support us. And we will support each other. So there is nothing to worry about. But there is one thing—until we release the footage, we must keep this whole project top secret. That means you mustn't tell anybody about it, Elena.'

'I won't tell anyone,' Elena promised earnestly.

'Good. That includes Sasha, whom you are staying with.'

'I will not tell him.' She began to blush, and was all the more anxious to dismiss the possibility. 'He is not... I am only staying with him for some days. I will not tell him.'

Ahishor gazed at her with thoughtfulness etched on his face. He was the calmest among us after the events of the day, pride and relief settling deep inside him. Drawn to his aura of leadership, I myself could well empathize with Elena's state.

As she began to blush again, turning to me (she was turning at random), he spoke further: 'It may be better if you come to Delhi in the meantime. We'll be preparing the video for a release in Delhi. Also I'd like to introduce you to the others there, who are part of our movement. I know they are all keen to meet the star of this show. You have done us proud, Elena.'

'I really support your cause! These people are cheats and all the things that are going on are not good. I know that!'

The words came out of her with terrible sincerity. She had experienced, read and heard many things in India and although (in spite of everything) her young mind burgeoned with cheerfulness, we had found in her—and struck—the chord of indignation.

But she was also shivering with excitement, desperate to please. As I looked at her, I began to feel a little sorry for her, for she was so plainly overwhelmed. I did not realize then that her innocence was also her shield, and that I, melting in with the other figures in the dark—Bharat, Mihir, Sushant, Malik—and smiling as one mature and knowing, was in the graver peril.

*   *   *

Two days later, I walked into the office to an unexpected sight. The main hall, where the two bosses usually sat, was empty. Looking around, I spied, through the glass doors of the conference room, Sushant and Malik, looking pensive and nodding their heads with gravity, while a massive figure in a checked shirt, whose face was hidden from me, gesticulated wildly and continuously. His speech sounded to me like a murmur, which meant that he was almost shouting inside.

Suddenly, I heard my name being called. Turning, I saw Bharat's head poking out of the screening room. He was beckoning urgently. When I joined him, I was further surprised. There, in the front row, crouched over a bright blue seat in an ungainly way, his head bobbing on his reedy frame as it swivelled to face us, was Jatin's young assistant, Arvind.

'Hey, man!' he waved at me. 'Long time no see!'

As I returned the greeting, I felt a sharp premonition of trouble. There were glances being exchanged between Bharat and Arvind. An unbidden thought entered my head that the two of them rather resembled each other.

'Arvind will be joining us on the tech end,' said Bharat.

'Great,' I said. 'We needed someone.'

Then it occurred to me.

'What about Jatin? Are you leaving Jatin?'

'That asshole?' replied Arvind, his eyes narrowing with hatred. 'You bet I am.'

Then he held my gaze with a set, steely look that I had never seen in him before. I had the sense of a changeling act taking place in front of me. But the truth was that I had never given any thought to Arvind's state of mind. Why would I? He was merely the laughing, cocky figure—too cocky to be affected by anything—who had replaced me at Jatin's office.

'Dhruv, you will understand what he is talking about,' Bharat was telling me. 'It has just gone on too long. If this guy is not taught a lesson today, he will kill someone tomorrow. I've told Arvind we are going to back him up completely.'

'So I'm filing charges,' said Arvind. 'Bharat thinks that's the way to go. And I agree.'

'But what happened?' I cried, though Bharat was right; I could guess already. 'Did he hit you?'

'He laid his hands on me,' said Arvind, nodding slowly. 'Grabbed my collar. I swear if he'd done anymore I'd have broken his jaw... Reason? There was no freaking reason, man. I told him I was quitting. His website wasn't going anywhere; I had got a better opportunity. That was it. I was even ready to finish this one thing I was supposed to, if he hadn't begun yelling at me. After that—no freaking way.'

Strangely, my first reaction was to feel bad for Jatin. I could picture him, toiling away at some doomed, esoteric project, with the rent and the bills for the air conditioning stacking up, and only one ally to alleviate the dread. No doubt, Arvind's departure would leave many things in the lurch. But he was forever wrecking his relationships.

And yet—

'He will apologize to you,' I said, though without conviction, for I knew what grudges he could hold. 'Wait a bit, he'll apologize.'

But Bharat was shaking his head furiously.

'He has not just attacked Arvind. He has been defaming Epochal for a long time. He abused us again when he learned Arvind was joining. He has abused you enough and more times too. Why are you defending him? I don't understand! You have moved far ahead in your career only because you left him. Do you want to be dragged back now?'

Suddenly, I had the sense of one dawdling, from sheer foolish perversity, at the edge of a precipice. Bharat was right—was I going to let my entanglement with Jatin trip me up even after I had broken free of it? It was necessary now only to mitigate my mistake.

'No, no, it's just that he is capable of good work too,' I said. 'He was the one who started Friends of Freedom to support Ahishor. I mean, that's how Sushant got involved too. But I agree completely. I agree he should be punished; that's the only way he will learn a lesson. What charges are you filing?'

Bharat sat down next to Arvind, who was breathing tensely and staring at the floor. He placed a hand on Arvind's shoulder, but looked up at me.

'Epochal has to be strong. Exactly because Jatin has been linked with us in the past, we have to act against him. We have to prove our principles by rejecting people like him, who are loose cannons and who abuse their employees. When such violent and unstable people claim to be libra—excuse me, liberal—Indians, this weakens the cause. Dhruv, understand this—I want to finish these Babas like nothing else! What did Ahishor say? If we ourselves have a divided camp, we cannot fight the enemy... I don't have anything personal against Jatin.

Theek hai[49], he abused me too when he was here. *Mere ko bura laga.*[50] But just because of that I would not encourage Arvind to file a case against him… We have to show our guts. It's not only the case of Jatin. We have to reject really powerful people too, if they are the elitist types. We don't need such liberals… Now see what is happening with Karim Azad! Our stand is going to shock weak people.'

The door had opened while he was speaking and Sushant had entered the room. Flopping down on one of the chairs in the last row, with his thin legs stretched out, he was chuckling to himself.

I had a sense of the surreal, for the little room suddenly felt packed with tall, thin men.

'Accha, you haven't heard about Karim…' Bharat continued, reading my expression. 'You haven't, na? Go check it out; the paper is on the table.'

I went up the steps to the door, brimming with anticipation. Outside, I glanced towards the conference room. Only Malik was still sitting there—on my favourite chair. He was staring out of the window. Then I picked up the newspaper. The page at which it was open carried the following report:

Legend in a Fix

Renowned lyricist Karim Azad has run into trouble for comments made by him during the gala night of the Sony Arts Festival last Saturday. Speaking in a session on 'Faith and Reason in Modern India' with Sadhguru Narayanan, Mr Azad was allegedly heard saying that 'lower castes are the

---

[49]Fine
[50]I felt bad.

biggest fools in India'. This allegedly defamatory and insulting comment has prompted furious reactions from Dalit leaders. An FIR under the SC/ST Act has also been filed by Shri Suresh Kumar, lawyer and activist, in Mumbai. Mr Azad could not be reached for comment.

I read through the whole piece with rising excitement and hurried back to the screening room, clutching onto the newspaper as though it might vanish like magic any instant. As I entered, I almost ran into Arvind, who was walking out. He skirted me politely. The other two were sitting as I had left them.

'It's so stupid!' I cried, when the door was closed. 'I was there in that session. He didn't mean it like that!'

'Then how did he mean it?' asked Bharat, standing up.

I plunged into an explanation of how Karim had been talking about god-men taking advantage of oppressed people—and the Scheduled Castes being the most oppressed, and therefore, the most vulnerable to such foolishness—and masquerading as saviours; and how he had prefaced his comment with a disclaimer that it would sound bad, but was not to be interpreted as an insult. Then I suddenly remembered (for I never gave such matters any deliberate thought) that Bharat Mishra himself was certainly not a Brahmin. So I stopped short—and he, with gleaming eyes, cut in.

'Those who are privileged never mean harm. It is their privilege not to mean harm.'

'Yes,' I began to nod. 'That's also true... Just that I wouldn't imagine Karim as a casteist.'

'*Haan, casteist nahi hai,*' Bharat shook his head. '*Kahne ko toh casteist nahi hai.*'[51]

---

[51]Yes, he's not a casteist... Supposedly, he is not a casteist.

'He's elitist,' said Sushant. 'You understand, bhai? It ain't about caste. It's about elitism and arrogance.'

I looked from one to the other, but I could not understand if they were in agreement. Nor could I read the smile that had appeared on Bharat's face.

'Suresh Kumar ji, the lawyer who has filed the case against Karim, he came to our office in the morning,' said Bharat. 'You may have spotted him when you arrived. We called him yesterday to hear his views, because Ahishor himself told us to. Ahishor has taken a very fair and firm stance on this... It's really inspiring.'

He was speaking truthfully, for it was only an hour or two later that the following note appeared simultaneously on Ahishor's Facebook and Twitter accounts, and his blog:

We, the upholders of the New Culture Manifesto, stand against casteism, classism and patriarchy alike. These are but many sides of the same illiberal oppression. And I wish to make it clear that my commitment to fighting them is without fear or favour. If my stepfather, Karim Azad, is proved to have deliberately belittled Scheduled Castes, as has been reported, I shall neither defend him nor remain silent. I shall be the voice that insists on his punishment.

Many Partings

That night, unusually for me, I dreamed vividly. In my dream, I was having lunch with Jatin at a place he loved, a South Indian restaurant called Banana Leaf, on the Juhu-Versova link road. He was in terrific spirits, smacking his lips, declaring the onion uthappam there to be the best in the world, and behaving towards me with extraordinary tenderness—as he often had. He was telling me of his confidence in me and that I was sure to become someone special if I retained my honesty and willingness to learn. Then he began to talk of his own failings, of his impatience and impulsiveness and how those two vices had wrecked him time and again—but also how, despite everything, he had never become cynical, and 'though my life is over, I still have the feeling that it is just beginning.' At some stage, he began telling me of Tara Krishna and how things could have been so different between them, had the timing only favoured him when they were young. 'But I have always loved her. She has been the only one in my life—and she knows that.'

As for me, though I was listening and nodding, my stomach felt like lead. I was trying to remember if I had given the waiter the wrong order for Jatin's next course. He had asked for a rava masala dosa but I, perhaps, had ordered something else? And then the waiter arrived with the dishes and Jatin's face went from smiling to apoplectic with rage, and a torrent of barbs were raining down upon me—I was spoiled, selfish, good-for-nothing and so was my whole generation. And then suddenly I had had enough. I threw the plates and the food, over the table, and stood towering above the incredulous Jatin, who had fallen over backwards. Then I began screaming in his face at the top of my voice.

When I woke up, the first thing I felt was a wonderful relief that no such episode had actually occurred. I was still half-asleep, when the previous day's developments came back to me and a fresh tension began to crawl all over me. And then, even as I lay in bed, I suddenly envisioned exactly what I was going to do. I saw that we were all ranged against Jatin and that I too was going to throw a stone at him. And that would be the end of our relationship—and so be it. I shut my eyes, as one might before a car crash. A few moments later, I got up.

It gave me a start to find five missed calls from Jatin on my phone, and a text message that began with the words: '*Dhruv, I am giving you one chance to—*'.

Without reading anymore, I deleted it.

*   *   *

The news of Arvind's FIR had reached him the previous night, and in the loneliness of his home, he had gone through a gamut of emotions. At some point, he went onto Facebook, full of bluster, striking out at us all. But perhaps the support he received online was too scanty and ambivalent, or perhaps it finally dawned on him that his fate would be settled in the real world. Then he began to dart glances at the door, feeling afraid. He felt he was not safe in his known address. With strange, uncertain feelings rising to his throat, he phoned Tara.

*　　*　　*

A scene was underway in the living room at Malabar Hills. Suraj Krishna, gripping the arms of his father's old chair, was staring at his wife, who sat on the edge of the sofa and looked at him steadily and silently, responding (he felt) to nothing he said, but turning over her own terrible meditations in her mind—and judging him.

'At least don't do anything suddenly,' he said. 'You know that doesn't make sense.'

'It's not sudden.' Very slowly, she shook her head. 'It's been building for months. You've seen that… Haven't you?'

'I have seen you upset about Maithili. We both have been upset.' When she continued to be expressionless, he could stomach it no longer and burst out. 'How can you even consider this, Tara? To go to the very person I am struggling and fighting against! It's bad enough that you have been aloof and unsympathetic while I've been waging this lonely battle!'

There was a sharp sound as she drew in her breath, and then, with her eyes still fixed upon him, began to nod to herself (maddeningly, he thought).

'Oh yes, I'm being insensitive, aren't I!' he cried out. 'Well, what do you expect? First my daughter is spirited off by a charlatan—to some den—where, God knows what! (his voice gave out and he took a long, shuddering breath). And now my wife wants to follow her there! And I'm supposed to—'

He uttered a sob, as the tears broke free of his eyes. Tara, watching, felt her heart tightening with a strange mixture of pity and stifled laughter. A wave of detachment passed over her. Suraj continued to ramble, with the cry rising and falling in his voice.

'It's not your fault,' she said at last. 'I'm not blaming you. You are who you are.'

'*Your husband!* Whom you are supposed to...' His voice trailed away as he stared at her with enormous eyes.

'I don't mean that,' she said—a little annoyed. 'I mean, you are an intellectual. You have your work with the Ministry. You enjoy debates and arguing; chatting with the Joshis. You are in your element in this climate... But I am tired. I'm sick and tired.'

'I am not an intellec... you are an intellectual too!'

'No, Suraj,' she laughed, 'I am not an intellectual. I never was. And now I hate it! I can't stand listening to the same old words and arguments and pontifications. There's so much noise all around me.'

'That's just politics,' protested Suraj. 'The country is going through a time of churning and, yes, there's too much noise, I agree, but the good people need to raise their voices too, to help it come through.'

'This is what I mean.' She had actually put her fingers to her ears, a pained look on her face as she shook her head. 'I am done with this. I used to be an artist. I abandoned painting— that was my biggest mistake! Now I need to find myself again. For God's sake, don't you understand? I want to live... Before my life is over. Just let me live... I beg of you.'

It was during the course of this speech that her phone began to ring. She quietened it without further ado. After some time, it rang again—and again she silenced it. Meanwhile, Suraj swallowed down fresh tears, which were like splinters in his throat. It seemed to him that he was up against some huge and unbeatable force, something vastly cruel and without a shred of human feeling, which had pounced upon him all of a sudden—bewilderingly.

'And what about Vishnu? What about your son's marriage?' he managed to ask.

She looked at him with dreadful calm.

'That's still some time away... I'm not thinking about it.'

'You're not thinking about it!'

'I can't. I have to go right now.' A trace of uncertainty had entered her voice. Suraj, who was feeling faint, suddenly heaved forward in his chair.

'Tara!' he cried. 'Even I want to be with Maithili! I want her back! But this is not the way... We have to be reasonable, for God's sake! Everybody has always said that we are a very reasonable pair of people!'

As suddenly as it had risen up, the energy began to drain out of him. He glimpsed Tara smiling, one eyebrow arching radically. 'Oh, Suraj, this is not what you think. It's something much bigger. I actually am grateful to Maithili. Can you believe it?'

She went on speaking, growing girlish in her enthusiasm. He was certain she did not know what she was saying or doing. *If she actually went to one of these ashrams* [he thought to himself] *she would not last a day from the physical labour they made people do. As for the pious satsangs and breathing exercises and mantras and contortions to get the chakras going—she would try—and then she would giggle! And time would prove him right. But at what cost! Both their humiliation! But she was bent on it...*

He glanced towards the balcony. The sky was bleached white, the city wilting in the heat. He thought of staggering towards the balcony—threatening to jump. *Would that shake her?*

But the only action he took was to clench and unclench

the thick tuft of hair above the nape of his neck. Tara's phone rang for a third time.

'Who is that?' asked Suraj sharply.

'No one,' muttered Tara, silencing the ringing. Irritated and embarrassed, she tried to switch off her phone altogether. *This was another source of stress, the endless chatter of modern life, phones ringing, doorbells ringing—but phones, most of all! And it would be Jatin calling; yet another demanding man in her life! And for how long!* In a sudden panic, she had a premonition that she would never be free. When she looked up, Suraj was staring at her with a pale face.

'You should get ready for your meeting,' she reminded him, rising briskly from the sofa. 'I'm going to lie down for some time.'

She went to the bedroom and closed the door, before going straight to the computer to check her flight ticket. While online, she came across an email from Jatin, telling her of the charges that had been filed against him and demanding a public testimonial and a show of support: *I am writing to all my friends—but to you first of all, for obvious reasons.*

In a postscript, he had issued an order: *Pick up your phone.*

As Tara's eyes rested on the message, something snapped inside her. She hit the reply button straightaway. Then the words came coursing out of her. In her email, she informed Jatin that while she was sorry for his plight, she had warned him about his temper many times herself. Perhaps it was best that he confronted this and other troubles on his own. She was aware that she may be sounding callous but he had pushed around and taken for granted far too many people—certainly her—for far too long. Now she was leaving the city for an unspecified period, and would like him, as a parting request, to respect her need for personal space. Then, before clicking 'send,' she added a last line, wishing him 'a more peaceful life'.

She had just logged off, when something occurred that made her gasp. A strange whimpering was in her ear, a familiar cologne was growing thick in her nostrils and a pair of hands was tightening around her throat, squeezing the very life out of her.

*　　*　　*

The case against Karim Azad was national news in no time. It was not only the gesticulating lawyer Suresh Kumar, but many other far-flung folk, who had rushed to their local police stations and magistrates to bay for the great artist's blood. By the second day, there were five cases against him, from Mumbai to Kerala. And more came later, though I gave up tracking them.

A state of shock prevailed in the apartment behind Yari Road. When the news had first arrived, it had seemed to Karim a mere joke. Later, he felt sure the matter could be explained away in no time, with a single statement of clarification. But the words, even to the wordsmith, would not come. The knot would not untangle. For the harmlessness of his speech was so obvious to him, he found he could not explain it to anyone who did not see it. But since the uproar refused to die down, it seemed others did not see even the simplest things the way he did. These people looked through alien eyes—wild, crazed and goggling.

Nalini was by his side during every trip to the lawyer's office and afterwards when the lawyer came home and they were closeted together in Karim's study. She too faced the media and defended her husband demurely but unflinchingly. But when the questions turned to Ahishor's stand on the matter, she offered no comment, and when they persisted, she fled.

Incredibly, many days elapsed, before they spoke a word

to each other about Ahishor. Perhaps Karim had been too perturbed. But to Nalini, it was a paralyzing nightmare—for Ahishor, true to his promise, was not silent. Even as an array of well-respected voices—fine old liberals, many of whom were his friends—spoke up for Karim, vouching for his egalitarianism, quoting from his lyrics to prove the point and protesting, indeed, that few Indians were more committed to social equality than Karim, Ahishor had stood up and denounced him. It was not commitment, but condescension, that he found in Karim. 'Elitism, by another name...' said Ahishor. 'Though I love my stepfather, I cannot whitewash his true colours as they are being revealed.' All of us, a whole generation, was echoing him, and bit by bit, we were turning the tide of opinion within the liberal community, because we were starting to look like the winning side.

Nalini, loyal to her husband, went all this while without speaking to her son (one aghast phone call had brought her no relief), but when Karim finally cursed him to her face, she went pale and retreated into her art. Accepting a long-standing request to do a set of theatrical monologues in Odisha, she began to spend all day rehearsing in a studio in Khar, returning home only late at night, when they were both exhausted.

Upon all these matters, the dust was still swirling, when Giri Joseph's new *Guardian* piece arrived, to peer confidently through the storm. It was titled 'The Fallen Liberal, The Rising Liberalism'—and this time I was impressed. It was an emotionally charged piece, mourning (with real excitement) the fall from grace of Pankaj Pande, Jatin Khanna, Ritesh Azad, and now Karim Azad. Joseph had lifted himself to see the greater good, for which these icons, esteemed by varying degrees, were being torn down—namely, that genuine liberalism, which was capable of fighting and was free of hypocrisy, and whose charge Ahishor was leading. The essay was both a lamentation and a celebration— the right notes for a revolution—though, Giri did close on his familiar note of detached superiority, reminding everyone that 'since India's majoritarian right wing continues to spiral dangerously, one hopes that the new liberalism will not stop at housekeeping.'

Some Kind of Priest

Jatin had bristled in the anticipation of being rejected, even as his email demanded help. But Sasha called him the same day.

'Can we meet?'

'What for?' asked Jatin. 'I don't need to meet anyone; I need people to go online and speak out! Show some damn support!'

'I will do that,' said Sasha. 'But let's also meet. It will be good for you to talk about this, I'm sure.'

There was a pause, before Jatin, to his relief, relented.

'Yes, alright. I'm busy till six. We can meet after that. But where shall we meet? I want to get out of the damn office. And I'm not coming to Versova. I might see those bastards there, and if I do, I will break their necks. I won't be able to stop myself.'

They decided, eventually, to take a walk in a park in Lokhandwala, a lengthy, oblong affair with a cement track laid upon the greens, open to the main road and the office buildings, but nonetheless one of the more pleasant parks in the suburb. Jatin was there before time, pacing up and down near the gates. His hulking shoulders seemed to ripple with strength and his eyes were set in a look of defiance. But lurking just behind them was something vacant and defeated.

He nodded slowly when he caught sight of Sasha.

'You're punctual,' said Jatin, smiling through pursed lips. 'It's one of your best qualities.'

In the ensuing pause, Sasha observed the state that he was in.

'Come on, let's not just stand!'

He swivelled and began to walk. He was silent for the first half-round, though he walked tremendously fast, leaving Sasha quite breathless in no time.

'I know what's really going on,' he said suddenly. 'This is not about Arvind really. Arvind is incompetent, smug and thankless. But he's also a coward! He doesn't have the guts to do this on his own. Epochal has put him up to it. All this only started after he joined them. Because I've been warning everyone publicly about Epochal and the kind of smarmy fakes they are. This is nothing but them trying to take revenge. It's so sick! Sick and underhand! But I'm not letting them get away with it. I've already posted about it on Facebook. Did you see?'

'See what? The new post? Yes I saw it.'

'Why do you keep silent then?' exploded Jatin. 'Why don't you comment?'

'I'm more concerned about the FIR,' said Sasha, but the strain was showing on his face, as he continued too, rapidly. 'That's happening in the real world. How will Facebook activities make a difference?'

'Don't be a fool, Sasha!' Jatin grimaced horribly. His voice became a wail of indignation. 'Are you trying to tell me that public opinion doesn't matter? This is the fucking age of social media! Why would the police even bother with such a childish FIR if there wasn't pressure being put on them? Or do you have a better idea? Do you know how to stop this?'

He stopped walking, for a desperate hope had lit up his eyes.

'Some people have suggested I file a counter FIR.'

'Against Arvind?'

'Who else? Against this excuse for a human being. Ah, I can't even take his name, it makes me sick! I gave him more independence and responsibility than he will get anywhere in this city ever in his life! I paid him twice what he was worth! You reckon I could file a case of cheating? Breach of trust? He refused to even serve a notice period, never mind completing the work he was supposed to!'

Sasha averted his gaze. The road outside the park was broad, and steady with traffic. The street lights were flaming slowly to life and soon they would be an incandescent row of white. From the distance, the office buildings looked neat and well organized. But his heart was sinking, as though beholding chaos, the ruination of things. He shifted suddenly to avoid the oncoming walkers.

'What have other people suggested?' he asked.

'Don't ask!' muttered Jatin, before lurching forward again. 'Come on, we can't stand here!'

Jatin's mouth continued to work, though he was no longer speaking. Stirred, Sasha saw the tears standing in the other's eyes, though he blinked them away briskly.

'I have been disappointed by the reactions of several people,' said Jatin. 'Hurt, actually.'

But he was thinking of only one. Tara's words had struck him numb. For he had done exactly what she had accused him of doing—he had taken her for granted. How could he defend himself? How could he explain that he could not but lean on her? She had written to him like a stranger. And though he understood, in hindsight, that the breach had been forewarned, still the pain of shock, the anger and the indignation had swarmed over him, overpowering him so much that he could only form feeble words in his own head. He had been unable to reply to her.

Now, however, he found relief in speaking, and, with overarching words, sought to mask the deeply private wound.

'There is no sense of loyalty. I've worked with many people in this town. They all know that I am far from abusive. Yes, incompetence and arrogance will always get my goat. And I am proud of this! But to be accused of being a criminal is patently ridiculous! I get impatient. And this has been the reason for my downfall on many occasions. But I have never been petty about praising people either. I have never been jealous of anybody else's success. I myself have backed so many others in this town. Have they forgotten everything?'

'You supported Pankaj Pande,' said Sasha, contemplatively.

'Of course! And I'm proud of that! Has it become the fashion to condemn people without even trying to be fair?'

'It seems to have become so,' nodded Sasha. The heaviness in his heart was growing. He began to slow down as they rounded a bend, and Jatin lingered too.

'You reckon it's because I'm not a big shot?' asked Jatin excitedly. 'If I was Mahesh Bhatt, I could say and do anything and a hundred chamchas would support me. But because, by conventional standards, I'm considered a failure and I still have the nerve to speak my mind...'

Sasha was shaking his head. 'It's more than that. Failure in conventional terms makes people pariahs; that is nothing new. But the yardstick here is new. It may be more courageous; it may be attacking the rich and famous too. But you are right, it is without loyalty. Without love. It is another kind of tribalism. Full of self-righteousness.'

Halting under the darkening skies, they stared at each other; each man grave and brooding, though according to his own lights.

'Well, they messed with the wrong guy!' cried Jatin, moments later. 'I shall file that counter FIR.'

'Why don't you listen instead,' asked Sasha, 'to the one who does love you? The one who is loyal!'

'Who are you talking about?' Jatin's eyes were narrowing, his lips curling incredulously.

'No no, not me. I'm talking about God! You are not alone. Listen to God, who does love you! He will help you through this!'

And then, glad tides of relief were flowing through him, as Jatin, whom he had feared would erupt into curses and abuses, grew subdued instead.

'What are you?' he muttered eventually. 'Some kind of priest?'

Sasha did not reply, but he felt a warmth in his chest and a steady lightening of his heart that made him almost want to shout for joy, quite unreasoningly.

'I don't really believe in God,' Jatin continued, looking away. 'At times like this especially I find it hard to believe in God.'

'*We* bring about such times,' said Sasha, 'because we have the freedom to turn away from Him and do evil. Without Him, even the best-intentioned people will turn to evil. Human love dries up; it runs out. It is running out everywhere in India, isn't it? It's being overwhelmed by all kinds of monsters. But the wonderful thing is that God's love is greater.'

'Please! In India, we talk all the time about God. It has got us nowhere.'

'Because we put our faith in corruptions, not in God. I think we always have. And those who are persecuting you right now, they do not believe in God.'

'Well, why doesn't He strike them down then?' bellowed Jatin. 'Ahh, but fuck it! I have to do it myself!'

He began to stride forward again. Sasha hurried to keep pace. The park, at that hour, was milling with walkers. Sasha spoke rapidly: 'He allows these things because He has made us free. But He turns even our evil choices to good. We only have to take His side to realize that.'

'I'm not talking about this anymore,' said Jatin, with an irritation that was exacerbated by his own sense of having lapsed into foolishness. 'If you have any practical suggestions, please come out with them. Otherwise just keep walking. I don't want to waste my time.'

Setting his jaw, he walked even faster, his upper body swivelling furiously as he bulldozed his way down the path. With a desperate, lunging gait, Sasha followed.

'That's the whole trouble,' he raised his voice. 'If we are like cogs in the machinery, and always moving, how can we begin to live? Look at this park—it's supposed to be an oasis, but even here, we can feel the traffic right outside... We can see the lights and hear the horns all around us. How fast everyone is walking! You yourself cannot pause for even a moment! I am talking about the only real and beautiful thing in existence and you think it is a triviality. I am giving you the most practical suggestion there is, and you say I am wasting your time! But I know that you know better, because you love life, Jatin! That is why you are able to live by your own conscience and be fruitful even after disappointments. Because you do rely on God!'

It seemed that Jatin was preparing to speak—but Sasha continued:

'I know you don't believe in the ways of the world and

worldly wisdom! So don't lose your faith now; make it grow! God has allowed this trouble to come upon you, but with God's help it will be a blessing to you! The very last thing you should do is hit back blindly. You will be destroying your own blessing.'

'Don't tell me what I shouldn't do!' exclaimed Jatin. 'I want to know positive steps!'

'Accept this, as though it is a blessing, with the faith that it is! The same way you admitted to me just now that you are impatient, admit it to whoever is attacking you. You can explain yourself when the time comes, if the case proceeds, but also admit the wrong you did. No matter how badly Arvind worked, it was not right to become enraged. Accept that first of all. It will disarm them and free you.'

But Jatin, pounding towards the entrance to the park, was reminded again of Tara's words. *She had told him the same thing, had she not? To suck it up!* She had said it, of course, to get rid of him—but he did not now consider the difference of spirit. In the oppression of the humid night air, as he gazed through a blur of sweat and tears, he saw no solace in any direction, but only many varieties of foes. He had fought the right-wing Hindutva brigade tooth and nail, while others equivocated; yet it had won him no favours from this grasping new generation. They had come at him with knives instead. Young and old had failed him—those whom he had befriended, those whom he had mentored (for I know how I had hurt him). Not even the one who had possessed his heart for years had thought it worth the saving. *As for Sasha* [Jatin looked into the shining eyes of the young man beside him], *he had known him a few months, but how he talked! How very upright he was—for a hunchback!* A bitter humour settled upon Jatin suddenly, his lips twisting in laughter.

But when he spoke, he was grave again. 'Never mind,' said Jatin. 'Seriously, never mind. We have talked enough. I'm going now… I need to work.'

*　*　*

When Sasha tried unlocking the door of his apartment, he found that it was bolted from the inside. He could hear a scuffling noise from within, which ended abruptly as he pressed the bell. In the silence that followed, the door opened a fraction and a suspicious face appeared in the crack.

'Elena, it's me,' he said, suppressing a smile.

She was wearing her favourite sleeveless white smock with blue sailor-stripes, and shorts and slippers. Her face was flushed with effort, for in the middle of the little room lay open a huge suitcase, half packed. Her clothes were in untidy piles on the mattress.

'I'm going to Delhi for some time,' she said impatiently, though Sasha had not spoken. Frowning, she turned back and resumed her packing.

'What for, and for how long?' he asked.

It seemed she had not heard him. He went to the kitchen for a glass of water. Upon coming back to the room, he asked her again.

'Why every time you want to know?' retorted Elena hotly, her eyes flashing with resentment. 'It's a new project, that's all!'

He was surprised, though not entirely taken aback, for she had been uncommunicative the whole fortnight. Yet, in the same period, he had seen her quite as herself, bringing home little gifts of fruits and ice creams, and becoming steadily excited at the prospects of the new city. He had not probed into the phase she was passing through. So much imponderable experience lay stored up at the bottom of Elena's young heart that he felt in her a holy mystery, to be loved rather than understood.

But now something had happened to tear aside that enchanted veil. A mean and narrow aspect—familiar in general but startling in her—had entered into her gaze.

'How come so suddenly?' he asked. 'You're packing already, and I had no idea.'

'It's not sudden; I've been working on it. But it's a secret project. It's a big project—with Ahishor Frances,' she told him, in a burst of pride. 'Don't ask me more. I can't talk about it.'

'He's making a film again?'

'It's not a film. It's a different project.'

'But you want films. You came here for that.'

'No films are happening! I need work first! This is still cinema in its own way,' she added.

'Is it something with Epochal Pictures?'

Elena hesitated. 'Yes.'

Sasha sat down deliberately on the edge of the takht on which she slept. He tried to hold her gaze, but she, though noticing his expression, continued to pack busily. Then he found himself at a loss for words, growing angry, though he willed himself into restraint.

'Why are you working for Epochal? You have already seen what kind of work they're doing. You came home crying that day! Don't you remember? And you had every reason to!'

'That was different project; this is different one.'

'But the people are the same!'

'So? Work is different.'

'But what is it?'

'I can't tell you; it's secret.'

'Yes, but why is it secret? Did you think about that? Good

work should not normally be secret.'

'I know why,' continued Elena, with every appearance of indifference, 'but I'm not gonna tell you. I already told you enough.'

Struck silent, he watched her move about the room, her face taking on the deep gravity that (like her unceasing excitement) seemed so natural to it. When she put her hands on her hips, lost in some minute consideration, he felt his heart going out to her. Simultaneously, the pangs of fear and danger were growing in him, assailing ever more insistently. But he saw no simple way to justify them.

'Man, stop staring at me!' she said, looking up suddenly. 'You're like a ghost!'

'Don't be rude,' he said softly, for he was stung.

'Man, what do you want?' demanded Elena. 'I should just sit here and suffer? It's very good opportunity with Ahishor. I am lucky to have got it!'

'You're just enamoured of the name,' said Sasha bitterly, suddenly unable to contain himself. 'Because Ahishor Frances is involved, you don't look at anything else. But Ahishor's talent was for films, and he is not the same person he was. In any case, Epochal is run by Bharat and Sushant. They are not good people to work with; they are very mixed up—dangerously mixed up. I mean, Sushant is going to hit on you for sure—if he hasn't already!'

To his astonishment, she began to smirk, her cheeks colouring quickly. It was a mystery to him what was on her mind. Then she seemed to shake off a certain train of thought, before pulling herself together and narrowing her eyes.

'Man, no. You are talking about things you don't know. Everything is fine.'

He took a deep breath and looked at her. 'I want you to tell me what the project is. Otherwise I don't want you to go.'

Elena's eyes widened, growing bigger and bigger. Before he knew it, she was running across the room and leaping over the suitcase and the strewn clothes. She pushed the door, flinging it open all the way, and went out onto the empty landing where the tube lights were glowing balefully. She then turned on her heel, exclaiming, 'I'm not your prisoner! I will go if I want to go!'

Sasha rose in shock. She was packing furiously now, throwing her things in. Her mouth was set in an awful manner that quite transformed her face.

'Elena,' he said. 'Of course you can go. I wasn't saying that…'

His voice gave way and he sat down again, as tears came pricking at his eyes. She threw a glance at him, but then looked away, her face staying queerly hard while she muttered justifications, addressed to no one in particular:

'I need to work. I can't keep sitting here waiting. I don't have rich father like you. I need to work with important people. It's my chance. I need to go.'

In between, she cast quick looks at him. He saw how firmly the suspicion of him had been planted in her. There was no doubt it had been planted—for it had not been there before.

Half an hour later, he was lifting her suitcase into a taxi waiting in the courtyard. Behind them, across the boundary wall, was the beach on which they had met, now shrouded in the dark of the night. But they could still hear the sea in its eternal rhythm.

'Have you got your ticket and passport?'

'Yes.'

'And your phone and purse?'

'Yes, yes.'

She had changed into her flower-patterned dress, in which she stood, with her arms by her side, waiting expressionlessly for her ride to be ready. Her thin hair stirred in the warm night breeze, which billowed about them in bursts of generosity. *Out in the street* [thought Sasha], *there would be autos cruising, people loitering, the clatter and the chatter of the continuous cafes, their air thick with dreams of money and love.* And now all these too seemed to him like the greetings of old friends. For he realized that, in spite of everything, Elena had been safe here, managing to grow in the turmoil of Mumbai, like the flowers that sprung up in the concrete dividers of roads. But she was leaving for a place where she had suffered much.

At the last moment, he saw a hesitation in her.

'It may not be a long trip,' she said. 'I'll let you know.'

'Come back soon.'

He stepped forward, ready to embrace her, for her eyes too were wet and frightened. But a spasm passed over her face and she ducked into the taxi, calling to the driver: '*Chalo, chalo, chalo!*[52]'

Everything was a mess, thought Sasha. The crashing sea was loud in his ears, as he watched the car with Elena inside it, make its way into the night.

---

[52]'Chalo' means 'Let's go'

Ahishor the Pure

I must say that we had not deceived her. When the 'sting' against Sadhguru Narayanan was broadcast, in the furore that followed, Elena's fame was no less than the Guru's notoriety. The tens of lakhs, who saw the footage on YouTube and shared it across the Internet with noisy comments of every kind, may have differed in their politics, yet each had eyes only for her. For hers was the face of the video, even more so than the Guru's. I felt that myself, when I watched it. Who could but wonder at the baby-faced white girl, perched on the sofa in front of the great Master, spinning out her tall tale in her endearing accent, asking careful questions and listening politely to the answers that were not only exposing the god-man's trickery, but shaking the very foundations of the government!

I know the mischief of the operation had delighted the child in her and I imagine she must have daydreamed during her difficult life, about the part we gave her to play. It was in the guise of the granddaughter of a Russian countess that we won her the appointment with Sadhguru. The story she told him—though she told it incompletely, breathlessly, and, thus, all the more persuasively—was as follows. Her great-grandmother had been a Russian noblewoman of vast wealth. During the Bolshevik revolution, she had been dispossessed of all her land, but managed to escape to California with her personal jewellery, which too was worth a fortune. After the perestroika, her parents had moved back to Ukraine, where (thanks to her mother working in Hollywood, and the family inheritance) they were able to repurchase their ancestral castle. This was where young Elena had grown up, on lavish grounds beneath stately turrets. Then one day, soon after her fourteenth birthday, Elena chanced upon the keys to a dusty old attic-almirah. Inside, all carefully preserved, she discovered her great-grandmother's journals alongside stacks of newspaper clippings about Madame Blavatsky and the Theosophists. From these papers, it transpired that the old lady had been highly spiritually inclined and had yearned to join the Theosophical Society, but had felt herself unable to, because of her parents' objections. (For this failure to follow her heart, she had considered herself punished when the Bolsheviks came marauding). But young Elena was hooked, and the more she read, the more she was drawn to India herself. A spiritual awakening had come upon her. It went on for two years, until two months ago, one night in Ukraine, she dreamed that she was stretching out her arms to the vision of a silver-haired man, floating above the sea. She had woken up, overcome with emotion. The next morning, she switched on the TV—and there, by an extraordinary coincidence, was Sadhguru, the very man from her dream, speaking at a conference in New Delhi.

In culmination, it had been explained to Narayanan that Elena wished to enter his ashram. Not only her, but her mother (the former Hollywood actress) would also be flying down to India shortly. For the Countess also had felt the pull of Sadhguru.

'And the father?' she had been asked.

He had died, in a car accident. Perhaps, Elena surmised, it was the shock of this death, which had kindled her mother's latent spirituality, for she had lived a rather wild life in her youth. In any case, neither woman wanted to live a moment longer in material abundance. They were already in the process of selling the castle in Ukraine, and everything in it. The proceeds would be transferred to the cause of the Spirit—meaning, of course, Sadhguru's foundation. That was what her great-grandmother would have wanted. There was only one hitch. The ladies did not wish either country's government to lay sinful hands on any portion of the money. Who could forget what the Bolsheviks had done during that mad time! It was not only the old lady's dispossession. Darkening the pages of her journal were hints of a rape as well. No—the money was intended entirely for the Spirit. Could Sadhguru suggest a way?

Such was Elena's 'backstory', and even now, when I tell it, I feel I must immediately share the proper credit for it, lest anyone think this masterpiece was all my creation. Malik and I devised it together, in consultation with Elena, and not only did Malik contribute to the plot, he also acted the part of the Hamolka family's Indian factotum. This performance, sadly, was not captured for posterity, because much of it took place behind the scenes, while afterwards, during the crucial backroom meeting with Sadhguru, it was Malik's person that concealed the secret camera. But we all heard his voice, eager, cajoling, loud and fearfully hammy in hindsight. (But so was the whole charade, and it seemed to sail through all the better for it.) Lines of his dialogue ('One sugar please,' he had told the god-man) became part of Versova parlance, like a second *Sholay*. It was Malik's finest hour. He, who had always been well-liked but revered by nobody—a movie buff, but no achiever himself—shot up overnight to the status of a legend, someone who had worked wonders in every aspect of cinema. For, they were all saying, a sting such as this was a work of art and the reinvention of cinema—just what India needed.

Of course, neither Malik nor I, nor any of us, had anticipated the extent of the catch we were going to haul up. It was beyond reckoning.

'You need not worry about the government,' Sadhguru had answered Elena, throwing back his magnificent head and laughing as he spoke. 'The ministers themselves come to me when the taxes become too much.' And then he took names. That became the first piece of breaking news, night after night. The second was, in the judgment of some, even more devastating. 'You have come to India at the perfect time,' he had said with great gravity. 'The whole country is being carefully realigned onto the correct spiritual path—the Hindu way. I have to tell you, for a long time the spiritual energies of this place were dwindling—going to the dogs. India had completely forgotten its identity. Now we are slowly recovering. When I met the Prime Minister, he himself gave me this assurance... Well, all politicians are incompetent; I don't trust any of them. But I think these guys are trying.'

It seemed to confirm every one of the worst fears that had been floating in the air for so long—and like a lit match, set them aflame. The government was far from secular; it was insidiously bent on transforming India into a Hindu nation of the most bigoted variety. The Prime Minister himself was behind this grand project. This, and not economic development, was the real agenda of the right wing. Moreover, at the very least, they were plainly crooks, who, in the company of their tribe (god-men, religious fanatics, rich devotees), were going to siphon off the country's wealth, while the rest of us stood about, overwhelmed.

I have already spoken of the fame that Elena and Malik garnered after the sting. But even Bharat, Sushant and I in Mumbai, Mihir in Delhi, and Alisha, Gaurav and the rest, were being written about, discussed in private and public, and even sought after for interviews, which, however, we abjured, as we did all gratuitous limelight—to begin with, I should say (while our collective discipline held). Only one among us was permitted to step forth—the man at the helm, Ahishor.

The feeling around him was indescribable. I realized just how special, when one afternoon, as I watched Ahishor speaking on television, my flatmate, who was passing through the room, stopped suddenly, nodded significantly and began to chant Ahishor's praises. This boy, an avid gamer and stoner, was the least political of all people I knew, but I saw him smiling that day, in a way I could never have imagined. It was a smile full of pride and shyness. Indeed, he was trembling with the kind of emotion I didn't think he had had in him.

We all felt heady, because we all felt pure, as our fountainhead was pure. I think what got most 'neutral' observers excited, was that Ahishor could not be slotted into any mere camp. He was not an immature young man, out to throw a tantrum for the sake of his whims, nor was he anything like a cynical old one. Soon, this negative intrigue became a positive sign of the genuine article, the unicorn—a rare, real revolutionary, who had not hesitated to take up cudgels against his own stepfather. And even now, when the whole country's media was listening, Ahishor talked as much about rescuing liberalism from liberals, as he did about the threat of the Hindu right. Indeed, he spoke at length about the false liberals. He pointed out that there was a pattern to the type, which he had identified in the Manifesto too. They were typically privileged and powerful men, grown smug in themselves, who had become accustomed to mistreating the weaker sections of society—especially women. He named names, which made people uncomfortable, but when they found his motives perfectly pure (his arguments, of course, were already compelling), they realized that they needed him all the more, to quell the very fear he had wakened in them. And his motives were indeed pure; what axe did he have to grind with the likes of Pankaj Pande and Jatin Khanna anyway? Even to this day, I entertain only a little doubt in one case—ironically, that of Suraj Krishna, whose offence was the most egregious, and who had just then become the latest false liberal to be unmasked.

All I knew at first (perhaps it was really all that mattered) was that Mr Krishna had tried to strangle his wife. This was incredible to me. Every time I had seen her, the impression Tara Krishna had left on me was that of the gentlest of souls, a decorous woman who wouldn't hurt a fly. Moreover, not only was violence against her unthinkable, but violence proceeding from such a man seemed doubly so. For he was sweet himself; an old-fashioned gentleman. No doubt he was a wordy bore (I remembered his speech at Maithili's Film Festival debut), who would grow tiresome to live with—but surely he was no Bluebeard! Yet I did not spend time wondering. In those topsy-turvy times, the nicest of folks were proving to be monsters—that too, in quick succession.

There had been no mistake. He did not deny the charge when it became public. Once I saw him on television, ashen-faced, in a suit and tie, trying to avoid the cameras as he scurried across a parking lot. In a way, Suraj Krishna was lucky, because in the smorgasbord of juicy developments, his case escaped the full feeding frenzy of the public.

In fact, I had almost forgotten about it until I heard it being talked about in a new light, on the day that Ahishor and Sasha came face-to-face in the slums off Yari Road.

I remember—it was the second Sunday of May. The previous night, I had received an invitation from Ahishor's maid, communicated to me by Ahishor. Kaushalya, he had informed me, was hosting a lunch in her jhuggi. This was notionally in celebration of the Easter just passed, but was actually (Ahishor explained) because she was a friendly soul who cherished having her own people in the midst of the city crowds. So she had insisted that Ahishor come, and not alone, but with the one friend she specified, which was me. I was amused, but I was also flattered that among all his visitors, I was the one the maid had thought of. Then, when the day came about, I suddenly shrank from the prospect, but at twelve o'clock Ahishor picked me up and ten minutes later, I was there with him, wrinkling my nose, squinting in the sun and wondering what I was doing with my Sunday. We were walking across an open field, with pigs, garbage and rows of shacks cutting off the horizon.

'That's her house,' Ahishor tilted his head, though I could not make out at what.

'You've been here before?' I wondered aloud.

'Twice before,' he said, picking up his stride. He was wearing a kurta, which was flapping loosely, with the top buttons open, and linen pants that ruffled in the rancid breeze that blew in from across the field. He looked cheerful and full of relaxed energy, eyes bright behind his scraggy beard.

'Kaushalya!' Ahishor called out, as we ducked past the plastic flap that was her doorway. Entering, my eyes adjusted to the dimness. There was a little cot and mattress, with shelves above and beside it, empty of all but religious icons; pots and pans in two shelves above the stove, where Kaushalya, who had turned to greet us, had been busy cooking; and rows and rows of onions and potatoes in a third shelf below these. Perpendicular to the stove was a rather fancy LED television, switched on currently to a Hindi soap. There was nothing else in the room, except bottles of beer in one corner, and two blue plastic stools placed in the shadows beside the door. Perched atop one of them—was Sasha.

He looked as though he had been expecting us, though we were startled to see him. He seemed to me altered and somehow much older, perhaps because he was wearing a plain pair of shorts and a T-shirt, whereas I always expected him to be dressed fancily. His thin, smooth legs were stretched out, and his hands were folded on his lap.

'What are you doing here?' Ahishor laughed.

But he was looking at us without smiling, in a way that discomfited me.

'I've come because Kaushalya called me, of course. She works at my house too.'

'*Bhaiyya bahut acche hain!*[53]' confirmed Kaushalya, looking proudly from Sasha to us. '*Aap donon bhaiyya acche hain! Aur aap bhi. Aapka name kya hai?*[54]'

'Dhruv…' I said.

'*Bhaiyya ke bahut acche dost ho!*[55]', she declared, and I blushed.

---

[53]Sir is very nice

[54]Both of you Sirs are nice! And you too. What's your name?

[55]You are a very good friend of (Ahishor) Sir!

'*Main Prestige Apartment vaale bhaiyya-didi ko bhi bulaya tha, lekin vo nahin aa rahe*[56],' she added.

She was standing before us—her dark, round person in a brightly patterned gown, her face wreathed in beads of sweat, smiling and showing a gold tooth in between healthy white ones; a happy and (to me) comic figure. She had a wooden ladle raised aloft. But as she spoke, her arm dropped limply to her side and a sadness came over her.

'*Mera idhar koi nahi hai*,' brooded Kaushalya. '*Apna koi hona maangta hai na?*[57]

'*Hum hain na*, Kaushalya!' Ahishor winked at me. '*Accha ab udaas mat ho. Bolo khaane main kya hai?*'[58]

Beer and spiced eggs, for starters, were duly brought forth. I was soon beginning to enjoy myself, sitting on Kaushalya's cot, drinking straight out of the bottle and staring at the surreal slumscape outside. Perhaps I made the immemorial remark that it was a great setting for a short film. I certainly thought so. But I was very quiet in general, and, for some time, there was no particular conversation around me either. I recall a general praise of the food, comments being offered on the television set, how much it cost and what a good deal it was, criticisms of the dreadful soap now playing, which Kaushalya, a fan, was content to smile at, and small talk about the price of vegetables (this was in relation to her hoarding of onions).

But in the midst of all the chatting and eating (chicken was now being served), I was surprised to note that Ahishor was getting annoyed. The reason was that Kaushalya continually

---

[56]I had called the Sir and Madam from Prestige Apartment too, but they are not coming

[57]I have no relatives here... But we should have someone to call our own, right?

[58]We are there, Kaushalya... Okay, now don't be upset. Tell us what's for lunch?

reverted to glumness—with a morbid thought here, a depressing prospect there—and (I was surprised, for it seemed insensitive) he was showing little patience for it. Pretty soon, she was on a roll, listing a litany of troubles—her rent, which was being raised; the neighbour's son, who had committed suicide; the demolition of a nearby slum, which had struck fear in her, for theirs could be next; and her physical illnesses, the pain in her joints and the bouts of extreme dizziness that assailed her, sometimes twice a month. What could she do, she bemoaned. She had no one to care for her. Her family was distant and may as well be dead. However, she was praying more than before and going to Church every Sunday.

Suddenly, Ahishor put down his plate and looked straight at her.

'If you people don't stop being foolish,' he said, 'you deserve your difficulties. I have told you a hundred times to go to a doctor for your joint pain. But you just want to pray!'

'I have been to a doctor,' protested Kaushalya, but Ahishor made a dismissive gesture.

'It's not just about going. You also have to do all the things he tells you. As for all these other things—demolitions and so on—God is not going to stop your house being demolished! You people will have to fight for it.'

'I have changed my faith,' she said suddenly.

'I know that.' He was further irritated. 'You have joined my faith—except it isn't really. I was baptized as a child, when I didn't know better. That's how religion gets all of us. What I'm saying is, it makes no difference what God you believe in. Your life belongs to you, not to any God.'

'Ahishor…' I heard Sasha say softly, yet there was something in his voice that made us all turn towards him. 'Why are you telling her what isn't true? Have you not read? "Except the Lord build the house, they labour in vain that build it. Except the Lord keep the city, the watchman wakes in vain"… Kaushalya is right to pray.'

When he finished speaking, Sasha turned his head and stared oddly in my direction. I felt as though he was trying to look into my soul, and was either failing to, or was confused by what he saw. I also saw a sheen in his eyes, as from tears. But I did not know whether to smile or frown, and so I turned my gaze to the wall.

'Well, well,' said Ahishor. 'So you are a fatalist. And you have read the Old Testament, which is full of fatalism. Here I thought you were writing scripts.'

'I've not written any after the one I showed you,' Sasha replied.

'That tends to happen,' nodded Ahishor, 'when you leave everything up to the Guy in the sky.'

'But you have been very active,' said Sasha quietly.

'Yes!'

Ahishor looked at Kaushalya, with a grin spreading over his face.

'O Kaushalya!' he exclaimed. 'You are not alone in your troubles. India itself is groaning in pain. But we will change the country; if not for ourselves, at least for the next generation. When a new culture comes to India, Kaushalya, then all work will be respected, including manual labour. You people will not be left, discarded, on the fringes. You will be taken care of! O Kaushalya, I promise you!'

He spoke in such a kidding yet earnest manner, that I think she could not help but smile in spite of herself. '*When* the country changes… that will take a long time,' she said. 'I am suffering today.'

'Ah! Don't worry.' He tossed his head. 'I will lend you money whenever you need it. You know that.'

For a moment, I saw an almost abject devotion passing over the maid's face. She clasped her hands and lowered her head. 'Thank you, bhaiyya.'

Sasha began to speak quickly, as though stamping something out. 'Are you going to form a party?' he asked. 'I heard it on the news.'

'Don't believe what they say on TV,' smiled Ahishor. 'We aren't forming a party. No, our ambitions are much greater than that. I must tell you—this very evening, there are simultaneous protest marches happening in four cities. We have brought this scam to light, we have the government on its knees, and now there will be no let up until we break through and heads roll. Why don't you be a part of the Mumbai march? Dhruv and I will be going to the venue straight after lunch. You are welcome to come with us.'

There was a moment's strained pause.

'Why did you choose Sadhguru in particular,' asked Sasha again, 'for the sting?'

'Ha! Are you interrogating me?'

'I would like to know.'

'Because we had done our homework on him. We knew his dubious links with the Cabinet.'

'I'm sure he's not the only god-man with dubious links.'

'Ha! Of course he isn't.'

Sasha raised his eyebrows. Ahishor had turned away from him, but now looked back, irritated, as though someone had tapped his shoulder.

'Try to get it! I care about the liberal community. This particular god-man has been making converts even among educated people—supposed liberals. He's a suave businessman—one of those who harps on about philosophy and is careful never to talk about religion, as though a culture of hierarchy by any other name is any better. So it was doubly important to strike him.'

'Are you sure you weren't trying to hurt Maithili? You know she has gone to this man.'

'Maithili? Don't be ridiculous, man! Her father wanted to get her back. I didn't care a hoot about Maithili's involvement or lack of involvement.'

'But now you have struck her father too.'

'He struck—as you put it—himself, the day he tried to strangle his wife. I cannot have hypocrites in my movement. Call it an idiosyncrasy. But one rotten apple—you know...'

'Who made the complaint against Mr Krishna? It wasn't his wife, as far as I know.'

By now, everyone had finished eating. Our plates were set aside. We should have been in a leisurely post-lunch period of digestion. For her part, Kaushalya was casting glances towards the TV, even though it was on mute. But I was listening, against my will. I could hear sounds from all about—a child crying, roosters cackling and the ceiling fan stirring the afternoon heat. They were peaceful sounds. But the conversation overrode them.

'Since you are so curious,' Ahishor smiled, closing his eyes, 'the police complaint was filed by Bharat, on my instructions. I issued those instructions the moment I heard of the incident from Dipankar Joshi, whom you may or may not know. He is a civil servant and a signatory of the New Culture Manifesto. After committing the crime, Mr Krishna had come to Mr Joshi for advice, you see; hoping to be bailed out of trouble. Now, that isn't how we do things... As for Tara, bless her, she must still be in shock. You are right, she filed no complaint. It is very difficult for the immediate victim to file a complaint in such cases—for all sorts of reasons. But we are all victims of violent, entitled men. Our whole society is. Don't you think so?'

Sasha frowned, and seemed to fasten his gaze again on Ahishor. 'I have no special sympathy for her father. But consider your own motives. You are now fighting Maithili's father as well as her guru,' he said. 'Perhaps you are taking revenge... for how she treated you.'

'I have misjudged you badly, again and again.' An unpleasant smile had forced its way onto Ahishor's lips. He was still sitting as before, cross-legged, up on the cot, leaning against the wall of the shack, but I had the frightening sense that he might lunge forward any instant.

'When I met you on the train last year, I thought you were a decent guy. Naive—but good at heart. Then I began to have some doubts about you. But I told myself I was being too suspicious. But now I see I was right to doubt you the first time. You are a low life, Sasha. Your mind is cramped. Your thoughts are in the gutter. How the—*fuck* (his eyes were bulging now)—can you even imagine—that everything I am doing—my Manifesto, my movement, my physical and emotional sacrifices—I have quit my *damn profession*—for the sake of this epiphany—this wonderful, crucial epiphany—put into *action*—which people all over are recognizing—how can you even imagine that I am doing it all, to get back at an ex-girlfriend!'

'I know you are not,' replied Sasha soberly, and surprisingly quickly. 'I said that *seems* to be one of your motives. I am sure it's the least of your motives. But I want you to understand that if this weak link exists in the chain, then the whole chain is weak. If this petty motive finds a place in your grand scheme, then the whole scheme is guilty. As you said just now—one rotten apple...'

Kaushalya, I was surprised to note, was enjoying the spectacle—smiling, as the two of them talked, with proprietorial pride. Now she looked at me and chuckled.

'*Bhaiyya jhagda kar rahe hain... Bhaiyya sabse jhagda karta hai!*[59]'

'*Kaunsa bhaiyya?*[60]' asked Ahishor at once.

After a moment, she replied. '*Donon bhaiyya!*[61]'

'Haha, she's a diplomat!' he laughed. But the moment passed quickly and he swept a hard look back towards his nagging interlocutor.

'Judge us by our actions, please. Or if you like your cynical theories, keep them. But what people need is hope. That's what we've given them. That's what the country was yearning for! Why did the right wing come to power in the first place? Because people were desperate for an idea. To give them an identity! A sense of their worth! The liberals had nothing to offer; only their own hypocrisy. So they attached themselves to the nearest idea at hand, and that was really an old, bad idea. But we only have to redirect those energies that have now been unleashed—those hopes and cravings—towards our idea—a true liberalism—and India will change! And this is happening! You have no conception what a wave we are riding. People believe in us, because they see our sincerity. They are not small-minded and suspicious.'

Sasha bowed his head, drawing his feet back under the stool

---

[59]Sir is fighting... Sir fights with everyone!
[60]Which Sir?
[61]Both Sirs!

on which he sat. I thought perhaps he was chastened, but I had misread the look on his face.

'I know you are sincere,' he spoke at last, in a heavy voice. 'As sincere as humanly possible. I know you are not small-minded. You stand above the politics of our times. You have sighted many truths. You are doing a great and courageous thing, which has not been done before. But you are doing it without God, and in your own impatience. And that is why I am afraid for you, Ahishor. That's why I pray for you.'

In the silence that followed, he continued apace.

'Yes, India is a thing barely breathing. It must die and be reborn. It needs an idea, but neither an old one dressed up, nor a new one. God is the one we need. God is the one that India is crying out for. Not Hindutva, not liberalism. Don't you see how similar you are to the people you are attacking? You have rightly called out Sadhguru for his bad philosophy. But any philosophy is bad, when it tries to establish what is good—because no one is good but God. Both of you are preaching a mere philosophy, a mere culture of living—and then mistaking it for a standard of goodness. They might say all good people should live in bondage with their extended families, and you say all good people should live in freedom, for and by themselves. They may say good women ought to stay at home, and you say they ought to go where they please. But you are both judging by externals, by the things that people say and do and wear; not the things that are in their hearts. Both of you are godless and so both of you are doomed to futility and hypocrisy.'

I saw Ahishor, baring his teeth in a near-growl, but Sasha went on with greater passion:

'Why do the liberals always disappoint each other with some or the other lack of liberalism? Why do the right-wing xenophobes secretly send their children to study abroad? Why does this mean motive of taking vengeance on Maithili exist even in you—*you*, who sincerely aim for grandeur? It is because truthfulness only comes from God. Without God, you are bound to betray yourself. If someone says "I will walk from here to there in a straight line", he cannot even do that without God, though he may not know it. But if he wishes to do a grand thing, then he must ask for God's help all the more.'

'God!' spat Ahishor. 'You fanatic! God is on everyone's lips! India ought to have been a utopia if God was not really a curse! The *world* ought to have been! But all over the world, God is behind terrorism, violence, the murder of innocents. It's amazing that even today, in the times we live in, you can say such a thing!'

'I say it all the more today,' said Sasha. 'Liberalism and secularism will not halt the tide of terror, because they don't have the strength. Has it never occurred to you, when you hear a terrorist calling on the name of God, and then you hear the world's feeble condemnation calling on nothing at all, that we have surrendered to them the better language? Because we have surrendered to them our only saviour! Oh, you can make your liberalism as radical as you like, but you will not beat the terrorists; you will only become one yourself.'

'And I am saying,' he continued, glancing towards Kaushalya, 'that it matters a great deal what God one believes in. This is not an arbitrary matter; there is reality here—*the* reality! Precisely because there are all kinds of ways to be faithless, so it is vital to change one's faith—by growing in faith. Or we just fall to worshipping ourselves—and then start wars with one another.'

Suddenly I spoke up, for I could take it no longer. 'Just shut up! ... No, man!' I cried. 'Let people enjoy their lunch in peace!'

I felt a hand on my shoulder. Turning, I saw Ahishor, with his face screwed up in distress, shaking his head.

'I apologize, Kaushalya,' he proceeded to say. 'We are bad guests. I must tell you, I like your house a lot. It feels spacious, even though it's just a shack. It feels like a shelter. Look, it's so hot outside. Just look at the sun, it hurts my eyes! But here it feels like home. The only problem is, you have to be very careful whom you invite into your home. One small-minded person can make an entire palace feel like a prison. And you only have a shack to begin with.'

He was recovering his humour, his eyes gleaming and his lips curling with self-satisfaction.

'Since you force me to say it,' he turned and stared at Sasha, 'I will tell you. You have a diseased mind. It's like something haunted. You remind me of a ghost! Sickly and obsessive. That's what you really remind me of. Now I can see why you were so hooked on Maithili, because she was the same. She used to see her demons, and you see your God. And neither of you see real people or the things they need to live this life, and be happy in this life. You are so unhappy, Sasha, it almost hurts me to look at you. You are—'

'Desolate,' said Sasha. 'Without roots. Without a home. Yes, I am. And so are you and Maithili and all of us, a whole generation—and our parents before us—who cannot find their place under the sun. Kaushalya has come from another country and taken refuge here, so she knows her condition, but we are like refugees in our own land. So we rage and we despair and we rush off in this or that direction. But all the ways lead nowhere. We are jostled from every side. We find no rest anywhere. Yet we are really blessed, if only we realize it. Others may be blinded to their need for God, but He exists especially for the homeless. Our poverty makes us fortunate, Ahishor. Because for us, it is certain—we will find no home until we find it with God.'

Something in his words was arresting even if absurd; they were not thoughts I had been confronted with before. When Sasha had finished, I turned to Ahishor, with my eyebrows raised.

Ahishor, his head cocked, was scratching his chin.

'I see your problem, Sasha,' he said, thoughtfully. 'You are simply unable to believe that everyone is not like you... You are the one who fell for Maithili so badly. You stalked—*yes*—you stalked her obsessively. You probably still do. So you think I must be the same. You can't even comprehend that a man can rise above such things. Because I had her, you understand? *I had her.* I'm not like you. And I moved on from her.'

Suddenly, as though embarrassed of it, he abandoned his measured tone.

'You disgust me!' he exclaimed. 'Stalking even a child!'

Sasha sat erect. 'What?'

'You know "what"! We know all about what you did with Elena.'

'What I did with Elena?'

'What you were trying, anyway. What you wanted to do. What you would have done, if we hadn't—'

'*Be quiet,*' breathed Sasha, in a terrible voice that I had never heard from him before. He was leaning forward, his eyes flashing, his body trembling. He swallowed, trying to master himself. In the meantime, we were indeed struck silent.

'You have much to answer for,' he said, 'but I cannot forgive you this. You have used Elena and thrown her to the wolves. It's all very well for you to cause chaos, because you want to—but how dare you drag in somebody who is completely innocent! Do you even know where she is right now? Have you thought about how she is coping with the abuse online? It may be easy for you, but not for her! You simply turned her head—you misled her.'

Ahishor got to his feet. I saw that he was grimacing; his mouth was twisted in pain, as though he had been slapped.

'Thank you, Kaushalya,' he said, not looking at anyone, but fixedly out of the door. 'I am sorry we can't stay longer.'

'I did not harass Elena,' Sasha went on with the kind of ferocious clarity that is near to a state of collapse, 'but my father did. My father molested her many times. He is Satish Dhawan, of Ozymandias, whose money is funding your work.'

Ahishor had his back to me, so I could not see his reaction to these words. There was only the briefest pause, before he said, in a seemingly normal voice.

'Come on, Dhruv, let's go.'

I made a distracted nod at our hostess, who was looking on in bemusement. As I stepped out of the shack, the last thing I saw was Sasha, his face suddenly stricken like a child's, staring at the shelf in front of him and the row of crosses upon them.

The Rumour

We did not go to the protest march that evening. Ahishor said nothing to me on the drive back, but after he had dropped me home, he turned and booked a flight to Delhi. As for me, I lay down on my bed, because I felt a fever coming on. So it was Sasha alone, who travelled to South Bombay.

Afterwards, he couldn't say clearly what led him that way. As one who hears a cry for help and goes towards it, he went to Malabar Hills, for he seemed, in his head, to hear the plea of all the Krishna family, and of Maithili herself—Maithili, who saw demons, and who spoke of them with utter frankness. He felt chastened, amazed at his own laxity, for until he had heard Ahishor scoff at it, he had almost forgotten what a curse she laboured under, and how significant it really was. He remembered the look on her face the last time she had laid eyes on him. But in that astonishing hatred, he now saw a desirable change. She was no longer lukewarm with indifference, but cold with rage, and it was no longer as a lovelorn boy that he was going towards her, but as one who had grown in a mystery himself, more profound than her occult talents—the mystery of faith. Whatever afflicted Maithili was coming to the surface, and when he had brought it forth, by the grace of God, he could put it down.

Even so, he did not know what he would say or do when he arrived at the house—but he was gripped with the premonition that there was not a moment to lose.

The watchman was not at his post and so he slipped by unnoticed to the elevator, and thence to the front door, where his ringing went unanswered for a long time. He was aware of an unnerving silence. When he put his ear to the door, there was only the echo of the doorbell dying unheeded. But he rang again, until finally, there came the sound of movement and, with much unlocking and unlatching, the door was pulled open.

A young man, about his own age, stood facing him.

'Yes?'

'My name is Sasha. I'm a friend of Maithili's.'

'Maithili isn't here.'

'Oh, yes… She's at the Ashram.'

The young man—it was Vishnu, Maithili's brother—began to frown.

'If you know she isn't here, then…'

'I had hoped she would come back,' said Sasha simply, and as he spoke, he knew what he said was true.

'Well, she hasn't.' Vishnu hesitated. 'Anyway, come in. Yes yes, come in!' He seemed to make up his mind all at once.

He was big and fleshy and, at that moment, seemed touchingly awkward in his appearance and movements. He had grown a stubble, there was drowsiness in his eyes and his hair was uncombed, for he had fallen asleep at twilight and only just woken up. Sasha watched him walk unsteadily to the living room and pause on the carpet, unsure of where to sit.

'So, how do you know my sister?' He was still pondering, and did not wait for an answer. 'Sorry, I'm jet-lagged. I only reached last night from America.'

'You're getting married soon,' nodded Sasha.

'That's right…Well, that's the plan! Let's see if Maithili shows up for that one!' Vishnu had finally plonked himself onto his grandfather's old armchair. There he stretched out, revealing his paunch. He was smiling in a bitter way, his sleepy eyes narrowing, which also brought out, for the first time, the resemblance between the siblings.

'I'm sure she will,' said Sasha firmly. 'You know, it isn't all her fault. The troubles she has had… But I think she is going to overcome them.'

Vishnu frowned and wondered at the earnest figure now seated opposite him, talking with strange presumption. But he was in no mood to be suspicious nor fastidious about manners, because for one, he was too tired to be, and secondly, he was grateful for the company.

As for Sasha, he would not have gone away for anything. Whether the kinship he felt towards the boy was on Maithili's account or Vishnu's own, he did not know. But it came charged with a sense of responsibility. There was something about the chubby young man, seemingly the lone person in the apartment, which acted on him like the sight of an infant in the woods. Yet his anxiety was all the greater, because Vishnu's face was not stamped with innocence, but a weariness and a knowingness.

'Sorry, I haven't offered you anything. It's been a rough day. My parents are actually home, but—anyway, never mind. Things are a bit strange at the moment.'

He did not even need to say so. Tragedy, like a thick pall of dust, hung in the air. Sasha saw the doors shut all around him, as they were everywhere in the house. In the closeted silence from somewhere within, the hum of an air-conditioner was just discernible. Tara was in her bedroom, and Suraj—an undertrial on bail—was in his upstairs study. They were subsisting thus, in shock and separation.

'But that's another story. I have to leave soon,' Vishnu sighed.

'Where to?' demanded the visitor, at which Vishnu uttered a laugh. But then, without demur, he simply answered, 'There's a protest march on Marine Drive.'

'I know about that. You're joining the protest?'

'Why else would I go there?'

'But you've just come back to India.'

'So?' Vishnu arched an eyebrow. 'That doesn't mean I don't know what's going on. Anyway, Sukanya—my fiancée—she really wants me to go. Her cousin is apparently one of the organizers— or something like that.'

He was referring, of course, to Anamika, who at that moment (I imagine) was with Satish Dhawan and the others, drinking triumphantly at Ozymandias.

'And I can do this much for Sukanya.' The bitter smile was on Vishnu's lips again. 'Considering everything else she's going to have to deal with. Anyway, I don't know why I'm telling you this; it's not your concern. I guess you'll be leaving now. I'll walk you downstairs.'

'I'll come with you,' said Sasha.

'Really? You don't have to, if you're not interested… Well, suit yourself.'

The evening was hot with that heightened, moist heat that yet gave hope for the monsoon. On the road, Sasha and Vishnu walked, perspiring heavily. There was no taxi in sight. Sasha remembered walking the same streets with Maithili (it seemed a lifetime ago) and how she had seemed to glide with otherworldly buoyancy. Her brother walked warily, as though stepping through muck. But impatience flickered in his eyes, as it often did in his sister's.

When at last they found a taxi, the driver said he would drop them a kilometre from the NCPA—the theatre building where the march was to begin.

'No cars can go,' he explained. 'There is a protest happening.'

'That's what we're going for,' smiled Vishnu.

They alighted in a lane that was already streaming with people. There were tall buildings on both sides and people who had come out to watch the march from the balconies. From the distance, where the dark sea merged with the horizon, they could hear the (still indistinct) chorus of sloganeering voices. After staring straight ahead of him with a blank expression, Vishnu suddenly grimaced, nodded several times, and began to press forth. Sasha hurried alongside.

They said nothing to each other, but both were darting glances about them as they went. The young and the middle-aged alike were on the street. Indeed, there seemed to be whole families that had come out together. But the young predominated. They were a smart and handsome set, in witty T-shirts and yoga pants and pretty dresses too—the kind of crowd that, on any weekend, might be found in a Bandra nightclub. As the lane connected with the boulevard of Marine Drive, cheers and laughter broke out from the dense knot of marchers, who were already waiting to proceed. Sasha spotted a vaguely familiar figure, enormously fat, with bulging eyes and a devilish grin, who seemed to be leading the cheers. Soon after, he placed the boy as one of the members of a group of young, urbane comedians, great votaries of free speech and mockers of the religious right, and Internet sensations too.

*   *   *

This was the unprecedented thing Ahishor had achieved. He had mobilized all those of my generation who poured their grievances onto Facebook and Twitter, and brought them to the street—as never before. Now they were physically marching together, connected to each other, no longer notionally, but limb to limb, body to body, their voices in unison, and moreover, doing so for a cause that was especially their own. For, some in that crowd had marched (in a desultory way) for farmers, slum workers, bar dancers and rape survivors, and had lent their support to particular plights of other communities. But how many had marched, until now, under the banner of pure liberalism, which was dearest of all to their own selves?

There was another striking feature of the protestors. Most of them were women. This was evident from the photographs I saw later (pictures that, even afterwards, filled me with mixed emotions and made me almost wish I had been there). I heard, also, that the timbre of the chorus had been feminine. It was women who had walked in the lead; women who had sung and shouted with the greatest abandon. Indeed, as the older generation had been led by their offspring, so the men seemed to have caught fire from the women in their lives, as they all came down the street with placards raised aloft.

*   *   *

At first, as Sasha watched, Vishnu only fell into stride with the others. He sported the same queer grimace on his face. There was sleepiness in his eyes even in the midst of the rousing scene, and his shirt was coming untucked to add to his dishevelment. Gradually, he began to murmur, and then to raise his voice, joining the chorus of slogans, most of which (another feature of the protest) were in unabashed English.

'Don't want god-men, don't want gold; we want the freedom of the bold.'

'Right wing, won't win!'

'Religion no more; we shall be pure.'

'The only solution, is revolution!'

And the exclamation most beloved of all, which was simply: 'Liberty! Liberty!'

The lights of Marine Drive were burning now, completing the beauty of the boulevard. Onward rolled the crowd of protestors, spreading over both lanes of the adjoining road. Somebody raised a new cry: 'Come together, take the cure! Ahishor, Ahishor!'

This sentiment was received with a certain ambivalence, for it was generally felt gauche to be glorifying or paying allegiance to any particular individual. That was considered a common failing of other movements. We, on the other hand, were committed to the ideal, rather than to any one man. It was true, of course, that the whole movement and each of its slogans owed their existence to something Ahishor had written down in the now-legendary Manifesto. Nonetheless, the protestors had their pride, and the cry in his name soon petered out. But then suddenly, it surged up again.

Sasha and Vishnu were deep in the crowd, surrounded by marchers on every side. They saw a young woman, who had been smiling a moment before, but was now hatefully staring at the intersection up ahead, where a small knot of police officers was watching quietly.

'Ahishor, Ahishor!' she screamed, enraged.

'What happened?' Vishnu asked, but she had slipped away from sight, as he felt himself being shoved from the back. Everyone seemed to be trying to move faster, but the space to move was shrinking as the crowd swelled and heaved forward in unison. Then he found Sasha, pressed to his side and brandishing a phone.

'It's this!' cried Sasha, though he was barely audible in the rising din. Vishnu snatched the instrument and peered at it.

On the screen was the snapshot of a woman, crouched on the dusty ground, her shirt torn, her shoulder and most of her back bare, and her hands covering her bosom. She was looking with frightened eyes at something that was not visible in the frame. Her face was shockingly recognizable. The caption said: 'Nalini Frances attacked by goons one hour ago.'

This was the news that was spreading through the crowd, angering every person it reached. The crowd itself was enlarging, as more and more people arrived in solidarity and the ones who now joined were streaming with fury, energizing the ones who were present. The slogans for freedom were becoming less orchestrated and soon they fell away altogether. Ahishor's name was chanted continually, in a heady, savage frenzy. This chant, however, was also like a pause; a shifting of gears; because when it ended, the curses began.

Now individually, people were chattering and yelling, for each one's blood was boiling. There rose up a discordant wall of noise. 'Thugs!' and 'Creeps!' were the gentler insults. But collectively, the word that stuck was: 'Goons!' This was the new roar of the crowd, as it kept coming, and the police—who had been standing by, already on edge—suddenly began to mobilize themselves.

The march was to go on till the Flora Fountain, where everyone was to sit down and speeches were to be made. All the relevant permissions had been taken for this programme. Now, however, some official (he was not named even afterwards) had decided on the spur of the moment that the crowd was too large and unruly to be allowed to proceed. A barricade was duly set up at the mouth of Veer Nariman Road, blocking the way past Churchgate.

Meanwhile, Sasha sensed the danger of a stampede. The smell of sweat and perfume was strong in his nostrils. Bodies were on every side and it was hard to tell where the mass of people thinned. He caught hold of Vishnu's arm, so as to not lose him, and as they moved, willy-nilly, forward, he tried to steer them sideways.

Vishnu himself seemed not to notice being held. He was pumping his fist at intervals and shouting feebly when everyone shouted, but his face was masked with weariness—and something else: a pale, dreamy aura that disturbed Sasha. In a burst of clarity, he became aware of how the young man did not react when jostled, how his breathing was slow and heavy, and how his eyes were not focusing on anything. Sasha was manoeuvring him steadily towards the fringes. The sea was just visible beyond the crowd, and the spray of water, over the parapets of Marine Drive. Then, even as he grew hopeful of escape, he heard a scream from the front of the crowd and saw smoke rising overheard.

*   *   *

When the crowd had pushed at the barricades, wild-eyed and continuing to repeat the lone word 'Goons!,' the policemen had lost their heads. Fearing (they said later) a terrible riot, tear-gas, water cannons and lathis were brought out in no time, and within minutes, the most brutal of crackdowns was in full swing. It was not stemming even though the protesters were fleeing; indeed, it was growing wilder in the face of their unexpected surrender.

On the news that night, I saw the Chief of Police at a loss to justify his force's behaviour. He went on about the 'dangerous look' of the crowd, the 'angry mood', and the 'threat perception' by the police, but it was obvious that he could not explain why unarmed protesters (howsoever angry, and many of them women), had been so violently dealt with. He was much-mocked for his comments, but he might have been mocked even more had he found the words to say what he really felt—which was that something in the sight of those young, smooth faces, contorted in rage, screaming words that were quite alien to the ears of his men, had simply shaken them. Perhaps it was impossible to understand, but the police had been in the grip of an instinct—a sixth sense—which had made them look upon that crowd of young liberals as the most terrifying danger.

Flipping through the channels the same night, I saw a clip being telecast, which someone had shot on a mobile phone. It showed two young men, both drenched from head to toe. One of them was wearing a Stanford University jacket and waving his fist at a lathi-toting cop, before suddenly buckling at the knees and collapsing on the ground. The one beside him (whom I recognized, despite him being completely drenched) immediately caught hold of him and they both fell together. At this point—in what seemed like madness—the policeman began to lash out. A reporter was using the clip to illustrate the cop's excesses, but I could not take my eyes off Sasha. He lay there, shielding the other's body with his own, writhing from blow after blow.

Like in the strange disconnections of a dream, where familiar faces come and go, the pictures turned to more breaking news.

I saw Karim Azad weeping on camera, the famous face marred and twisted, while men in uniform held his arms and herded him into a van that had grills over the windows. His son, Ritesh—the anchor informed us—had also been arrested the same day, on separate charges.

The Crashing

All these events took place that same night, in the third week of May. It was only the next morning, however, that the media picked up on the story that had swept through the crowd and so infuriated it—namely, the assault and molestation of Nalini Frances at the hands of right-wing goons. And now, the general understanding of what had happened on Marine Drive began to change completely.

For the story had been a hoax. Nalini was unharmed. She was in faraway Odisha, getting ready for her performances and was as shocked as anyone to learn what was being said about her. It was soon discovered that the picture that had been shared on WhatsApp was the result of somebody's morphing together two photographs that had been in the public domain: one, from a famous theatrical portrayal of Sita, by Nalini; and the other from a French soft porn film.

This was enough to swing the mood of the discussions. The Chief of Police was back on the channels, insisting that the crowd had indeed been frenzied, their passions whipped up by this pernicious rumour, that there was no telling what they would have done, and that the culprits for the debacle were not his men, but whichever 'miscreants' had spread the falsehood. He further cautioned all members of the public not to be deceived by such messages in the future and, in no circumstance, to share them.

As I watched this drama unfold, lying on the mattress in my bare living room, I remember laughing to myself. Everyone on screen was so agitated! But it seemed to me quite beside the point. So, the picture was a fake; what difference did that make in the larger scheme? If not today, Nalini might have been attacked tomorrow. When I had received the photo the previous evening (from Bharat's phone), I had shared it at once with practically everyone on my list, and I did not feel guilty even then. In fact, what I felt most of all was annoyance—that a triviality was being harped on to obscure the bigger picture.

But this matter of the hoax refused to die down. By evening, the discourse was peaking with excitement. Officials from the Cyber Cell of the Mumbai Police had arrived on the scene. They would be focussing on those who had spread the rumour in bulk, in order to zero in on the original culprit. A breakthrough was expected shortly. When I heard this, I felt a knot in my chest. The police were not going to let it go, I realized, because they were trying to cover up their own mistakes. So I got up from my bed, retrieved my phone, deleted the entire message history, and then slipping on my sandals, simply left, with no aim in mind.

On the road, in the pageant of lights and people, I began to feel better. But then suddenly I felt resentful. As usual, in a time of crisis, there was no word from anyone—neither Ahishor, nor Mihir, nor Bharat! I walked on, remembering the first time I had visited this part of Mumbai in the company of college friends. How quickly I had lost touch with them. I thought of

Jatin and wanted to call him, but I remembered how impossible he was. Then I found myself standing at the busy intersection between Four Bungalows and Seven Bungalows, staring at a homeless man, who was playing with a dog. I felt I was losing my bearings completely. I was drowning in a wave of sheer sadness.

In this state, I made my way down J.P. Road. As I passed Sasha's apartment building, I remembered him and thought of calling on him. But who knew what condition he was in! I hoped he was alive and I moved on.

Somewhere during the course of my walk, my phone started ringing. I was relieved to see that it was just my mother calling. However, the next moment I was disappointed that it was not somebody else. I let the phone holler silently and quickened my stride. Though I was barely conscious of it, I already had a destination in mind. Yari Road's eternal jamboree passed me by; the lanes narrowed after Mandir-Masjid, and grew more squalid, even as the residences improved. Walking with sureness now, I reached the compound of Ahishor's rented flat, a little out of breath.

The flat was on the ground floor. I saw from a distance that the door was open, presumably for the sake of letting the breeze in. As I approached, I thought to myself how strange it was that open doors had the contrary effect—that of making a visitor feel like an intruder.

Inside, the place was bathed in orange lamp-light. The furniture looked hunched and ghoulish. In the middle of the living room, on the bare floor, I saw Sushant lying flat on his back. He was smoking a joint and staring at the ceiling. The sickly smell of weed was everywhere. I called him and he raised the hand that held the joint, trailing smoke.

'Bhai.'

'Why are you on the floor?' I glanced at the empty mattress alongside.

There was no answer, but a wheezing sound. I realized he was chuckling.

'Don't worry, bhai, you can sit on the chair… I like it here.'

I remained standing, however.

'Where is Ahishor?' I asked, for I did not know at the time that he had flown to Delhi the previous day.

'No idea,' said Sushant. '*Kal se nahi dekha*[62]… Where were you yesterday?'

'Oh, I was sick, man. I didn't go. How was the protest? I mean, I saw what happened on TV. That's why I came to check on you,' I lied, and Sushant began to chuckle again, his thin shoulders bobbing up and down.

'*Main bhi nahi gaya, bhenchod…*'[63]

A nasty smile lingered on his lips. He turned his head towards the furniture. Then realizing that I wasn't there, he looked around and saw me standing. He grinned and jerked his head off the ground.

'But I contributed, haan! You saw, na?'

A prickling sensation was coming over me. 'What? The message about Nalini?'

'Ya, ya. I made that, bhai. Photoshopped! It was a fake!'

'I know!' I was staring in disbelief at his exultant face. 'Everyone knows now. It's all over the news!'

He scrambled to a sitting position, smiling all the while.

---

[62]Haven't seen him since yesterday
[63]I also didn't go, damn it…

'*Idea mera nahi tha.*[64] It was Bharat's idea, originally. See, anger is very important, bhai. The kind of people we have convinced, they are posh people; it takes a lot to get them off their asses and onto the streets. That's why it was very important to make them angry. If, after everything, this protest had flopped, it would have been a disaster. The whole movement would have really suffered. So we came up with this plan. But I made the photoshop! *Kaisa laga?*[65] It was good, na? It was realistic! She was looking hot, na?'

His eyes twinkled lasciviously.

'I thought it was real,' I said. 'You never told me.'

'Sorry, yaar, Dhruv. I mean, *tu humaare saath hain*[66]. *Aisa nahin hai ki*[67] you wouldn't have shared it if you had known.'

I said nothing, for I was unable to demur. But I could not understand his nonchalance.

'Dude, we're in big trouble now. The police are looking for the person who made this.'

'The police have better things to do,' Sushant retorted. '*Vaise bhi*[68] they can't trace a viral message. It's not possible.'

'I don't know, man, but they are trying. Have you seen the news?'

'Dhruv, *tu itna darta kyon hai*?[69]'

He was getting angry. I was almost relieved to see this, though I was startled as well; so sudden was his ferocity.

'Even when everyone is with us, you're still scared! When

---

[64]The idea wasn't mine.

[65]Did you like it?

[66]You are with us

[67]It's not like

[68]Anyway

[69]why are you so scared?

will you not be scared?'

'I'm not scared—'

'You are!' He was glaring, with bulging eyes. 'You are always scared. What we are doing is not for scared people! If you have the balls—if you can be the Übermensch—the Overman—if you have that belief in yourself, then you can do these things. No power in the Universe is stronger than you! And we are seeing that! This is just the beginning. Bharat told me ki[70] don't use the photo of Nalini, because Ahishor may not like it, but I told him this is not about Ahishor. I am my own person and nobody's will is greater than mine. I do what I *will* to do. The only reason I am part of all this—here is the point!—hear me carefully!—is for the expression of my own will! But if you are scared, you betray your own will, and that very act leads to your failure. Are you getting it?'

Having spoken thus, he looked ecstatic, but I stepped back, for a fanaticism was in his eyes. He must have noticed, because the very next moment the irritation was pumping back into him. It occurred to me that my doubts threatened him like a disease; he thought they might infect him. His mouth was trembling in petulance. I had the impression of a tremendous, childish anger. I had seen tantrums from Sushant before and they had made me roll my eyes. But now I was half afraid.

'Anyway, just wanted to check on you,' I said, with my feet turning to the exit.

He continued to stare, sitting up on the floor in a white undershirt, the joint falling to ash by his side. I had almost left and was about to close the door behind me, when he shrieked: 'Leave it open!'

---

[70]In this context, 'ki' means 'that'

'Sorry!' I cried out, pushing the door open again. The night breeze blew past me. I swivelled once more, but I had not yet left the scene when I received another jolt from within.

'Motherfucker!' His voice was as though writhing. 'You pitiful motherfucker!'

* * *

No doubt Sushant's door was open all night and into the dawn, when two policemen entered and put him under arrest. He did not go quietly, which was worse for him, because he had his limbs broken after he struck one of them on the nose.

In the Epochal office at 10 a.m., we had not yet heard the news. The atmosphere was weary and hung-over. I was alone with Bharat at the central table. Arvind was in the pantry, fetching tea. I understood that Malik was not expected because he had been at the protest and needed the day off after his exertions.

'Was he hurt?' I inquired.

Bharat shook his head briefly. 'Why didn't you go?'

'I was sick,' I repeated, and thought of asking why Bharat too (as it seemed) had stayed away from the march. But he was not really paying attention. There were dark circles under his eyes and his sallow face was turned to the window, where, under the sweltering summer sun, the city crawled.

'Ahishor has been unreachable since yesterday,' he said. 'Where is he?'

'I don't know.'

I explained to him how I had last spoken to Ahishor at Kaushalya's lunch. He opened his mouth to say something, but fell quiet. Then he said: 'Something bad is going to happen.'

He clasped his head and I stared at his thin, sharp profile, tense with thought. I was growing more discomfited by the minute. His voice had sounded oddly strangled.

I gathered the strength to speak. 'Spreading the rumour about Nalini Frances was a big mistake. Everyone's only talking about that. Why did you guys do it?'

Bharat looked up and fixed me with a baleful stare.

'That's not what I'm referring to.' His voice had dropped. 'Arré Dhruv, I am organizing everything. All the content we have uploaded... The sting operation... The march... You think it's easy to control people like Sushant? ... I am talking about Mihir,' he continued. 'The Delhi people were just waiting for something like this to happen. I got his email yesterday itself. Demanding answers. No congrats on organizing the rally; no concern for us after the police atrocities... I need to talk to Ahishor. But he is not taking my call.'

Suddenly he looked so morose that I felt a pang of sympathy. But I was too anxious myself to say anything supportive. I looked on, with a hollowness gnawing at the pit of my stomach. I saw Bharat sigh and turn his head away from the window. His eyes were glazing over with a familiar fatalism. He was even beginning to smirk. Suddenly, however, he was staring open-mouthed, in utter terror, trying to rise from his chair.

I spun around, exclaiming. I could hardly believe my eyes. A huge figure in a black, flapping shirt was charging down the corridor. A cricket bat was bobbing beside him.

'Jatin, wait!' I cried.

'Dhruv, get out of the way!' he roared. There was a sound that felt to me like an explosion, and our table lay shattered. Bharat's laptop had been utterly smashed, with bits of wood, plastic and metal scattered in every direction. Both Bharat and I were ducking for cover. Meanwhile, Jatin, I glimpsed, was scrabbling in his pocket for his phone. Like a marauding animal, preternaturally agile, he wheeled around the wreckage, almost casually swinging the bat to shatter the window next. Shards of glass fell ten floors. All the while, he kept speaking in a normal, if slightly breathless tone.

'I warned you,' I heard him say. 'But you are too fucking smug. You deserve this. Your whole generation deserves nothing but this. I will make an example of you... Where's Arvind?'

'Police! Hello, police!' Bharat was screaming into the phone as he stood up and ran towards the door. But Jatin was there to intercept him. I stared in horror; I had started to cry. He had thrown aside the bat and with his bare hands was squeezing Bharat's throat. I saw Bharat flailing wildly, kicking hard as he was lifted off the ground, though Jatin didn't flinch.

What happened next made me believe I was assuredly in a dream. It was impossible—because it was only seconds after Bharat's phone call. The front door opened and one after the other, three men in uniform entered the room. After a moment's stunned pause, all three immediately pounced upon Jatin. It took all their strength to break him loose from Bharat, who fell to the floor like a discarded toy.

They had come, of course, to arrest us, not to save us. But on that day, they did both.

*　　*　　*

As a great wave eventually breaks, so our work was crashing from revelation upon revelation. It was bad enough that a false rumour about Nalini had spread through our supporters, but that it should have been concocted by a founding-member of Epochal Pictures, who was also Ahishor Frances's own flatmate, and disseminated by every other member of Epochal, was devastating in the eyes of the media and the public opinion that they moulded. In the space of two days, we had gone from heroes and martyrs to cunning schemers, who could not be trusted—who, in fact, had all been arrested! The one person who could have salvaged the situation was Ahishor, on whom no personal stain had yet been found (for police had confirmed that he had not spread the rumour) but 'Ahishor could not be reached for comment,' echoed every reporter.

With the help of Alisha, Mihir's lawyer-friend, we were bailed out in twenty-four hours—all except Sushant, against whom the charges were the most grave. When I returned home, I was able to see for myself how our cause was dying. I could not understand how every voice that had praised us only two days ago, was denouncing us now—but I realized that they were also being driven by a strange sense of relief.

The fact was, Ahishor had made everything uncomfortably rigorous. Our intelligentsia was—sincerely—for a sincere liberalism, for the end of privilege and dynasty and for the exalting of proper behaviour over all else. Yet, the arrest of Karim and Ritesh Azad had really been a hard jolt to them. 'Was it not going a bit too far?' people were beginning to murmur—first to themselves, and then openly—as their fears and misgivings came to the surface. If Karim Azad was bad, then who was good? Surely a fine, modern liberal like him and a man so accomplished ought to be treasured rather than punished?

Many of those who were turning on us were also, of course, friends of the Azads. And all those networks of social connection and cultural capital, which Ahishor had hoped to break down into individual consciences, were reasserting themselves with their age-old resilience.

Considering that spectacle then, I had felt nothing but sadness. Looking back to it now, I feel the same.

*   *   *

In Delhi, Bharat's apprehensions were being realized with a similar, disorienting quickness. One evening, in the Greater Kailash home of the Joshis, Dipankar, Ira and Anamika all waited in the living room, as Mihir entered through the glass-and-wood sliding door and closed it carefully behind him. With a rucksack on his back, he looked not unlike a young boy coming home from school.

He greeted them with his usual big grin, but their smiles were brief and forced. Anamika did not smile at all.

'Come, sit,' said Dipankar, although Mihir had already taken a chair. 'You're nice and punctual today,' he continued in a blustering way, for he was settling his own nerves. 'What will you drink? Whisky? Rum?'

'Uncle, what's the matter with you?' laughed Mihir. 'Lemon squash, of course. You know I don't drink.'

'Even now?' muttered Dipankar.

After the servant had brought in the tray and everyone had a glass in their hands, Dipankar took a sip of his favourite single malt. Fixing Mihir with a portentous look, he tried to speak casually.

'Mihir. Is Ahishor staying with you?'

'No. Actually I haven't even met him. He's staying at Ozymandias. '

'Oh! You mean he's with Satish?'

'I suppose so.'

Dipankar and Ira exchanged glances. But it was Mihir who continued: 'I know, it's all a bit strange. I myself don't know what's going on. Is Satish still backing him after what's just happened? I really don't know. But I know I'm not. This has been the last straw for me. In fact, I wanted to tell you that today. I was going to land up for dinner even if you hadn't called me.'

Again, the Joshis took quick looks at each other—but they had both sat up alert.

'What do you mean?' asked Ira. 'Do go on.'

'I just think it's a bad idea for me—or for anyone—to continue to be a part of this movement. I'm really sad about saying that. But with the way things have been run from Mumbai, the kind of people Ahishor has allowed to be in charge, frankly a disaster like this was always on the cards. In a way, I'm surprised it didn't happen sooner.'

He looked steadily at Anamika to make his helplessness known. Her eyes, however, were shining, and her face had come alive. Across the room, on the sofa, Dipankar Joshi was smiling dazedly.

'Well! I see!'

'Well that's a relief,' broke in Ira. 'We were afraid we'd have to convince you.

'Oh!' Mihir, looking astonished, began laughing. 'Oh, no, no!'

'Yes, we underestimated you. You've a good head on your shoulders,' smiled Ira.

'What we wanted to say,' Dipankar Joshi wriggled his plump body happily, settling back into the cushions, 'is that this has been a very important, very significant endeavour. It's brought us all a good way forward—it's certainly done a lot for you, Mihir, I'll tell you more about that. But now it does look like it's going off the rails—and that's the time to exit.'

'He knows, Dipankar!' Ira scoffed merrily. 'Oh, but Dipankar must still recite the speech that he's prepared!'

A shared mood of relief (that there was to be no conflict) and pride (that they understood each other so well) had settled over the room—along with a becoming embarrassment on the part of the Joshis, that they had ever entertained a contrary fear. After a moment, Ira looked gravely at Mihir.

'Listen. Are you worried about what to tell Ahishor?'

'I can't even get through to him,' Mihir shrugged. 'But I've drafted a press statement; I'll send it to you. I thought you would like to sign it too? It's to explain to the general public that we condemn what the Epochal team has done. And that our own communication with Ahishor has broken down, and we regret that we can't associate with the movement any longer in the form that it's taking. And there are some other points in there too.'

'Excellent! Do send it to us both!'

'But it's true,' continued Mihir. 'I had already told Ahishor before that Epochal was being run badly. He didn't listen. He has too much a soft spot for his Versova boys. They all worship him, you know. Bharat Mishra has been a long-time sycophant.'

'That's right,' Ira nodded several times eagerly, 'But listen— don't feel bad about this. It's not your fault; he's brought it upon himself. The sad thing is, it's such a common failing. The adulation has gone to his head. He's become power-mad.'

'Every revolutionary becomes the worst enemy of his own revolution. History proves this,' said Dipankar, between thoughtful sips of his drink.

'For instance,' continued Ira, 'even apart from the dubiousness of the Versova people—whom I don't know much about, though their problems are quite obvious now—what was the need to hound poor Suraj? The man came to us for help. And now to get Karim arrested! It's all become simply tasteless. I don't see any method or strategy in any of it.'

'You've put your finger on it,' said Mihir. He darted a look at Anamika. 'Ahishor has no sense of strategy. He is all emotion and passion. That was necessary in the beginning, of course.'

Dipankar leaned forward, with a stubby finger jabbing the air in front of him.

'*You* need to pick up the baton, Mihir. The beginning has been made, we are all thankful for that. Now *you* need to take forward these principles of liberalism—with a proper sense of strategy. We must add that to your press statement, if you haven't mentioned it already. I'll tell you what—I'm going to speak to Satish about this. You two should work closely now. Satish has developed a high regard for you, Mihir. Through this whole business, many people have.'

Ira, who had been nodding along, suddenly appeared troubled. Turning to her husband, she said, in a low voice: 'But what is he doing with Ahishor? Apparently Ahishor is with him.'

'Not to worry!' Dipankar drained his glass and smacked his lips. 'Satish will do the right thing in this situation, I'm sure of that.'

'Satish drinks too much,' said Ira suddenly.

'Satish does nothing by halves,' Dipankar laughed. 'But he's nobody's fool.'

*　　*　　*

After dinner, as usual, Mihir went upstairs to be with Anamika. Their alone time was a tradition that dated back to their childhood. Indeed, as he entered her room, they were both remembering that time spent together, and the secret world they had always shared. Neither spoke of it, but it manifested in them in the form of a heightened alertness to one another; paradoxically, like that of one interesting stranger's towards another. But that was the virgin ground on which a new impulse was sprouting.

She was lying on the bed, flanked by pillows. A smile came to her lips as she watched him move, strangely deferentially, to sit near her feet. Then he turned to her with his big, bushy eyebrows raised. She pulled a serious face.

'Are you ok?'

'I think so.'

'I feel guilty,' she said, her eyes widening. Few people were privileged to see the stern-faced Anamika in this mould—of an ingénue.

'Why should you feel guilty?' Mihir laughed again.

'I'm the one who encouraged you to stick with him, na?'

He recalled, with a little surprise, that she was right.

'Yes, you did. But it was very good you did. And I'm the one who started this whole thing, remember?'

'Yes,' nodded Anamika.

'This had all been very good,' said Mihir, 'until it went bad... I think this is when we say: Ce'st la vie.'

She propped herself up eagerly against the headboard of the bed.

'I agree! You know, I realized something about myself. I like people, but I don't like politics. I don't like causes and marches and fighting. I just want people to be nice. But people seem to like all the *other* stuff; not being nice.'

'That's because very few people are simple and clear-headed. They're all twisted somewhere.'

'But *I* am, right? Clear-headed.'

'Yes, you are good.'

'You are good too.'

As they gazed at each other, their breathing strangely laboured, an inarticulate excitement was creeping over them both. They kept talking with rapidity and rapt attention, though neither thought much over what they said or heard.

'Maithili was such a meanie!' said Anamika suddenly. 'She didn't even get in touch when she was in Mumbai.'

'Just as well,' said Mihir, his voice low and full of a staccato rhythm. 'It might have caused another scandal if you two had gotten friendly while we were busy exposing her guru.'

'Aww, but I'm friendly with everyone. Unless they are total bitches. Ahishor and Maithili should really have stayed with each other. They were just like each other.'

'Well, they were both power-mad. But I think Ahishor had a little more sense.'

'Ha! You're just taking the man's side.'

'No, no.'

'Ahh no, you're right, you're right. At least he was doing something in the real world. And it has helped you, right? You got to meet Satish Uncle and impress him, and now you will work with him. So Ahishor was good for you.'

'We are talking about him like he's dead!' smiled Mihir, shifting forward on the bed.

'And it's all because I encouraged you at the right time,' Anamika said, pouting. She moved her leg to nuzzle his hip. 'But you still haven't thanked me.'

'I am thankful to you.'

'You haven't thanked me... Nobody thanks me.'

For a moment she felt a real stab of pain, perhaps because she was still thinking of Maithili. Then she let her regrets fall away like sheer silliness, and gazed hard at Mihir. Her eyes were bright with something unmistakable. Her foot continued to move over his hip, his lap—now quicker, and with intent. She leaned forward and stretched out her arm. He took hold of it. She pulled him close. They were both breathless with excitement. She bent her large head and kissed him on the mouth.

Mihir's eyes were closed, but he murmured, through parted lips, 'What about Alisha?'

'She's like the others... Do you care about Alisha or me?'

This time, without hesitation, he pressed his lips on hers and pushed her backwards, probing for her tongue. Their arms moved to enfold each other and they fell away onto the bed, their limbs entwined, gorging on forbidden ecstasies.

Reunions

Sasha lay in bed, drowned in a world of pain. Twilight was the most difficult time of the day for him. In the mornings, Kaushalya would come, aghast to see him thus laid up, but in between her lamentations, she would look after him. In the afternoons, he slept, for his fever was still consuming him, but he was cheered by the day burning brightly outside. During the night, he found himself best able to pray. But in the interim, when the sun began to set, his heart was pierced with woes.

The bruises he had suffered from the police were painful, but not crippling. He had fractured an arm, and one hard blow near his left ear had diminished his hearing, at least temporarily. He had fallen ill, however, in the aftermath of the water cannon attack, and medicines had not prevented the fever from soaring. Now he lay in bed, swaddled in blankets at the height of summer, and each day at twilight was bombarded by otherworldly sensations that enveloped him like a fog of horrors.

These visions—though he knew they were only that—seemed to bring him news of the others. Often he saw, as had really happened, Vishnu fainting in front of him and then convulsing on the road. They had been separated in the hospital, where he had heard someone saying that the young man had suffered an epileptic fit. He saw Malik running, wild-eyed and shaking, and heard Jatin's voice hollering curses in his ear. Ahishor came to him in the white robes of a monk, but with eyes open and fanatically staring. All through, he felt whispers and murmurs hovering about him, unintelligible and haunting.

One evening (he had scant notion of how many days had passed since his illness), his reveries were interrupted by a noise that, at first, he took to be a part of them. It was a soft, insistent knocking. But it persisted, even in the lull of his dreams. Suddenly, Sasha sat up with the realization that there was indeed someone at the door.

And now his heart began to pound with new anxiety and excitement. A most unexpected feeling had taken hold of him. He felt certain that it was Maithili, who had come to visit him! Maithili, whom he had just now seen in the disturbances of his mind, walking from the beach, deeper and deeper into the sea, had softened in actuality and come to him! She had seen and heard everything—her god-man's corruption, her parents' plight, her brother's misfortune, Sasha's efforts to save him—and she had not stayed away! He struggled to get up, calling out: 'One moment please!'

He made his way to the door. The knocking had stopped a few moments ago and he was afraid she had turned and left. He knew how she hated to be kept waiting. He had lost the use of his right hand and so he struggled with the latch, cursing his own clumsiness. When he finally managed to open the door, he peered hard at the landing, which, at twilight, was still unlit.

In the first instant, his heart sank slowly, because the shadowy figure outside was far too large to be her. Then the stranger stepped forward and the hair on Sasha's arms stood on end.

'My dear boy!' said Satish Dhawan. 'What has happened to you!'

The face, shockingly familiar, was marked with an expression of horror and concern. But he had seen that before too, and he remembered when and how. Waves of emotion buffeted Sasha. He stepped backwards.

'What are you doing here?' he managed to ask.

'I came to see you, of course! Can't a father come to see his son?'

'Don't be absurd.'

'Oh Sasha, you are wounding me! I do particularly want to have a talk with you! I saw you on television, being attacked by those mad policemen.'

As the man was speaking, the lights came on. When Sasha saw his father standing in the light, in a red-and-gold batik shirt, with his face crumpled in distress, he felt overwhelmed. The knot of resistance dissolved in him. Anything was possible. He did not really think this or believe it, but, in a hollow fashion, was aware of it.

'Come in,' he said. 'Sit anywhere. But I'm very ill. I have to lie down.'

As he walked back to the bed, he caught sight of his own face in the mirror that covered the wall. He looked unhappy and haggard, as though he had aged two decades in two days. But an elemental energy, sparking with vitality, seemed to roll into the room with his father.

'I can see that! Of course, you must lie down. You've seen a doctor, haven't you? You're taking medicines? Ah, but they broke your arm, the bastards! Oh gosh, aww shucks! Sasha, my Sasha... Well this is a lovely little apartment you've got yourself! Very cozy and intimate, and a nice sea view, I see!

You've made good use of our money! Ah! You're giving me a look! Our money, I said—not mine alone. We are father and son, Sasha, even if you've always harboured ill will towards me… I can understand, of course—but—we shall come to that. Pity about that construction outside. Is it always noisy like this? Ah, well, it's the same in every city. This whole damn country is perpetually under construction!'

He had seated himself on a chair by Sasha's bedside. Looking at him with glassy eyes, Sasha could not help but note how comfortable and at ease he appeared, though the chair was too narrow for him and the apartment, for its tiny size, must have taken him aback.

'Are you sure I can't get you anything?' he continued. Sasha shook his head. 'No? Hmm. Well, I won't nag you then. However, I can use some refreshment myself! One moment please!'

Sasha saw him put his hands on his knees and rise. He closed his eyes. The hammering from outside continued, as did the pounding in his head. When he looked again, Satish Dhawan was seated in place, leaning back with a glass of Sprite resting near his paunch. He was smiling.

'The one good thing about your being laid up is that I found you at home! Didn't have to hunt around! Haha! It's nice to see you smiling too.'

'I'm not smiling,' said Sasha.

'I thought you were. We need to talk. Now, where shall we start? I think…'

A moment passed.

'I think I should start by cautioning you—by telling you something—about young Ahishor Frances, the gentleman in whose cause you have suffered these dreadful injuries. I don't know if you're aware of this, but I have been funding everything he's been doing... You were aware?'

'I made inquiries,' said Sasha. He was staring up at the ceiling fan. A hot flush crawled over his skin.

'You were aware,' repeated Satish, with minor puzzlement. 'Well, I'm glad my association with the movement didn't put you off it. Does that mean you have softened towards your father at last? ... You're not saying anything? I hope it *does* mean that! You have always misunderstood me. But look here—I wish you had been wiser about getting so involved. I mean, I funded him, but I wasn't facing lathi charges for him! Anyway—you will understand why I feel almost personally responsible for what's happened to you... Sasha, my boy, Ahishor has turned out to be a crazy idealist and a fool. Please have nothing to do with him!'

'He's not a fool,' said Sasha slowly. 'He's very brave.'

Satish Dhawan began to smile. A faraway look crept over his face. It was a large, good-humoured face, and he might have been cherishing, with all sweetness, a wistful memory—except for the particular way the corners of his mouth curved and the glint that he could not keep out of his eye.

'Ahishor,' he intoned, 'stormed into my office some days ago... threw a cheque at me... and swore that he would send me to jail. Was that brave or foolish? Perhaps it was both. However, I consider bravery to be that which ultimately wins. Now I'm sure you're wondering what he was so upset about. I was too! At first I thought he'd discovered that Sadhguru has dinner with me every time he's in Delhi. But it wasn't that. It was something even sillier that had got him all het up.'

Suddenly, his eyes seemed to well up with emotion. He cocked his head and gazed down at Sasha's face, pale and glowing over the mounds of bedclothes.

'Sasha, you are my son, and I cannot see you like this! Surely you are wiser than the Ahishor Franceses of this world! I know I am to blame because I wasn't there for you enough when you were younger. But I've come to talk to you—about life. Yes, life. Humour me now, because this is important. Answer this for me: What—what in your view, is the purpose of life? Indulge me!'

Outside, it seemed that a lavish silence had fallen, because the construction workers had finally finished toiling for the day. The sounds on the street, too, were growing faint, drowned beneath the rhythm of the ceiling fan. Sasha reached out and pressed a switch. Strong yellow light filled the space around the bed.

'I can't talk much,' he said.

'Don't bother then! Let me—'

'Truth,' said Sasha.

'Truth?' Satish Dhawan looked surprised. 'Is that what you said? Truth! That's your answer... Hah!'

With the back of his hand, he made a sharp, sweeping gesture, as though to bat away what had just been spoken.

'I won't even ask, as that wise Roman once asked: "What is Truth?" However ironically he said it, he left himself open for an answer—which came afterwards, unfortunately! But I am here to teach you—not to be taught by you.'

His composure was a little lost. For a moment or two, he stared out of the window sombrely, taking gulps of Sprite in between and licking his lips. Gradually, once again, a kind of beatitude settled over him.

'As you know, I am fond of many philosophers,' said Satish Dhawan. 'But there is a sentiment by Carlos Castaneda, which you might say I live by. Castaneda asked us to think of the world as a host, and ourselves as its guests. A good life, therefore, consists of being a good guest. Now I like that, because there is another thing that's said about guests. A good guest must eat wisely, but not well, and talk well, but not wisely... Just dwell on that a moment, Sasha... *Eat wisely, but not well, and talk well, but not wisely...* I'm afraid, young men like Ahishor—and you too, I'm afraid—do exactly the opposite. You eat well and you talk ever so wisely. You eat your fill of something or the other, ignoring the other dishes. You eat obsessively, not seeming to notice the looks you're getting from the other guests. Then you turn around and you call that one thing you are eating—(here he made his voice tremulous with mockery) *The Truth!'*

'But then you get indigestion,' he continued, smiling. 'Now, what I do, is that I try everything on the table. I don't turn up my nose at anything—anything that this world of ours offers me. I don't call it good or bad. I let you greedy eaters do that labelling. But I don't argue with you either. That is to say, I can and do argue, because argument is one of the pleasures of civilization—but not to the point where I'm getting beaten up for it. I have absolutely no interest in being beaten up. Dinner time is too short and there are too many other things on the table... Including my fellow guests... some most attractive women, don't you think? Or should a guest not try to sleep with other guests?'

Sasha looked stony-faced.

'You're giving me that look again! It's "bad," is it? Hahaha! I say a guest should try to sleep with the hostess too! I have done that a few times; it's quite a pleasure you know—a real pleasure—because when you have taken so much from someone, and then by way of thanking them, you take even more, it is delicious! Women are such delightful creatures! But that's another subject. You know what is most attractive about them? Their unstoppable curiosity! Ah, but why am I talking like this? I think it must be your apartment, Sasha—it's so cozy and intimate. I hope you've been making good use of it?'

'I'm not like you,' said Sasha, but in the next moment he was annoyed with himself, for he had spoken showily.

'Are you sure?' asked his father. 'Are you absolutely sure? Even in this matter of women? But why fight it, Sasha? You're doing yourself no good. This runs in our blood. You must not argue with your own blood!'

He shifted in his chair, as though to cross his legs, but he was too fat to do so comfortably, so he stretched them out instead.

Sasha felt the air in the room growing oppressive, his fever marauding him, the bed too hard and the sheets slick with sweat. He heard his father's voice bounding along, lively and self-absorbed. He was wilting under the strain of it, but he felt compelled to listen.

'There's another interesting thing,' Satish was saying. 'I'm telling you this, since you all seem to be quite passionate about India—I mean Ahishor and you, and all you young revolutionaries. No doubt you think a man who follows my school of philosophy can't be much of a patriot. Well, the funny thing is—the answer's "yes *and* no". I myself have often wondered why I came back to India; and why I continue to live in India. It's not because I feel any sentimental or even cultural attachment to these parts. Oh no... I've lived all over the world and I can truly say that I am at home in any fine city anywhere in the world. So, why did I choose India, where there are no fine cities at all? All we have are little outposts of civilization, don't we? I think the reason is—and I've given this a lot of thought—the reason is, I feel a philosophical affinity to India. My philosophy of life, I have realized, is really the Indian philosophy—quintessentially! India is its home—its guru, if you please. Are we not the only land that has shunned Truth—

the way you said "Truth" just now; with that capital T—as a matter of *principle*? We have always valued sophistication, even if very few of us have gained it. Who is a Brahmin really?—an evolved soul; a good guest at the world's supper. But when it becomes a matter of who your parents are, it loses sophistication. When it becomes a matter of meditating and unleashing your chakras—or whatever it is these modern god-men do—it loses sophistication. Because it starts to *fixate*, you see. Now, your Abrahamic religions—I'm no expert, but I know a few things— they fixate. But a good Hindu doesn't! He's infinitely flexible! I once told this to Sadhguru too. He thinks Hinduism points to him as an exemplar. But I think it points to me. And I don't even call myself a Hindu. Because why fixate on a name? Haha!'

He paused, as a fulsome smile spread over his face. Then he became thoughtful.

'The modern man, anywhere in the world, is the true Hindu. And the true Hindu is the modern man; put him anywhere in the world. That is why, despite all our misery, India really is the vanguard of the modern world... Or is it the forerunner? Let's say, both. And so there's no need to *stress* and *strain* over changing this country. When you do that, the joke's on you. You're missing the point—like poor Ahishor. I was frank with him. I let him understand that I was simply betting on him. And I *was* betting on him! I wished very much to back a winner. But he became so awfully involved. Ah well... You'll say I should have known from that Manifesto of his. Oh, but I sincerely loved the Manifesto! I thoroughly enjoyed it. In a—shall we say?—sadomasochistic way. Haha! How was I to know he'd be daft enough to get married to it?'

As he lay there, though he had done nothing but endure, Sasha felt his sickness and vulnerability draining away. He raised himself upright, resting his head on the wall. A magical new strength was flowing into him.

'Why did he want to send you to jail?'

Satish Dhawan contorted his face and waved the question away. Yet he was unable to stay silent. He began to speak quickly.

'Why did he want to...? I don't know why you're asking! It was embarrassing for him. And for all his blind supporters, I imagine. Ahishor had some rather quaint ideas about women and honour. Ahem! I had had a very pleasant, albeit brief, relationship with a young girl from Ukraine. Some years ago. The same girl has now become famous for this Sadhguru sting operation. Small world! Well, that's how she met Ahishor. Now, I suppose at some point she complained to him about me—I gave her money to help her along, but she wanted more, poor thing. For some reason, he seemed to think I had done something shameful, just because the girl was younger than me. Came storming into my office—as I've mentioned already. Ah well... He wasn't as broad-minded as he thought he was. Young men hate old men who won't stop living. Young women, thank heavens, are fairer...'

'A god complex,' he continued, resuming his equanimity. 'That's what Ahishor had developed, by the end of it. He saw himself as a sort of avenging angel. But let's not keep talking about him. Sasha, look here. I want you to come home. There— I said it. Come home to Delhi. Let your father look after you.'

'My father?' asked Sasha, in a strange tone.

'When you were a child, you saw the world in black and white. Whatever you thought about me—the truth was more complicated. I loved your mother dearly! I still think of her. You have her eyes. Though I wasn't worthy of her. I say so myself! However, let bygones be bygones. I see how you are living here, sick and alone. The watchman told me nobody has been visiting you, except the maid. Is this the life you deserve? Come, don't be stubborn. I think you will grow to appreciate me. Just look—what a set of coincidences have led me back to you. I am, of course, no believer, but sometimes I get an uncanny feeling that there is a sort of exterior agency guiding the course of our lives. Do you ever feel that?'

'Yes,' said Sasha. 'I wasn't at the protest march to support Ahishor. I was there because I was guided there—to look after somebody.'

'Well, that's a bit unfortunate! I would be having second thoughts about that kind of guidance! ... What do you mean "look after somebody"? ... But listen—this is good to know! So you *weren't* supporting Ahishor. Then I think you already understand the things I've been saying to you?'

'You are mistaken about my attitude to Ahishor,' said Sasha. 'And you are mistaken in another thing you said. When you raped Elena, she was a child. She was not merely younger than you... Not a young woman... She was a child.'

For a few moments, the room felt utterly still, while a look of amazement transfigured the cherubic face of Sasha's father. Suddenly, he was staring grotesquely.

'What are you saying?' he began muttering. 'You're not well. Lie down.'

'I know what really happened, because she told it to me herself, in this very room. It was I who told Ahishor.'

Sasha went on in a controlled tone, while Satish Dhawan's face continued to alter.

'Those are the fruits of sophistication. You molest a child. Why? I'm sure she was attractive to you. It must have given you some pleasure. But why, after all? Just to pass the time? Just to amuse yourself? A tree is known by its fruits. Look at your actions. Your endless subtlety—what *you* call your endless subtlety—it's a cipher. Don't you see? The heart of your philosophy of committing to nothing—*is* nothing! A thunderous nothingness—that's what I see in you. Maybe you are right and that is the "uniquely Indian" philosophy, but if it is, India must change. We must learn to believe.'

'What are you planning to do?' His father's voice, always deep, was now a low growl.

'You talked about being guided in your deeds...' Suddenly, Sasha's own voice wavered. 'Papa,' he pleaded, 'come to your senses. You have taken the devil as your guide.'

A silence fell, like a thing in the balance. Then came a noise like the gnashing of teeth.

'You snake!'

Satish Dhawan was rising to his feet. His face was filled with savagery.

'It wasn't rape!' he snarled. 'You know nothing about women! You know nothing about life!'

He loomed above his son, staring with smouldering eyes, and asked, 'What are you planning to do? Be frank. What is it?'

Just then, it dawned on Sasha that his father was afraid.

'You think you can trap anyone! I'm not one of your movie directors. I showed Ahishor. Now what about you?'

Even as he watched, his father's eyes turned dark and hollow, like flames dying out into utter emptiness. He was flexing his fingers with some macabre intention. Then, still standing and staring, he began to talk aloud, not to Sasha, but to himself. His tone grew thoughtful, as he reasoned openly.

'Hmm... What about him? Should I do away with him

too?... But he says he didn't support the other one... no, and he's not like him. He's got no drive. No capacity. A passive person. Like a woman. Of course, he takes after his mother. Supine—that was the word for her. He's not dangerous in the sense that he needs to be crushed. Should be kept tormented though. Made to writhe. Yes, certainly. That's justified... for the way he talks, if nothing else...'

Frissons of revulsion crawled up and down Sasha, as his father continued to discourse aloud, with the same insane reasonableness, which soon turned to weariness—until suddenly he was smiling again.

'I am going to leave now,' he said brightly. 'I owed you one opportunity to save yourself. Now, I owe you nothing. You may think you disowned me a long time ago, but you never suffered for it. Now I disown you, Sasha, and now you will realize what it means to spit in your father's face. You have been living off my money. From today, you shall have no money. But it won't end there. I shall continue to take a special interest in you. In all your endeavours, Sasha—my erstwhile son—I will lend a hand—to lay you low. It will be instructive for you to learn just what powers your old father has. Oh, you have made yourself a fine old enemy! I am almost sorry for you. But you deserve it, and so I shall sleep soundly, very soundly. Au revoir—but not farewell.'

Sasha said nothing, but watched his father make his way to the door, his flesh quivering with every step. Satish Dhawan turned a last time. Sasha saw the awful smile still fixed upon his lips and the void-like eyes.

When the door had closed and the noises from the landing died away, he took a long, shuddering breath. He felt the hatred that had welled up in him drowning slowly. He swung his legs off the bed and raised a hand to his forehead. To his surprise, it was cool to the touch.

*   *   *

It was well into the night when some knocks rang out again—once, twice, thrice. They were desperate.

'Who is it?' cried Sasha. He had eaten and was about to lie down.

There was no answer. He stood near the door, a dreadful feeling growing in him. Then, on a sudden impulse, he pressed his ear to the wood. There came a faint noise, oddly repetitive. But it seemed to Sasha that he recognized it.

'Elena!' he cried, pulling open the door.

She stood outside, beneath the glaring white tube light, weeping and gazing at him with unreadable eyes. Before he could say more, she had flung herself into his arms. Her embrace tightened about him, as though it would never break away.

'Elena, Elena!'

'Sasha!'

There, on the threshold, she clung to him. For a while, he knew nothing but her cleaving muscles, her young heart pounding near his chest, and the smell of her hair, like gentle, throbbing magic. It filled him with the certainty that one spot in this mad world was soft and good—and that was enough.

But her tears would not stop. Suddenly, it seemed to him that there was more to her emotions than he could ever guess. He drew back, staring at her.

'Elena, Elena! Why are you crying?'

Epilogue

I hear that Giri Joseph is writing his account of the whole affair. I am already dreading the breezy tone; the clichés dressed up as incisive, insider analysis; and the absence of caring for any of the people involved, but only for the impression he is making—which, no doubt, will be great. But I will finish my story.

I was in my parents' home when I heard the news, via a text message from Bharat. I called him, but he couldn't speak. When he tried to, I barely recognized his voice; it was so queer with grief. On the TV, however, no one could stop talking and it was from there that I learned the details.

Ahishor had been shot three times in the chest, while walking down a road in South Delhi, close to the private club, Ozymandias, where he was lodging at the time. This had happened at ten o'clock, on a typical smog-shrouded Delhi night. He had probably just had dinner in a nearby market. There were no eyewitnesses to the actual attack, but the assailants were presumed to be two masked men on a motorbike, who had been spotted speeding away from the scene. The police were hard on the case, giving out assurances that they would track down the killers as quickly as possible.

In the meantime, in the media and across social media, reactions were pouring in—and a near-unanimous theory taking root already. One did not need to be a genius—it was pointed out—to recognize the handiwork of the fanatic far right. No one, in recent memory (if ever) had done so much for liberty and rationality in India as young Ahishor Frances. Other voices of reason (older, gentler voices) had been silenced before, in much the same way. Was his murder really so surprising then? But how long, it was demanded, would this terror continue? How long would violent young men, pumped full of hate, be allowed to kill, and slip away into obscurity—and no one be held responsible?

Thus, in front of my eyes, I saw Ahishor's name exalted higher than ever. The episode of the fake WhatsApp rumour, which had led to the arrest of the Epochal team, was quite forgotten. Similarly put aside were the criticisms of his zeal in prosecuting men like Karim and Ritesh Azad. All these, it was finally declared, were mere distractions (which no one ought to advert to any longer) from the central issue, the thing that Ahishor had lived for—and now died for: the new culture of liberty.

I received all that was happening with a kind of paralysis. It passed my mind that I ought to return to Mumbai for the funeral, but I had no strength even to begin such a journey. I was overwhelmed, laid low by my emotions—and in that fashion, equanimous. I merely continued to observe the goings-on from the bosom of my childhood home.

The funeral procession was a massive and star-studded one. I remember seeing the traditional top-angle snapshot of the coffin, surrounded by a sea of mourners. It was incredible to realize that on this occasion, the one who had died was a friend of mine—and to witness the extent of the celebrity he had attained. But perhaps his very celebrity had obscured him, or perhaps the fault was mine. Though many moods and thoughts came to me, I allowed very little into my heart. I only continued to scan the coverage. There were pictures of Karim, stamped with his signature dignity that seemed to have only grown from his legal ordeals. He was carrying the coffin along with other known personages, including Ritesh Azad (in dark glasses—was it to hide his grief, or the lack of it, I wondered vaguely) and also Bharat Mishra. This I was pleased to see, for Bharat had been loyal from beginning to end, and he deserved the pride of place. In another photograph, he was consoling Nalini Frances, tears streaming down both their faces, while a famous Bollywood actor stood nearby, deferentially.

It was, of necessity, a political procession too. In the newspapers I read a quote by Mihir, vowing to carry on the banner of the movement, which, he reminded us, owed everything to Ahishor. When I read this, I became truly disturbed for the first time. I had promised my parents I would have nothing more to do with politics and I fully intended to keep that promise. I knew I had had a lucky escape. With the public mood as it was, the cases against us would probably be dropped. (Sushant too was out on bail.) So I could go back when I was ready... pick up the pieces of my career.

However, it was not that I feared being dragged back into the net. Stranger still, it depressed me to simply escape it.

Then, two days after the funeral, my phone rang. It was Malik, calling with an invitation.

'Few of us are meeting in Bandra tomorrow. It's a memorial meeting for Ahishor. Please come. We are meeting outside American Express Bakery at 5 p.m.'

'I'm in Delhi,' I said.

'*Aaja re!*[71]'

Suddenly, for the first time in days, I felt energetic. The fog in my head began to clear.

'Ok!' I exclaimed in desperation. 'Ok, I'll book tickets and come!'

The next twenty-four hours, which included a tense, difficult conversation with my parents, passed as though in a dream. I called a taxi and reached the airport. I stood in queues without any luggage at all, feeling a delicious irresponsibility as well a sense of distinctness from every other person around me. It seemed to me, that unlike them, I was close to something fundamental and that I was getting nearer to it, while they, perhaps, were travelling further away—though our destination might look the same. I was calm and excited all through the flight. When we landed, I walked straight out of the airport, and sans haggling, climbed into an auto.

It was a beautiful evening. My ride rolled its way through sparse traffic. The breeze danced about me as I gazed upon my beloved city. All around, there was an atmosphere of lull. The heat had abated for the day and so had the frenzy of work. Come night-time, the traffic would swell again, surrounded by an electric glare, and the restaurants would swing into renewed activity. But for now, it was almost peaceful.

I got off at the bakery, paid the driver, and turned to find the others there already—for I was late. They were standing on the pavement, shoulder to shoulder, like a welcome party. My eyes swept over Malik, Sasha and Elena. There was nobody else—except for a stray dog seated between Sasha and Elena,

---

[71]Come, man

who too was regarding me with a solemn expression.

Sasha stepped forward, catching my gaze. I stared back at him, aware of a smile forming over my face. There was something odd and comic about the three. Perhaps it was their markedly different shapes and sizes; or maybe it was the dog, whose presence was surely surreal. A laugh itched in my throat. But as Sasha continued to look at me, a new emotion swept over me.

I felt I was being understood, not in the way I understood myself, but mysteriously, and as though from a much grander vantage point. There was a steady sympathy in his eyes, like a fathoms-deep ocean. Whether he had changed, or my perception had sharpened, I knew I had not seen him thus before.

'Let us go,' he said.

'Nobody else is coming?' I asked, surprised. 'Where are we going?'

'They will join us later. Come on.'

I sensed a faint censure in his words. I began to follow him, along with the others. The dog did not come along, but watched us go. Nobody talked much. It was only a short walk, but I remember the moon, unusually big and sharp in the dusky sky, and how the old buildings looked melancholy and beautiful in the light. We began passing by familiar cafes—places I had often been to; places much talked about. But we ended in another world that I had never visited.

Past the great facade of the church where, in the presence of hundreds, Ahishor's coffin had been brought forth, we entered a garden of crosses. He lay there by himself now, in the company of all the ordinary dead, though his grave stood out, for it was bedecked with flowers, great heaps of marigolds that reminded me (ironically) of Hindu deities being venerated.

When Sasha and Elena strode up to the grave and stood

by it in a deep quiet, I began to feel uncomfortable. I looked at Malik, but he was staring, heavy-hearted, at the epitaph on the tombstone. I glanced at it myself. It was a polished white tombstone, beautifully engraved. Below Ahishor's name, and the dates separated by a dash—that revealed, with perfect brevity, the pathos of early death—was inscribed the following verse:

He makes my feet like hinds' feet,
And sets me on my high places.
He trains my hands for battle,
So that my arms can bend a bow of bronze.

A breeze blew over the mud and grass, laden with moist, secret life. I felt my skin crawling. Suddenly, it seemed to me strange and even unsafe to be standing in that place. Some distance across the boundary walls of the cemetery (which were criss-crossed with niches for more bodily remains), the city was visible. I must have looked with yearning at that jumble of buildings, or even wandered away unconsciously towards them, because Sasha called out: 'Dhruv! Come here!'

I turned in surprise. He was looking straight at me.

'Why are you so hesitant, Dhruv? Why do you always stay on the outside? Come! Don't guard yourself! Come! There is nothing to worry about!'

What had begun with Malik's phone call was suddenly completed. His admonition first humbled me and then I was flooded with blessed relief, because I knew that Sasha was right. I was always lingering on the edge of things, always wary. For instance, I had wanted to get to know Sasha for months, but I had never reached out to him. Something had held me back—a self-consciousness I was proud of; calculations that I considered precious—but now that they were falling away from me, I realized they amounted to nothing.

'What has all your fearfulness done for you?' I listened to Sasha with a glad and fervent yielding. 'You have simply gone ambling along, Dhruv, like a lamb, only worrying about yourself, while so much slaughter has happened in front of your eyes.'

'I know,' I cried suddenly. 'I feel disgusted. I feel like—I haven't had a bath—for months! But I don't know what to do!'

Trapped in his gaze, which seemed to respond to everything I said, and yet never alter, I realized with dawning amazement, the insincerity of even my last complaint—my besetting insincerity! Then a quiet came over me. Indeed, it came over us all.

'We must be able to stop the work we are doing,' Sasha was speaking in a clear, calm voice that reached us easily, as we gathered about the gravestone, 'to remember what lies beyond it. Ahishor taught this, by his example. He cared for truth more than he cared for comforts and achievements. He wanted to do the right things more than he wanted to impress people. To work, and not just to be busy. God gave him great talents and he recognized them and wanted to make good use of them. That was his goodness. He lost his way when he forgot where his strength had come from. Then he slipped into false actions, violent plans. But he was still always attracted to truth. He was drawn towards the truth that overcomes the whole world. That's why he made enemies on every side—not only on one—as he would have if he had been entrenched in one or the other ways of the world. For the time being, he spoke against all faiths. But I believe he was on the path to true faith. It is, after all, a miraculous path! I want to say to all of you—remember Ahishor's example, and remember truth, in your own lives. Don't lose sight of it in the work you do. Don't be ashamed of serving the truth you see, just because the world hates truth and loves to make all talk of it meaningless. Whenever you find that your work is not truthful, stop it and come back to the truth that you can see. This way you will grow in faith and in your understanding of truth, which is the object of faith.'

He continued:

'I also want to thank you. I owe each of you, and others too, who aren't here today. I came to Mumbai not knowing what work I was meant to do. But you welcomed me amongst yourselves. You allowed me into your lives. (Yes, you also Elena—*you* most of all!) Then I saw your hopes and your troubles… Your afflictions. You are soldiers—all of you in Versova. You have the courage to go to war for an ideal. Didn't you show that even with Ahishor? And you showed that you want to help each other, to lean on each other, as good soldiers do. But you must avoid being turned into pawns by those who want to exploit your need for guidance. They make you pawns of money, pawns of power. That, in reality, is what has been happening with you. When that happens, you use and neglect each other, as even Ahishor used and neglected Elena. But I think he was sorry for it… Be guided only by the truth! Help each other to speak the truth together. Remember that everything but the truth will make a slave of you. But the truth will make soldiers and artists of you. As for me, I am preaching to you with such authority, only because you have given it to me.'

Then a smile, which was almost shy, appeared on Sasha's face. Simultaneously, it seemed the very sky was growing lighter as the sombre mood lifted and my heart leaped with unreasonable happiness. He looked at us in turn, with that mixture of love and pride, whose name is appreciation. I felt I was bathed in it.

When had I last prayed? … Not since my childhood. Truthfully, then, I did not know what I was doing. But I prayed as best I could—for Ahishor, for myself, for each of us and for everyone I could think of. I lost track of time. As I stood there, my eyes closed, there came to my mind the story that Jatin had once told—his dream of the country's richest and vilest people gathered together at a party, into which, by and by, a pride of lions is released. I thought to myself how it had really happened; how Ahishor had been the king of that pride. But Jatin had dreamed naively. The king had been overmatched.

My eyes opened onto a sudden resolve. I would go to meet Jatin and build our friendship again. For I too was beginning to appreciate the things that God had made.

In the last light of the day, as the trees about the churchyard were losing their shapes, we began to leave. We walked in silence and were full of a sort of peace that would not quickly dissipate.

*   *   *

Sasha, however, stayed awhile. He lingered in the cemetery grounds. A dim corridor stretched alongside the garden of graves. In an alcove at the end of this corridor was an empty tomb, over which hung a life-size statue of the crucified Christ.

He stood before these for a long time. His right arm throbbed with pain, while his thoughts travelled dimly to angels and demons, to curses and prophecies—a boy lying on the ground, convulsing; a girl with a face like a mask, with proud looks and a lying tongue; the sound of footsteps running to do mischief and the play of hands shedding innocent blood—and the redemption of them all hung before his eyes.

He stood there, while the darkness gained thickly, until a moment arrived that, perhaps, he had been waiting for—when he realized that he was not alone.

Turning, he saw her standing a few paces away from him.

'I'm sorry I am late,' said Maithili.

Yes, it was her in the flesh—that face, those eyes. She took a step towards him, and he felt—or thought he felt—such a pull and a surge of emotions that it seemed a miracle that he did not dash forward and take her in his arms.

However, he knew he never would.

'Come and pray,' said Sasha. 'We don't have much time.'